D1260341

Producing the Modern Hebrew Canon

New Perspectives on Jewish Studies

A Series of the Philip and Muriel Berman Center for Jewish Studies
Lehigh University, Bethlehem, Pennsylvania

General Editor: Laurence J. Silberstein

Producing the Modern Hebrew Canon: Nation Building and Minority Discourse
Hannan Hever

Mapping Jewish Identities
Edited by Laurence J. Silberstein

Interpreting Judaism in a Postmodern Age
Edited by Steven Kepnes

The Other in Jewish Thought and History: Constructions of Jewish Culture and Identity
Edited by Laurence J. Silberstein and Robert L. Cohn

Jewish Fundamentalism in Comparative Perspective: Religion, Ideology, and the Crisis of Modernity
Edited by Laurence J. Silberstein

New Perspectives on Israeli History: The Early Years of the State
Edited by Laurence J. Silberstein

Producing the Modern Hebrew Canon
Nation Building and Minority Discourse

Hannan Hever

NEW YORK UNIVERSITY PRESS
New York & London

NEW YORK UNIVERSITY PRESS
New York and London

Library of Congress Cataloging-in-Publication Data
Hever, Hannan.
Producing the modern Hebrew canon : nation building and
minority discourse / Hannan Hever.
p. cm. — (New perspectives on Jewish studies)
ISBN 0–8147–3644–0
1. Hebrew literature, Modern—20th century—History and criticism.
2. Israeli fiction—History and criticism.   3. Jews—Identity.
4. Hebrew literature—Minority authors.   5. Authors, Arab—Israel.
I. Silberstein, Laurence J. (Laurence Jay), 1936–
II. Title.   III. Series.
PJ5020 .H48 2001
892.4'09006—dc21   2001003986

New York University Press books are printed on acid-free paper,
and their binding materials are chosen for strength and durability.

Manufactured in the United States
10 9 8 7 6 5 4 3 2 1

To Tal, Yaar, and Shir

Contents

Foreword

This volume marks the first book by a single author to be published in the Berman Center series New Perspectives on Jewish Studies. Like the previous five volumes in the series, Hannan Hever's book provides a theoretically informed, interdisciplinary discussion of a basic dimension of the field of Jewish Studies. Imaginatively using insights derived from literary theory, philosophy, and postcolonial studies, Hever frames a new and provocative interpretation of Hebrew literary production. Sensitive to the role of power in cultural production, a role usually overlooked in conventional studies of Hebrew and Israeli literature, Hever explores the dynamic formation of what emerged as the "canon" of Israeli literature. In the process, he provides a fresh and exciting perspective on Israeli culture.

I am pleased that the Berman Center was able to provide a context in which the author could test several of the arguments more fully elaborated in the book. This was done both at the continuing Berman Center colloquium on Judaism and Postmodern Culture and in several of the previous volumes in this series. Thus, the publication of Hannan Hever's book represents a continuation and elaboration of ongoing discussions taking place at the Berman Center for almost a decade.

LAURENCE J. SILBERSTEIN

Acknowledgments

Earlier versions of some chapters in this volume were published elsewhere. The author and the Philip and Muriel Berman Center for Jewish Studies thank the following publishers for allowing us to reprint these works:

Gordon and Breach Publishers for permission to reprint "The 'Other' Will Arrive Tomorrow," by Hannan Hever, © *Contemporary Theater Review* (vol. 3, 2, 1995) and the Overseas Publishers Association N.V.

Indiana University Press for permission to reprint "Israeli Fiction of the Sixties," by Hannan Hever, which appeared in *Prooftexts* (vol. 10, 1990).

University of Minnesota Press for permission to reprint Hannan Hever's "Hebrew in an Israeli Arab Hand: Six Miniatures on Anton Shammas's *Arabesques,*" first published in *Cultural Critique* (vol. 7, 1987).

University Press of New England for permission to reprint "From Exile-without-Homeland to Homeland-without-Exile: A Guiding Principle of Hebrew Fiction in Interwar Poland," by Hannan Hever, © *The Jews of Poland between Two World Wars,* edited by Y. Gutman, E. Mendelsohn, J. Reinharz, and C. Shmeruk, 1989.

A Hebrew version of chapter 2, "Nationalist Satire and Its Victims: The Politics of Majority and Minority in S. Y. Agnon's 'With Our Young and Our Old,'" was published in *Iyunim BeTkumat Israel,* 1995.

A Hebrew version of part of chapter 8, "Of Refugee Gals and Refugee Guys: Emil Habibi and the Hebrew Literary Canon," was published in *HaMizrah HaHadash,* 1993.

Introduction

Amos Oz was once questioned about the critical acclaim that greeted Anton Shammas's novel *Arabesques*. Did Oz, asked the interviewer, consider the publication of this novel, written in Hebrew by an Israeli Arab, to be a turning point in Israeli society?

Oz responded: "I think of this as a triumph, not necessarily for Israeli society, but for the Hebrew language. If the Hebrew language is becoming attractive enough for a non-Jewish Israeli to write in it, then we have arrived" (Twerski 1986, 27).

Oz recognizes the importance of *Arabesques*, although he is less sure of its place in a particular Israeli context. Despite his slightly patronizing tone, Oz simultaneously and publicly acknowledges a certain lack of strength in the Hebrew language. The admission that it is the Arab writer who is proof of the success of "having arrived" reflects an insecurity, as if "we"—the Jews—could not have achieved such success on our own. His words can also be interpreted as setting Shammas apart as an Arab and not according him his full cultural rights as a member of Israeli society. But observe that Oz's answer sounds almost like a direct quotation from decades of Zionist writings that expressed the unflagging hope that the persecuted Jewish minority would someday achieve the status of a majority and, with it, political sovereignty in Israel. Oz presents the Hebrew language in a dual light: as the language of the ruling majority and as the language of a minority compelled to fight for cultural and political recognition.

This perspective, coming from a major Hebrew writer such as Amos Oz during the mid–1980s, provides powerful testimony to the stability of perceptions regarding Hebrew literature over the course of the twentieth century. At its core, this orientation places the Jewish ethnic identity of the literature together with its writing in the

Hebrew language as two (undeclared) necessary components of Hebrew literature, establishing a complex and conflictual taxonomic combination. The stance that Oz takes, still deeply embedded in this complex intersection, raises again the question of the modes of construction of modern national Hebrew literature. How did the literature's dynamic relation to its being the literature of a national majority facilitate its dramatic role in the constitution of the national Hebrew subject in the twentieth century? How did the complex attitude of the national Hebrew subject toward its own power, whether as a national minority or as a national majority, determine the structure of Hebrew literature in the twentieth century? The central role performed by literature and by writers in the politics of the new Jewish nationalism makes their study a crucial element in understanding the cultural dynamics of Jewish nationality.

The construction of national imagination, as Benedict Anderson has taught us, involves the writing and rewriting of historical memories and shared narratives that seek to shape the reader's understanding of the nation and of national identity. The development of modern Hebrew literature provides a dramatic example of the production of one such national imagination. Since the end of the nineteenth century, Hebrew writers in Europe and Palestine/Israel have produced texts that consolidate moments of nation building. Within the dominant modes of Israeli literary interpretation, this process of nation building is depicted as a coherent and progressive one in which the widely dispersed Jewish people is configured into a sovereign nation. As I shall show, however, a careful reading of the literary historical narrative can pressure it to reveal moments of rupture and reversal that have the effect of undermining and diverting efforts to construct a hegemonic Zionist story.

Drawing on recent studies of literary canonization and minority discourse, I show how the construction of the tradition commonly referred to as Hebrew literature entailed the suppression of heterodox discourses. The conflict of discourses that produced what is taken as the canon of modern Hebrew literature (that is, the corpus of texts which, since the end of the nineteenth century, have been valorized as occupying a special place in the repertoire of national culture) is evident as far back as the earliest expressions of a Zionist literary sensibility and continues to the present day.

The earliest phases of the creation of modern Hebrew literature were the work of a group living as a minority amid, and on the margins of, other national groups. With the destruction of most of European Jewry and the establishment of the State of Israel in the land of Palestine, however, the concept of minority status underwent a dramatic change, as Jews in Palestine emerged as the national majority of the state, with the Arabs relegated to the role of minority population. This situation is forcefully represented in the discourses concerning Arab otherness that, as we have begun to see, emerge vis-à-vis the Hebrew writings of Anton Shammas, as well as the Hebrew translations of the writings of Emil Habibi (see chapters 7 and 8). Drawing on postcolonial theory and the examples of other newly emerging national literatures and cultures, I read the specific conditions of the growth of Hebrew literature in terms of the conflict between what Gilles Deleuze and Félix Guattari have described as major and minor literatures. That is, Hebrew literature is viewed here in the explicit context of power relations. Such relations, commonly overlooked in hegemonic treatments of the Hebrew literary formation, become visible when we focus on the ways in which diverse, conflicting discourses participate in formation of modern Hebrew literature— rather than seeking to emphasize the putative "unity" of the latter.

The special case of Hebrew literature as the descendant of a rich, ancient, mythic and archaeological heritage called on to function in a modernist national situation, as a literature that had a major role in Hebrew culture before it came to serve modern national project, complicates such readings beyond the problematics to be found in other national literatures. Contrary to the widely accepted demand, however, to read the formation of Hebrew literature as being a uniquely Jewish phenomenon, I read it as a Western modernist national phenomenon. Such a reading, rather than seeing this literature as the natural product of a emergent nation, views it as a political apparatus serving the production of a national culture. Thus, despite its case-specific focus on Hebrew literature, this project also generates insights that can be applied to the creation of other national literatures that are similarly marked by struggle, ambivalence, and contradiction.

This book, then, offers an alternative reading of the historiography of Hebrew literature and of major narratives in modern Hebrew literature. This alternative reading becomes necessary once the dichotomous status of Hebrew culture as incorporating both colonial and postcolonial cultural consciousnesses, both majority and minority relations, is recognized. At the same time, however, it is crucial to see that the opposing sides of these dichotomies can overlap in a dynamic interchange that makes the very notion of tradition an ambivalent one, open to continuous changes.

The reading of the historical project of Hebrew literature by postcolonial theory helps expose the hegemonic Zionist "cover story" that represses and excludes social, ethnic, and national minorities. It further reveals the violence involved in the transformation from Hebrew culture to Israeli culture. The transformation from a nonterritorial culture to a territorial culture always involves violent acts of occupation. But every act of territorial conquest invites reterritorialization on the part of the deterritorialized. Silent and marginal narratives subvert the exclusivity of canonical authors by creating texts at the periphery of the culture that may penetrate to the very core of canonical writing. In other words, the specters of heterogeneous subjects and "unaesthetic" writing, both of which threaten to undermine the supposed "naturalness" of canonical writing and its sanctified place as the sole inhabitant of the realm of consensus, are always present. It thus becomes clear, for instance, that the case of Hebrew literature has an important role to play in enriching postcolonial theories and theories of nationality. This is particularly evident in my discussion of the writings of the Palestinian Israeli author Anton Shammas, whose texts create a discourse that necessitates a reworking of the account proposed by the leading theorists of minority discourse, Deleuze and Guattari.

The critical reading elaborated in this book may serve as a vehicle for exposing the dynamics of the political and cultural development of Hebrew literature, especially with regard to the transition from Hebrew literature written in the Diaspora, in exile, to Israeli literature written in the Israeli nation-state. This transition now appears to be very different from the linear and teleological account that Zionist rhetoric promoted and reproduced over the course of the last century. Given its focus on repressed and silenced narratives, such as national (Palestinian) and erased ethnic (Mizrahi) narratives, my approach reveals the ways in which such discourses, like anti-Zionist or

Canaanite narratives, threaten the Zionist hegemonic narrative. In the consensual self-construction of the Jewish collective, any narrative that differs from the sanctioned metanarrative challenges the unity and authority of the Jewish Subject. When divergent texts, such as those mentioned above, come to threaten this authoritative unity, subverting efforts to depict national Hebrew literature as homogeneous, countermovements arise in an attempt to repress or co-opt these texts. At the same time, efforts are made, within the dominant literary narrative, to conceal or erase the processes of reaction and accommodation that inform hegemonic literature.

Notwithstanding such efforts, as the reading undertaken here clarifies, Palestinian and Arabic Jewish (Mizrahi) minority literary discourses, together with nonhegemonic Ashkenazi Jewish literary discourses, play a significant role in the creation of the national canon. I claim that the mode of reading developed here, which draws on but simultaneously refines current theories, can profitably serve as a model for the interpretation of processes of canonization in other national cultures, where the conflict between the colonizer and colonized, settler and indigene, majority and minority, occupier and victim, plays a significant role.

The present study traces the development of oppositional currents in modern Hebrew culture from its origins in Eastern Europe and in Eretz Israel/Palestine at the beginning of the twentieth century to the present. Hebrew fiction was institutionalized and canonized within the context of Zionist culture, a culture that itself rebelled against Jewish existence in the Diaspora, which it perceived as subservient and inferior. The ideological negation of the Diaspora and the harsh criticism directed toward the Eastern European Jewish "mentality" generated expressions of longing for political and social sovereignty. The national Hebrew literature of *hatekhiya* ("renaissance" or national renewal) played a major role in this process. Its critiques of the materialistic and spiritual foundations of Diaspora Jewish life were the vehicle of central assumptions about modern Jewish identity posited by Zionist discourse.

At the core of the *hatekhiya* literature was a utopian program for creating a normal national culture for a national majority living in its own historical territory. This program also constructed the image of an autonomous, homogeneous Jewish Subject, schooled in universalism but nevertheless implementing the realization of the national coherence and historical continuity of the Jewish people. Such a projection was incommensurate with Hebrew literature as the possession of a minority group living in the Diaspora.

This image of a national Jewish subjectivity lay at the center of the Zionist national canon that dominated Hebrew literature for many generations. It was, moreover, taken as a given in the dominant historiographical interpretations of Hebrew literature. Thus, the Zionist principles of the negation of the Diaspora and the creation of a national majority culture became the central criteria of the aesthetic that dominated Hebrew literature and culture.

My book portrays attempts to create alternatives to the Zionist canon. In so doing, it also describes some major canonized writers, as the targets of oppositional struggle on the one hand or as unrelenting fighters against the narrowing of alternatives presented by hegemonic culture on the other. The intersections of canonical and alternative texts become junctures where alternative registers of difference emerge, instances in a broken and fractured narrative of the struggle for national sovereignty, fraught not only with obstacles but with ambivalence. A case in point concerns the efforts made to produce Hebrew literature on the part of oppositional Jewish intellectuals living as members of a national minority in the Diaspora. These writers accepted neither the radical negation of the Diaspora nor the exclusivity of a Zionist utopia for the sole benefit of a national majority on Zionist territory. Contrary to those who regarded Zionist activity in the Diaspora as no more than a means to Zionist settlement in Palestine, supporters of the slogan "Laboring for the Present" (affirmed at the Helsingfors Convention of 1906) argued that national activity in the Diaspora, including Hebrew cultural activity, was necessary as well as sufficient in itself, rather than being, as later dictates ruled, merely a means of preparing Jews for emigration to Palestine. These intellectuals, I argue, were trying to develop a cultural stance as a national minority and a critical position toward the all-encompassing ideology of the national majority. The detailed study of other such junctures carried out in the readings that follow must be seen as a necessary stage in reworking the map of modern Hebrew literature, in a manner that undermines the hegemonic authority of the national historiography of Hebrew literature and culture.

Chapter 1 portrays a major phase in the canonization of the literature of the national majority, involving a struggle between conflicting interpretations of the nature of modern national Hebrew literature and centering on controversies over the boundaries of the Hebrew canon. It contains a detailed analysis of the efforts, beginning at the turn of the century, to exclude Hebrew authors in Galicia from the canon. The discussion of the energy invested by prominent writers Y. H. Brenner, M. Y. Berdichevsky, and others to delegitimate these Galician writers is used to map the power struggle in Hebrew culture at the beginning of the twentieth century.

Chapter 2 traces the manner in which a canonical author such as S. Y. Agnon dealt with the option of a national minority literature. As is well known, those who favored or at least legitimated the cultural existence of the Jews as a national minority in Eastern Europe failed historically. Yet to read the texts of Agnon from the retrospective position of the historical "winners" is to miss the severity of the struggle—whose outcome was not a foregone conclusion at the time—between those who hoped that Jews could integrate as a national minority in the Diaspora and those who opposed this quest. A critical reading of S. Y. Agnon's story "With Our Young and Our Old" (1920), a story at the very center of the Hebrew canon, serves to focus the discussion. This story can be read as satirical commentary on the minority position. My reading exposes a rich array of strategies aimed against the idea of a national minority, which had become a major political option for a Jewish existence in interwar Europe.

Chapter 3 describes the development of fiction in the Hebrew cultural center in Poland between the two world wars. In the complex multiethnic situation of a newly independent Poland, a new Jewish politics developed and, alongside it, a politics of Jewish and Hebrew culture. The publishing houses, literary salons, and intellectual discourse of Warsaw were outstanding manifestations of modern Hebrew culture as a national minority culture. The great force, however, of Zionist activity—political and cultural—made Poland into a conflicted arena. The Zionists equated Hebrew culture with the Zionist negation of the Diaspora. Consequently, despite the development of Hebrew culture in the Diaspora, its more Zionist adherents abandoned Poland for Palestine and, in so doing, developed a paradoxical cultural praxis that broke up the very community that had produced their literary identity in the first place. As Zionist He-brew writers and readers left Poland, the increasingly impoverished Hebrew literature there reacted in complex ways to its abandonment and became part of the practice of a dying cultural center.

In chapter 4, the discussion moves to the post–World War II pe-riod and to Palestine, then in the process of becoming a national state—Israel. In an effort to portray the way in which the Israeli sub-ject was constructed through the process of gaining political sover-eignty, the chapter concentrates on the representation of the Pales-tinian Other in Hebrew fiction of the time. To expose the strategies involved in forming the central Israeli Subject, the chapter focuses on representations of the Other in anti-Zionist, nativist, "Canaanite" fiction. Although writing from the perspective of a minority located outside the Zionist canon, the Canaanites of the period adopted the perspective of a national majority. This chapter focuses on the reverse dialectic that characterizes the relevant power relations and repre-sentations of the Other: the Canaanites, members of the major Zion-ist culture, which had won its war for independence, took the posi-tion of a weak minority but unconsciously also assumed a hegemonic position. Such a cultural practice, which operates ambivalently as the false political consciousness of the powerful parading their weakness, became a widespread phenomenon in the discourse of the young Is-raeli state. The quick transformation from patterns of a national struggle for independence to a sovereign situation left conflicting residues in Israeli discourse, attesting to both national strength and weakness.

Chapter 5 concentrates on Natan Shaham's play *They Will Arrive Tomorrow* (1949), based on the short story "They Were Seven" (1949). The play was written and produced immediately after the end of the 1948 war and exposes the lack of cohesion and internal unrest that characterized the Israeli Subject in the interim period after the war. The often self-contradictory imagery of power and weakness in the play is revealed as a complex arena where national culture determines its dominant and dominating identity while it comes to terms with its Palestinian Other. The chapter describes how the mythical subjects of the period of the struggle for inde-pendence were seen and analyzed in the period of national sover-eignty after the war.

Chapter 6 begins by interpreting three stories from the center of the canon of Israeli literature of the sixties. These stories, by A. B. Yehoshua, Amos Oz, and Amalia Kahana-Carmon, are presented as three alternative ways of representing the Israeli Subject between the poles of minority and majority. The Israeli culture of the sixties is often conceived of as the time when, after the heroism of the war of independence, a new Israeli was born. Reading its major modes of representation, however, exposes these modes as the outcome of a slow, tense, and contradictory process. Despite their differences, these three options are finally revealed to be equally hegemonic. All three pertain in one way or the other to a particular Zionist, Ashkenazi elite and require a foil to bring out their sameness. It is Shimon Ballas, an Iraqi-born writer, who presents this foil. The discussion concludes by examining how his work subverts the unified front of Ashkenazi writers of the sixties.

The long process of creating a modern national Hebrew literature began at the end of the nineteenth century and the beginning of the twentieth century with the active attempt of a Jewish Zionist national minority to constitute a utopian, imagined community poised to become a national majority. The establishment of the State of Israel, with its Jewish majority, reversed this situation. The narratives of the oppressed, who in the past aspired for national liberation, turned into narratives of the oppressors. The cultural oppression of the Palestinian minority in Israel created a confrontational arena in which Palestinian counterefforts were perceived as hostile.

Against this background, some Arab writers tried to enter the Hebrew canon and to become equal partners in this "imagined community." A central figure in this process is Anton Shammas, who, in his novel *Arabesques* (1986), challenged the ethnic boundaries of the Hebrew literary canon. Through this novel, the ostensible identification of Hebrew literature with Jewish ethnicity was broken in an unprecedented manner. Chapter 7 offers a close reading of this revolutionary novel as a test case of writing from the position of the minority attempting to enter the heart of the literature of the majority.

Chapter 8 expands the range of this process and looks at the radical changes that took place in the Hebrew canon during the 1980s through the indirect influence of Israeli Palestinian literature and in translations of this literature into Hebrew, focusing on the work of

Emil Habibi. The translation of Habibi's literary works from Arabic into Hebrew by Anton Shammas has turned Habibi, a central intellectual figure in Israel, into a distinguished literary figure in contemporary Hebrew literature. This is the latest stage in the long and complex process of the constitution of modern national Hebrew literature, a process that is closely associated with the immense changes in modern Jewish national identity.

I am used to telling the story of the development of Hebrew literature in Hebrew. It has therefore been a salutary experience to discuss this minority literature in the global medium of English, the language of a vast majority. I thank all those who have assisted me in this endeavor: the translators Haya Amir, Shai Bar-Yaacov, Louise Bethlehem, Oren Gensler, Peretz Kidron, Sonja Laden, as well as my English style editor, Doron Narkiss. I thank Eric Zakim, Irit Rogoff, and Larry Silberstein for their encouragement and support during all stages of writing. Thanks also to Jennifer Hammer for her fine editings, to Martin L. White for the indexing, and to Shirley Ratushny for help with devotion and care to the final completion of the manuscript. Some of the chapters that appear in this book were published in slightly different form in various journals, and I thank the editors for their permission to reprint them here.

Chapter 1

The Struggle over the Canon of Early Twentieth-Century Hebrew Literature: The Case of Galicia

The "Culture Debate" in the Zionist Movement

The aesthetic discourse in and through which the Hebrew canon was constructed embodied power struggles that took place in the cultural and political arenas of the early twentieth century. The rise of the Zionist movement as a modern political movement was inextricably bound up with modern Jewish national culture. Questions concerning the role of culture in the emerging Zionist nationalism were regularly addressed and deliberated from the inception of the movement. Debates focused on the extent to which Zionist culture should be based on tenets central to Orthodox Judaism, the *haskalah* enlightenment tradition, or a new form of secular, Jewish modernist culture. Another version of the new Jewish cultural nationalism saw Zionism as linked to the internal dynamics of Jewish daily life in specific Diaspora communities and developed a conception of "labor culture" as a way of grounding Zionist ideals (Almog 1987, 84–176).

The discussion within the Zionist movement about cultural affairs, known at the time as the "culture debate," became a major political issue among Zionists at the turn of the century. Many regarded the instruction of Jewish history and the expansion of the Hebrew language and literature as foundational to a national Zionist education (Luz 1988, 137–58). In these fields of cultural activity, political dissension was rife; yet it was precisely this dissension that ultimately fashioned the Zionist movement, for it shaped the inventory of new national symbols and the newly emergent national literature. The cultural significance attributed to this emerging national literature lay in the aesthetic presuppositions that informed

Zionist thinking. The call for a national revolution was frequently postulated as the need to transform the drabness of Diaspora life into ideals of beauty, zest for life, and national pride. Beauty, it was believed, was crucial to the formation of the new national culture coming into being at the time. Martin Buber perceived the nationalist movement as heralding a "new culture of beauty" among the Jews, while Markus Ehrenpreis noted that a cultural revival occurred as a result of "our revived desire to release beauty incarnate, our own self-beauty, which was imprisoned for thousands of years, and let it soar to previously inconceivable heights" (quoted in Almog 1982, 83–84).

What, precisely, was the nature of this beauty? How can it be gauged, and in what ways was it woven into and reflected in the newly forming national literature? These questions are addressed as we outline the emerging literary canon, whose very selection reflected a new concept of national beauty. The formation of the literary canon can be described as the result of political struggle, at times fierce and violent, between different concepts of literary practice. The literary struggle over the construction of modern Jewish Hebrew subjectivity was thus part of a larger cultural ideological struggle. One well-known locus of this debate may be observed in the confrontation that took place at the end of the nineteenth century between Ahad Haam (the pseudonym of Asher Ginzberg) and Micha Yosef Berdichevsky, concerning nothing less than the future of modern Hebrew literature. Their ideological differences set the parameters for the entire debate about the canon of modern national Hebrew literature at the time. We have a convenient date for the opening of the culture wars: in 1896, Ahad Haam wrote "Teudat HaShiloah," the manifesto, or statement of purpose, that opened the first issue of *HaShiloah*, a monthly journal edited by Ahad Haam. The opening statement and Berdichevsky's reaction to it provide us with two main literary categories. On the one hand is the literature of the center, the "major literature," which posits itself at the core of national culture. On the other hand is the "minor literature," the subversive literature, which undermines the values and concepts of the center. I first review the Ahad Haam–Berdichevshy debate and then turn to Galician literature as one case in which the dynamics of culture and political ideology can be clearly seen.

The Ideological Debate between Ahad Haam and Berdichevsky

Ahad Haam's primary claim in "Teudat HaShiloah" was that modern Hebrew literature must "instruct us in the ways of the inner world" of the people (Ahad Haam 1943, 126). Ahad Haam wanted to publish only material with explicitly Jewish content. Anything accepted for publication had to be directly relevant to the Jewish experience and concerned with the Jewish "national will for survival" and ways to secure it: "knowing ourselves, understanding our lives and wisely molding our future" (127). Ahad Haam had no doubts whatsoever about what the moral purpose of modern Hebrew literature should be; his positivist views led him to believe that its most significant contribution lay in "arousing our national considerations and expanding our knowledge thereof" (127). Worthwhile literary work was expected to extend the knowledge and understanding of the Jewish people. What he wanted were "good stories from the past or present of our people that provide a faithful portrait of our conditions in various times and places" (127). Accordingly, Ahad Haam had little regard for belletristic writing. Although he did not categorically reject such writing, he did consider it frivolous and contended that it should be set aside until the plight of the nation had been adequately settled.

> Yet even a work of art conveying nothing but its own beauty, arousing emotions for the sake of pleasure only, even such works of art must be valued alongside the intellectual things in life; but in *our present circumstances*, we feel that our feeble literature should not disperse its limited strength on such works, lest there be more urgent matters that require attention. For this very reason you will not find many poems in this issue. After all, most poets no longer follow in the footsteps of Yehuda Leib Gordon, who tried to combine in his poetry reflections on our various needs in life. And leave poesy per se, that overflow of emotions about the wonder of nature and the pleasures of love, etc., to those pursuing the languages of the world, for they will surely find enough of it. (127–28, my emphasis)

Addressing his readers in the first-person plural, Ahad Haam represented the collective community and exploited the literary and editorial options open to him accordingly. Firmly embedded in a positivist concept of the nation as a historically conditioned, organic entity, he believed that the national spirit prevails throughout history and that its lasting manifestations assume the form of a "national will for survival." As a biological phenomenon, he believed the national spirit would guarantee Jewish survival, in much the same way that religion had in the past. Given the large-scale historical changes in Europe, it was now up to the national will or spirit to ensure the survival of the Jews by establishing a contemporary, secular national culture and introducing it into Jewish Palestine by means of a spiritual center that would both create a new sense of cultural cohesion and meet the spiritual requirements of the emergent national culture. In the shift from the notion of shared territory to that of a spiritual center as the prerequisite for the Jewish nation, some of the deep conceptual differences between Ahad Haam's cultural nationalism and Berdichevsky's more radical Zionist stand can be seen.

These differences were clearly expressed in the second issue of *HaShiloah*, which contained a response by Berdichevsky (who was then coeditor with Ahad Haam) to Ahad Haam's manifesto. Most pointedly, Berdichevsky protested against Ahad Haam's distinction between Jewish and universal values and against the singularity ascribed to the Jewish Diaspora, which he believed subjugated aesthetic norms to pragmatic moral and social collective norms. Against Ahad Haam's collectivist approach, Berdichevsky regarded the individual as a universal entity. He wished to replace Ahad Haam's positivism about the Jewish national spirit with the vigor of romantic vitalism. Berdichevsky chided Ahad Haam, "You are, indeed, a serious thinker, Mr. Ahad Haam! Which is precisely why you make light of poesy, for you fail to discern its value to man or nation, just as you fail to note that a nation's survival is grounded in its poetry more than in its thinking" (Berdichevsky 1960, 155).

Part of Ahad Haam's positivism was his belief that the "national will for survival" was a hard fact, given in history, while Berdichevsky clearly distinguished between historical events and their subsequent reconstruction: "Our heritage is a burden and we, the last of the Jews and the first of the new Hebrews, must now construct a new nationhood for ourselves" (Berdichevsky 1960, 30). Thus, when Ahad Haam declared that *HaShiloah* would steer clear of aestheticism, he was conveying the desire to conserve Jewish intellectual energies rather than squander them on belletristic writing. Berdichevsky, in contrast, believed that the fact that Jews had failed to master such literature did not necessarily justify ignoring this mode of writing; neither did it condone distinguishing so unequivocally between Jewish requirements and universal needs: "Indeed, we have too few literary works! And the few there are should no longer be attributed to our founding writers exclusively, so do not force us to place Judaism on one side and mankind on the other!" (Berdichevsky 1960, 127).

Reassessing the polemic in terms of representations of power reveals that Ahad Haam believed will and desire were closely linked to the practical availability of options and to the nation's ability. Berdichevsky, however, keenly distinguished between the capacity to do something and the desire and need to do so. To him, as an antipositivist, these were distinct, independent conceptual categories. Hence, he was able to reverse the hierarchy proposed by Ahad Haam and subordinate ability to need: "when people feel a need for something it means they have the ability to obtain it, now or in the future" (Berdichevsky 1960, 157). Nonetheless, in a response to Berdichevsky, Ahad Haam reiterated the positivist subordination of "need" (*zoreh*) to "ability" (*yeholet*): "There is little doubt that our people, like all others, has the need for all sorts of science and writing, even if these have nothing to do with Judaism. But as for the ability to nurture this need, we know that our literature comprises only lean ears of corn" (Ahad Haam 1943, 130–31). In response to charges by HaTzeeerim, a group of young intellectuals led by Berdichevsky who were attempting to redefine the future of modern Hebrew literature, Ahad Haam called for accepting the collectivist national stand, which for all intents and purposes reflected his own view as a member of a national minority. In the following statements, Ahad Haam links the weakness of national minorities with the need for a collective discourse:

> It appears that what I first conveyed in "Teudat HaShiloah" failed in its mission, for the younger generation perceives it as total "heresy" as far as "humanity" is concerned. "We wish immediately to belong to the Hebrew people, in one fell swoop, a shared genesis." "We need to site human enlightenment and its requirements on a par with our own history." "There is not enough room!"

"We want! We need!"—*But are we able?* Unfortunately this question is not being addressed by the younger generation, and cannot be asked, for it is not the kind of question our people generally ask about national matters (indeed, the people of Israel *do know how to inquire* into their ability when it comes to private affairs), which is why everything is about-face, we are panic-stricken, our aspirations coming and going, our work bearing no fruit, for the road between the lofty objective and limited action is always extremely long. (Ahad Haam 1943, 131; my emphases)

Whatever led Ahad Haam to protest "'We need!'—But are we able?" led Berdichevsky similarly to conclude that while "we *expect* the Hebrews to surpass everyone else, yet our capacity to do so is extremely limited" (1960, 41; my emphasis). Both Ahad Haam and Berdichevsky, however, accepted that in the context of the nationalist debate at the time, "need" and "desire" were no substitutes for "capacity" and "ability." But Ahad Haam sought the harmonious survival of a nation, while Berdichevsky was fueled by the apparently paradoxical historical circumstances of the Jews at the time. It was within the overall attempt to balance the "need" of the Jews in their present condition with their "ability" that Ahad Haam saw fit to banish belletristic writing from the emerging Hebrew national canon, for he was convinced that such works could always be read with profit in other languages or could even be translated. Berdichevsky, however, thought the newly emerging national canon should be grounded in emotive, belletristic writing. In the midst of this debate about national "needs" and "ability," Berdichevsky postulated an aesthetic concept that cast aspersions on the naturalism (which he refers to as "realism") prevalent in Hebrew literature at the time: "Realistic writers are convinced that poetry is meant to poeticize life, as it were, and to reveal its covert characteristics; they forget, however, that the very core of poetry lies in revealing the hidden" (1960, 154).

In an alternative to the naturalistic approach, Berdichevsky (and, as we will see, Yosef Haim Brenner) favored highlighting the plausible in representation (though he did not always follow his own advice in his writing), for he believed that precisely the play between the overt and the hidden would provide the political basis for their aesthetic perception. Furthermore, according to Berdichevsky, the apparent disparity between a nation's need for poetic–fictional and lyric representation and its ability to produce such writing did not have to be resolved immediately. This "torn heart" phase was thus perceived as a natural and necessary, even vital phase to be experienced by most young Jews; for realism, as already mentioned, itself embodied hidden forces of utopianism. In taking this anti-positivist approach, Berdichevsky believed that the discrepancy between "need" and "ability" would not lead to abandoning hopes for a national utopia. What could not be attained collectively could be accomplished, in a limited way, by the individual. In effect, it is the tenuousness of the national collective that imposes on the intellectual avant-garde, especially on a few particular writers, the central function of sustaining hope for the collective national objective:

> When it is asked: "Why doesn't our artistic writing include praise-worthy works of excellence?" We must reply: "Because in our lives we are misbegotten; yet life itself is misbegotten, for we have raised some pitiful writers. The shepherds are not without sheep, it is the sheep who are without shepherds." (Berdichevsky 1960, 155)

Relating solely to the yardstick of romantic vitalism, Berdichevsky was not really concerned with the potential benefits of realizing a national utopia. He was content with the presence of the ideal itself and with plentiful allusions to its desirability. Any resolution of the discrepancy between "need" and "ability" was thus contingent on his universalist concept of individuality:

> Is it any wonder that things seem so disrupted? Is it any wonder that we bemoan our sons who "tend other vineyards," finally leaving us one by one? . . . The existence of our nation, the very possibility of creating a nation must be based on encompassing a unity of individuals within an overall social framework and on their ability to merge into a common receptacle to be sustained throughout the ages. The nation will only become a reality when we cultivate an adequate spiritual and material climate for its artists and makers. . . .
> Let us mold the life of a single individual, and the rest will follow suit. (Berdichevsky 1960, 41)

Hence, Berdichevsky viewed the construction of a national Subject as contingent on the sovereignty of the single exceptional individual. This was illustrated most clearly in Berdichevsky's attack on

Ahad Haam, whereby he paradoxically formulated his idea of national identity, itself based on his most recent conception of the individual's exclusive authority. Indeed, in an essay titled "Contradiction and Construction," Berdichevsky stated that "there is no Israelite Hebrew thinking, there are only thinking Israelite's Hebrews." The historical consciousness underlying Berdichevsky's conception is that of an ambiguous, indecisive historical moment, marking concurrently the end of one era and the beginning of another. Since the historical moment itself cannot determine how it should best be understood, it is up to the individual inhabiting it to do so:

> All the basic conditions, both internal and external, which have determined our existence to date, have disintegrated. . . . And the fear in our hearts is real, for we are not on firm footing regarding our next move—and we are now facing two worlds in collision: to be or no longer to be! To be the last of the Jews or the first of the new Hebrews. (Berdichevsky 1960, 29)

In another essay, Berdichevsky added: "If I might say something about the beliefs and values handed down to me by my forefathers, I must be free to choose to appropriate or entirely reject them, without severing the ties between myself and my people" (38). This paradoxical situation also underlies the dilemma of national identity signified by the doctrine of the "torn heart," another reference to the opposition between universalism and national particularism. The persuasiveness of this dilemma and its implicit authority emerge from the fundamental ambivalence embodied in the notion of "internal rupture," which merges even as it distinguishes between notions such as apportionment and fusion, the particular and the general, the Jew and the Gentile. Even as he is positioned within this ambivalence, however, Berdichevsky repeatedly undermines the collectivist identity of the national Subject. Instead of the collective authority that typically signifies that a minority national consciousness has come to terms with its marginality and other limitations, the national Subject Berdichevsky chose to construct subjugated the general to the private, and in so doing accorded universal authority to a particular form of nationalism.

Jewish Writers in Galicia—The Dispute

Toward the end of 1908, Yosef Haim Brenner left London and made his way to the Eastern European region of Galicia. By then a well-known writer throughout the Jewish Hebrew-speaking world, Brenner had just ended a brief yet significant chapter in his career, during which he set up an extensive program of literary activities in London (Bakun 1975; 1990). Returning to the Galician capital Lvov early in February 1908, where he remained for about a year before setting out for Eretz Israel, Brenner soon became involved in the local literary scene. Before long, local Galician writers sought his comments and views, which were subsequently published in the local literary periodicals.

The Hebrew-speaking Jewish center in Galicia was, at the time, at the beginning of a revitalization. Throughout the Jewish enlightenment, Galicia was an important center of Hebrew literary activity, yet a significant decline in its cultural and literary practices took place toward the end of the period, relegating the region to the cultural periphery, especially with regard to the emergent corpus of Hebrew literature. Galician writers had often since been treated with scorn and derision, and Galicia's cultural production throughout most of the nineteenth century was generally regarded as inferior. Toward the end of the nineteenth and early in the twentieth century, however, the region began to show signs of revival and was reinstated as an operative center of Jewish culture. The rise of Zionism and its attendant Hebrew culture began to restimulate cultural life in Galicia, especially in the realm of literary activity. Veteran and young writers alike, including Yitzhak Fernhoff, Reuven Fahan, Avraham Levensrat, Asher Barash, Avraham Ben-Yitzhak (Sonne), and S. Y. Agnon, had published their works in local Galician literary journals, especially in *HaMitzpeh*, which was under the editorship of S. M. Lazar. Occasionally some of these writers were lucky enough to have their works printed in major Hebrew monthly journals published in other, more prominent centers. "Beware the Galicians," cautioned Galician critic Rabbi Benyamin in an essay published in 1909, foreshadowing the success of such reputable writers as S. Y. Agnon, master of modernist prose fiction, and Avraham Ben-Yitzhak (Sonne), master of modernist poetry.

All things being equal, a writer of Brenner's caliber was bound to make waves in Galicia, and indeed, before very long he became embroiled in a bitter literary dispute in which he launched a frontal attack on the entire body of Hebrew literature being produced in Galicia at the time. Focusing especially on works by Reuven Fahan and Yitzhak Fernhoff, Brenner ruthlessly denounced them. "Heaven protect our literature!" he cried. "This is nothing but idle banter and rubbish!" Brenner stated:

> Many Jews in Galicia have a command of the Hebrew language (in its practical sense); Galician Jews still seem to be strongly affiliated with Hebrew works from the past, . . . nevertheless, no literary work has been produced here for many years, and there is, to all intents and purposes, no Hebrew literature in Galicia at all! (Brenner 1985, vol. 3, 250–51)

While this diatribe attests to Brenner's contentiousness, it also urges us to inquire why he would take it on himself—being, after all, just a passing visitor—to attack so viciously writers whom he regarded as nonentities as far as literary competence was concerned. Moreover, Brenner was not the only literary figure to voice such criticisms, making one wonder why a group of reputable literary critics should bother to attack the Galician writers and their works if they considered the quality of the writing so unquestionably inferior.

What I here try to show is that, despite their negligibility in the eyes of the critics, the political stances and corresponding poetic resolutions manifest in the literary texts produced by the young Galicians genuinely jeopardized the hegemony of the emerging national, modern Hebrew literature. Regional Hebrew literature in Galicia at the time was thus significantly molded against the existing literary canon, that is, the corpus of new national literary works that comprised the standard literary yardstick for all modern Hebrew literature at the end of the nineteenth and the beginning of the twentieth century.

"Before the Elections," by Yitzhak Fernhoff

Among those works produced in Galicia that were attacked because, I believe, they formed the beginnings of an alternative literary canon was a collection of stories titled *MeAgadot HaHayim* (From the Legends of the Living), by Yitzhak Fernhoff (1908). Fernhoff was a prominent Hebrew writer active in Galicia toward the end of the nineteenth and the beginning of the twentieth century, who spent most of his time editing and publishing local literary productions. These included a series of *Sifrei Shaashuim* (Books of Amusements), followed by the periodicals *HaIvri HaHadash* (The New Hebrew) and *HaYarden* (The Jordan).

Generally speaking, universal suffrage had led to stormy debates within the Jewish community, as illustrated in Fernhoff's story "Lifney HaBehirot" (Before the Elections) (1908), written against the backdrop of the 1907 Austro-Hungarian general elections. The questions that arose related to the participation of Jews in the political arena and the modes of such possible participation. An extremely important political issue for Jews in Galicia at the time was whether they should be represented as part of a unified national party of the Jews of the Hapsburg Empire or as a separate political entity of Galician Jews. "Before the Elections" depicts and juxtaposes a number of Jewish characters representing a variety of political views: one character represents the radical Jewish nationalist position and argues for unconditional civil rights for the Jews; another is doubtful about how the Jews will conduct themselves as a national minority during the course of the elections. On the one hand is apprehension regarding any form of Jewish political activism that might increase the political weight of the assimilationists, while on the other hand is the religious, Orthodox position favoring a Christian candidate over an assimilationist or a Zionist one. Yet, toward the end of the debate, an "extremely skeptical pessimist" voices his opinion:

> Whom the Jews will vote for in heterogeneously populated areas I have no idea. They may vote for the nationalist [that is, for the Zionist], for the assimilationist, or for the Christian. Anything can happen. But as for the other quarter in this city—I have no doubts whatsoever that an antisemitic candidate will be elected. (Fernhoff 1908, 32)

And when asked what this view is grounded in, the pessimist replies: "Because *all* those living in this quarter are Jewish" (32).

This story clarifies the author's position. The pessimist is convinced that the Jews will inevitably act against their own interests. The underlying political assumption concerning this irony is unequivocal: the author dismisses the idea of rejecting the Diaspora and urges the Jews to take full advantage of their civil rights in the Diaspora. The question raised by the pessimist is structural rather than quantitative, that is, it has little to do with whether the Jews, wherever they might be, statistically constitute a minority or a majority. It pertains rather to the idea of Jewish political consciousness and how it may be structured. Is this the same consciousness generally ascribed to national minorities who, fully aware of their political weaknesses, are yet intent on fully realizing their civil political rights? Or is it the consciousness of a statistical minority that has already relinquished its political potential, either out of sheer indifference or as a result of a radical Zionist stance that calls for the rejection of the Diaspora? The paradoxical formulation of the latter point underscores the fact that the political dilemma facing Galician Jews at the time was more a matter of frame of mind than of numbers and percentages of Jews in different districts.

In this story, Fernhoff grants political legitimacy to a Jewish political activism that extends beyond the act of a single individual, in the name of collective rights for a national minority in the Diaspora. For Brenner and his fellow critics, who totally rejected a Jewish presence in the Diaspora, the subversive component in Fernhoff's position lay precisely in its potential relevance for Zionists and had little or nothing to do with the anti-Zionists or a-Zionists. Pointedly addressing the cultural and political implications of Zionist participation in the general elections for the Austro-Hungarian parliament, "Before the Elections" implies a relatively low commitment to the extreme, anti-Diaspora Zionist position. This suggests that, in Galicia, the more extreme version of Zionism was gradually being incorporated into what was then becoming known, in Zionist political discourse, as "laboring for the present." Laboring for the present stressed an evolutionary process of bringing Zionism to fruition, acknowledging the needs of the Jews while they still lived in Diaspora and that nothing was expected to be resolved immediately or cataclysmically.

Brenner's and Berdichevsky's political critique of the Galician option of Jews surviving by fashioning themselves into a "national minority" paved the way for their cultural critique. Following the well-known formulation of Johann Gottfried Herder, the essential prerequisite for all modern discourse on national identity became the relation between a national language and a national territory. According to Berdichevsky, "a spiritual and material culture, self-nationalized, cannot exist without the fundamental national territorial claim to land, or without a socially- and historically-material reservoir from which both spirit and matter can be refreshed" (1960, 62). Similarly, Brenner pointed out that the inadequacy of Galician literature stemmed primarily from its lack of territory, its "landlessness," as he put it (Brenner [1908] 1985, vol. 3, 223).

Nonetheless, both Brenner and Berdichevsky present their political critique largely as an aesthetic critique, in which their aesthetic standards are determined a priori. They thus *appear* to be divorced from any political interests that may have been predicated on the historically specific political struggle they were fighting. By historically relocating these aesthetic standards, however, we may be able to uncover some of their implicit political uses at the time.

From the Karaite Lives, by Reuven Fahan

A stance similar to Fernhoff's may be noted in several narrative texts written by Reuven Fahan (1908) and appearing in *Mehayei HaKaraim* (From the Karaite Lives), a form of ethnographic prose. These stories address the lifestyles of the Karaite community in Galicia. Having lived in Galicia since the sixteenth century, toward the middle of the nineteenth century the Karaites obtained full civil rights throughout Russia. Yet Fahan refers to the Karaites in these narratives primarily by evoking a sense of their frailty as a disappearing ethnic minority. For instance, one story titled "Ever Meduldal" (Limp Organ) focuses on Kazimir Shmuelowitz, a converted Karaite who rises to prominence in Polish society (Fahan 1908, 48–51). Oscillating between the two worlds, Kazimir Shmuelowitz appears to be completely at home among the Poles yet never seems to feel that he has betrayed his own people. He is thus able to maintain ties with his family by purchasing a house for his father "so that he himself would always be one of them, part-owner of the property along Karaite Road, and so his mother would know that the ties between them could never really be severed" (50). Interestingly, this "territorial" solution to Kazimir's ambivalent standing is textualized in standard Zionist terminology, as the house, for instance, is referred to as *nahalat haavot*, "the land of the forefathers" (51).

The Karaites themselves view Kazimir's move favorably; as the narrator adds when reporting the news, they "display feelings generally articulated by a relatively 'powerless' community observing one of its proselytized members with pride—for he does not bear signs of being a traitor" (51). The Karaites thereby seem to have come to terms with their vulnerability as an ethnic minority.

Fahan's decision to recount this tale of the Karaite Other from a distinctly Jewish perspective reveals something of the Jews' sense of their own patronage (Feitelson 1970, 156) and represents the Jewish minority as the more powerful of the two minority communities. At the same time, if this portrayal is in any way indicative of the Jews' attitude toward the Karaites, it probably suggests Fahan's support for a Jewish national minority in the Diaspora. By way of deduction, then, the text urges the historical Hebrew reader to come to terms with the historical reality of the Jews, whose existence as a national minority in the Diaspora is presented here as a feasible option for Jews at the turn of the century. Fahan's view, in short, is not far removed from those who believed in "laboring for the present."

"Sheifa LaHutz" (Reaching for the Outside), another story in Fahan's collection, presents a rather different Karaite case (Fahan 1908, 52–57). Here the protagonist betrays his original Karaite identity. Having suffered from lack of identity as a child—being neither Jewish nor Christian—he is later proselytized into Christianity, yet resorts to his Karaite origins in order to secure a legal career. Given the prevalence of Polish antisemitism, not admitting one's Jewish descent was an advantage, and the said protagonist is finally able to secure a court position. Unlike the empathy evoked in "Limp Organ" toward the Karaite who chooses to withdraw from his own community, this story criticizes how this Karaite uses his ethnic identity for personal gain yet renounces his immediate family and community at large. The author seems to be implying here that despite the Karaite community's ostensible powerlessness, the Karaite protagonist in question should not have forsaken his birthright. Adopting an ambivalent stand, the author suggests that even if exploiting one's status as an outsider can be excused, disregarding the commitment to his or her powerless minority community cannot be equally excused. Displaying different attitudes toward each Karaite, the author seems to be urging Karaites to come to terms with their position as members of disadvantaged minorities in alien surroundings.

Zionism and the Canonization of a National Literature

Literary canonization was integral to the establishment of the ideological consensus of modern nationalism (Parush 1992, 110–11). Constructing a national literary consciousness among the Jews took place concurrently on several fronts. In the overall endeavor, Haim Nahman Bialik was to play a major role, yet perhaps even more central were Brenner and Berdichevsky, who systematically precipitated the construction of a Hebrew literature as a corpus of modern national literature. In the early years of the twentieth century, Brenner and Berdichevsky, renowned writers, critics, and readers, came to function as standard-bearers of literary taste. Once their position as key cultural agents was acknowledged, both their professional and personal relationships were enhanced. The affinity between the two writer-critics was reflected in their agreement over the boundaries determining the emergent literary canon.

Viewing Galicia's marginal writers from today's perspective allows us to reassess the cultural significance of writers and literary works that have been excluded from the canon of modern Hebrew literature and relegated to its edges. This act can be perceived as an attempted redress for the historical process of marginalization and a recuperation of texts within the dynamics of a modern Hebrew literature that at the time was in the process of shaping a new Jewish national identity. By reinterpreting formerly suppressed literary practices, we hope to extend the range of past literary options. We also hope to describe what these texts have imparted to us as a range of historically determined and politically selected literary products, and not as an accumulation of selected and given, authorized texts. Pointing out what mechanisms led certain leading agents to exclude particular texts from the canon entails uncovering the cultural and material circumstances in which these texts were produced and is bound to expose clashes of interests and power struggles between the parties involved. This form of criticism was advocated by Walter Benjamin when he described the task of the critical materialist historian as "brushing history against the grain" (Benjamin 1969, 259–62) of official historical writing, which, by its very nature, reduces and limits the possibilities available and constricts them within a linear and unified official historical progression from the national past to the present (see Anderson 1991, 161–62).

The primary issue on the agenda of those who constructed the emergent modern Hebrew canon was the formation of a Hebrew narrative that a wide public would regard as paradigmatic and "naturally" true. As noted by the feminist critic Lillian Robinson, the issue of a literary canon in general was considered a gentlemen's agreement, secured by an elite to whom it was valuable and was not really perceived as a vehicle of oppression (Robinson 1989, 572). Accordingly, many cultural practices in the hegemonic culture shape standard national Subjects, which are perceived as perfectly natural, commonplace products of literary writing. The practice of historiography, for instance, is central to constructing the canon of a national literature. Throughout the "revival" era, Hebrew literary historiography maintained a systematic linearity, which, over the years, coincided with a more or less stable image of the standard national Subject. At the same time, historical writing removed from its index those who cast aspersions on the hegemonic version of the Zionist canon. Yet, as I hope to show, this does not imply that the criteria determining the inclusion or exclusion of an author in the canon are contingent on a writer's overt political stance. Constructing a standard Subject has more to do with the representation of a desirable image for human existence, one that prescribes guidelines and values within the context of the hegemonic culture.

The linear progression of modern Hebrew literary historiography is predominantly grounded in the concept of "Revival Literature"—*Sifrut HaTehiya*—which integrates the idea of a literary revival with a national renaissance. The reversal in Hebrew culture that took place at the advent of modern Jewish nationalism is almost always marked by the historical writing known as "Storms in the Negev," which followed the 1883 pogroms that so abruptly dashed the "enlightened" hopes of Eastern European Jewish intellectuals for a Jewish existence in the Diaspora (e.g., Katz 1979, 3–12). The shift from "Enlightenment Literature"—*Sifrut HaHaskala*—to modern Hebrew literature is thus located around the end of the 1880s and the beginning of the 1890s, and modern Hebrew literature is considered, often by some of its own producers, to have been contingent on the historical events of the 1880s (Shaked 1977, 25).

A Universalist Canon versus Regional Literature

As I have previously suggested, the conception of a national literature is generally based on a presupposed yet constructed, desirable national Subject. If we perceive a national literature as a form of historical description based on a constructed image of subjectivity and reality, rather than as a natural, inherent narrative, we can "isolate" the components of the historiographical description and examine its delimiting power structures. The aesthetic notion underpinning most Western hegemonic views of a national literature can be referred to as universalist; and this universalism locates the point of departure for the construction of the national collective in the free individual. According to the universalist view, the free individual is bound to undergo the experience of a national Subject during the course of building a new nation. The Western nationalist ideology on which this view is based evolved in the wake of the Western Enlightenment. Relocating the modern national Subject within a new national framework, Western national ideology highlights the individual's constituency as a free and equal individual within the national collective. This collective is perceived as a "typical" national collective, no different from any other (Talmon 1982, 14). "The nationalist idea," claimed Brenner in the early twentieth century, "is only important insofar as it renders us free, proud, sure, rich in spirit, and creative" (Brenner [1908] 1985, vol. 3, 234). The literary representation of universality, however, must be realized by representing individuals: "Precisely those who experienced 'nationalism,'" wrote Brenner, distinguishing between Hebrew maskilic literature of the nineteenth century and that of the era of national revival, "will sing unto their people the song of the Hebrew 'individual,' praise and protect the individual" (vol. 4, 1403–4).

Hence, it is clear, for example, why the political, anti-Zionist stance of writer and literary critic David Frishman did not exclude nationalist literature from the canon but functioned centrally in his own realm of activity, thereby contributing to shaping the canon of modern Hebrew literature (Parush 1992, 10–11). To be sure, Frishman was extremely negative about the prospects of the Zionist movement as a political movement that would cure the Jewish people's afflictions. Yet, at the same time, where the standard Subject was concerned, his position was not very far removed from that of Berdichevsky and Brenner; for he, too, held collective Jewish redemption to be contingent on the spiritual redemption of the Jewish individual (Parush 1992, 11–12, 17–43, passim).

The sort of universality mentioned above, which is embodied in the concept of a national Subject, occurs regularly in the rhetoric of what Antonio Gramsci (1971) has identified as the "ethical state." The idea of the ethical state is represented, first and foremost, in a cultural consensus regarding the universal status of hegemonic institutions, which are perceived as natural and universal bodies through which mutually exclusive interests are reconciled. Issuing from these hegemonic institutions is a "moral gaze" that claims the right to judge, as it were, from the standpoint of "archetypal man." Literary products were a critical component of Western national consciousness because the aesthetic experience authorizes us to control the archetypal standpoint almost as though it were unmediated. Authors, then, come to be considered as representative, and literary works are read as testimonials of typical human experiences. These authors generally do not regard this type of ethical universalism as personal, biographical experience but rather as a manifestation of basic human desires and values. The authors are hence perceived as both representative and canonical (Lloyd 1987, 20). In this way, a historically determined approach to nationalist ideologies is shaped by a range of universal values linking the particular to a transcendental aesthetic reality. To this end is evoked a range of imagined, constructed attributes, traditionally shared in standard nationalist reality, whose very authority derives from its universality. These shared attributes provide the spectator/reader with a fixed range of metahistorical criteria by means of which specific moments in reality can be evaluated (Gramsci 1971,

240–41, 258–59, 261–63; Forgacs 1993, 177–90; Hall 1986, 5–25; Lloyd 1993, 9).

It is the spectator/reader's vision of the "ethical state" that enables us to posit the opposition between canonical and noncanonical literature as a struggle between what Gilles Deleuze and Félix Guattari have named "major" and "minor" literature (1986, 16–27). The power of major literature is grounded in the "common property," representing shared human possessions (which effectively embody essential human desires), and the universality of human nature. Because the representation of common human nature is implicitly "moral," major literary works belonging to the national majority claim that they are "disinterested." As David Lloyd (1987) has shown, the realm of the aesthetic in which a major literature is sited is thereby linked to the moral transcendence of political, racial, and class differences. It should, however, be noted that the hegemony of major literary works can be determined by both "disinterestedness" and overt commitment. Grounded in the concept of universality, major literature acquires its own moral legitimacy while imposing a dominant ethnocentric ideology (imperialism, in Western history). Typically, minor literature is conceived as a literature seeking to contest and to overthrow the canon and its values. Despite its attempts to violate the canon, minor literature can never fully appropriate features that are central to canonical literature; it thus always remains on the edges, or margins (Lloyd 1987, 20).

Literary works produced by a minority, especially by a national minority, can purport to be minor literature even as they pose as a majority literature, seeking to obscure group differences of race, nationality, and gender. Minor literature, too, seeks to undermine prevailing aesthetic criteria and to propose an alternative aesthetic. Thus, at times, minor literature will find itself in a condition of what the literary critic Myra Jehlen, in speaking about women's literature, calls the paradox of women writers—namely, being "torn between defending the quality of their discoveries and radically redefining literary quality itself" (Jehlen 1981, 592). This paradox may ultimately be resolved only if it is perceived in terms of a historically determined power struggle.

In the case of Galician literature, it would appear that Fahan's and Fernhoff's valorous attempts to propose an alternative to the mainstream Zionist canon were followed up not by a revision of mainstream aesthetic criteria but rather by the unequivocal denial of a place in the canon for most of the Galicians. Only years later, after Reuven Fahan died in the Holocaust (Fernhoff having died just before), did these Galicians become symbols of Judaism destroyed and undergo reassessment by proponents of the canon. Yet, for all the compassion they eventually evoked (Sadan 1964, 118–29) as tokens of a forgotten culture (Fernhoff 1952), they were finally excluded from the aesthetic arena, and the mainstream canon was reinforced.

Unlike major literature, which strives to construct a Subject in possession of autonomous moral identity, minor literature is typically faced with the ongoing task of negation. Whereas in a novel embedded in major literature the narrative continuum will peak when a plot is realized or destroyed by desire, in minor literary works, such as Franz Kafka's *The Castle*, the consummation of desire is always deferred. K.'s identity as quantity surveyor is always cast in question, and he is never really equal to the other characters in the Castle. Subsequently, he unremittingly, yet to no avail, strives for a recognition, which he hopes might grant him a clear-cut role in society (Lloyd 1987, 21).

The "minor literature" of Fahan, too, addresses the social and national identities of the Karaites yet finally never clearly delineates or accounts for these identities. Writers and readers of major literature consider the narrative of minor literature to be unproductive, for it does not bring to fruition the desired collective objective. Indeed, radical Zionist criticism views the Karaites as laboriously striving toward a purposeless and unethical end. And yet we may see this as a function of Fahan being charged with having "sinned" simply because he dared to empathize with the Karaites and because he tried to represent their collective narrative in terms similar to the Jewish national one. Fahan's narrator is careful not to abrogate the frailty of the Karaite presence in the Diaspora; he thus authorizes Jewish survival in the Diaspora and so violates a sacred principle of Zionism. In contradistinction, Berdichevsky and Brenner formulate narratives that climax with the construction of the individual Subject as a force to be reckoned with. "What struck me more than anything," Berdichevsky wrote to Brenner in February 1908, after reading Brenner's play *MeEver LaGvulin* (Beyond the Crossroad), "was that your hero's sorrow is not what humbles him, nor his cry for pity following his distress and suffering, but rather the pride he manages to muster" (Berdichevsky and Brenner 1984, 38).

The Majority as a National Minority

The radical tendency toward obliterating Jewish existence in the Diaspora led to reconceptualizing the most desirable future for Jewish survival. The mode of Jewish existence in the early twentieth century, as a national minority in the Diaspora, was formulated in standard utopian terms of a national majority. This thrust, which presents a minority as a national majority, led to the representation of Zionism as the political avant-garde of the Jewish people. The concept of a national minority nestled among the nations of the world, crystallizing its political thinking and strategies in terms of a national majority, became part of the internal politics of Jewish life. The concept evolved as part of a broader internal nationalist avant-garde thrust that awarded the Zionists, a statistical minority among the Jews of Europe, the unusual status of trailblazers for the entire Jewish population of Europe solely on the strength of their inner convictions. In effect, one might be expected to view the entire concept of "Zionism as avant-garde" as totally opposed to notions of Jews as minority communities remaining in Europe and "laboring in the present" (Almog 1987, 206).

Indeed, the perception of Zionism as an avant-garde movement proved greatly advantageous to Theodor Herzl and to other adherents of political Zionism who sought to reconcile the enormity of movement's transnational mission, soon to be realized, with the fact that only a minority of Jews were Zionist flag bearers. "Zionism," claimed Herzl, "is not a party, for it encompasses all the parties in the nation's life. Zionism is the Jewish nation-in-the-making" (Herzl 1897, quoted in Almog 1987, 137). Zionists frequently attempted to ground the avant-garde position in history, as in the case of Max Nordau, who presented himself as one of Gideon's three hundred warriors (Herzl 1897, quoted in Almog 1987, 137).

Knowingly or not, Brenner and Berdichevsky embraced the avant-garde approach to Zionism, and by the end of the century they had provided a canonical framework for several versions of a universally normative national literature. Brenner perceived the utopian slant of modern Hebrew literary production as essential to its future development. Moreover, he noted in an article written during his stay in Galicia that the local writers did not conform to the norms of "heroic literature" ("in spite of everything"), a literary model that became the basic foundation of Gershon Shaked's project of the history of modern Hebrew fiction (Shaked 1977, 32–34). Therefore, for Brenner, the products of Galician writers could not really be considered literature in the sense of an everlasting building, assembled brick by brick over generations; a self-generative entity progressing of its own accord, drawing new, revitalizing strength from its many readers:

> But here are a number of gifted Hebrew writers who carry the light of the Lord in their hearts, and simply write regardless . . . deeply-spirited writers, who seek to state their views regardless, and whose literary circumstances make them appear like flies trying to climb up a flat, slippery pane of glass—there have always been precious few such writers among us, yet there are still some. (Brenner [1908] 1985, vol. 3, 237)

A rather different attitude was adopted by Reuven Fahan, Yitzhak Fernhoff, and their young Galician colleagues, who sanctioned the idea of a local rather than a universal literature and preferred not to take a clear-cut stand on the Diaspora dilemma and the demand for a Jewish nation with its own history, language, and territory. Against the universalist views of the canonizers, who sought to ground nationalist norms in individual rights, those in favor of regional or local autonomy and some of those who privileged "laboring in the present" wished to secure the political rights of the Jewish community and its status as a national minority.

The Politics of Laboring in the Present

Fernhoff's and Fahan's works entered an arena fraught with dissension about the future of modern Hebrew literature. Within the overall context of Zionist politics at the time, some of the most heated debates on this matter took place shortly after the Helsingfors Convention, held in Russia in 1906, which legitimated the Zionist policy of "laboring in the present" and extended the concept of national responsibility to include the right to a Jewish life in the Diaspora alongside demands for "laboring for the future" of Eretz Israel (Almog 1987, 177–237). While the "catastrophic" view of Zionism regarded a one-time, permanent solution as mandatory, the view promoting laboring in the present sought a gradual series of evolutionary steps toward Zionist goals.

From the year 1900, the notion of Zionism as a "political strategy" began to appear. According to this position, the dissolution of the Diaspora was limited by major historical constraints. Members of the Zionist movement were urged to reconsider their objectives in view of the movement's newly conceived transitional role, which would eventually bring about the dispersion of the Diaspora. Aware that this might be a rather lengthy process, certain parties began to consider the strategy of Zionists becoming politically active in their respective countries of residence. Galicia, which at the time belonged to the multinational Hapsburg Empire, had an extremely pluralistic population, comprised of people with many different national identities. Jews in the Hapsburg Empire were awarded civil rights in 1868 and subsequently were allowed to vote. While this move led to an increased number of assimilated Jews, it also strengthened support for the Zionist movement.

The new Austrian government that was founded in 1906 elicited hopes for democratization and inspired new directions within the existing framework of the Zionist organization. For example, Jews who were stuck between the Poles and the Ukrainians were forced to attempt to acquire some kind of political autonomy. At the Zionist Conference held in Kraków in July 1906, there were demands for a party that would pursue "political structures for the Jews within the Austrian monarchy which would protect their national, cultural, and political rights" (Gelber 1958, 526). Those Zionists who countered this initiative grounded their views in the overall rejection of the Diaspora as even a partial solution for the Jews. Assimilationists, too, were highly critical of the demand for regional autonomy, choosing rather to fight it to the death. Yet, unlike the 1906 Helsingfors Convention, where similar decisions were taken on rights for Jews as a national minority and where the importance of laboring in the present while living in the Diaspora was weakly acknowledged, the Zionist conference in Kraków had some real political consequences. Most important was that the support for the regional autonomy of the Jewish national minority was established and continued to grow (Gelber 1958, 522–28). And to the dismay of the Zionist Executive (under its president David Wolfson), Galician Zionism, which had never really enjoyed much attention, began to flourish independently of the Vienna Zionist center (530–50).

Brenner arrived in Galicia shortly before a struggle between the Zionists and the assimilationists took place, in which the former gained the upper hand. For example, in numerous communities the Zionists obtained the decisive vote on issues of Jewish education. This followed a disagreement between the two camps concerning the marked wave of antisemitism in the educational system at the time and the assimilationists' refusal to take a definitive stand on Jewish education (Gelber 1958, 165). This struggle peaked during the 1907 general elections, when the Zionists won a most impressive number of electoral votes among the Jews.

Works by Fernhoff and Fahan were thus produced in a specific context of Austrian Zionist culture, which had a firm tradition of laboring in the present (Almog 1987, 217). Austrian Zionism was concerned with the economic prosperity of the Jews in the Diaspora and desired to prepare them, culturally and mentally, for life in Jewish Palestine. Some of these Zionists were not merely committed to recruiting financial resources for future immigration to Eretz Israel but sought to buttress Jewish life in the Diaspora economically and to secure political rights for the Diaspora Jews as well. Thus, laboring in the present had practical consequences in the form of programs designed to ensure autonomous Jewish life in the Diaspora (Dubnov 1937, 52–82). These programs rested on the assumption that Jewish existence in the Diaspora as a national minority was wholly legitimate. This is why the Jews could not be satisfied with equal civil rights as individual citizens in their host countries but sought further to secure their identities as distinctive groups. The Austro-Hungarian electorate, especially the Austrian Socialists, supported the idea of national autonomy for communities sharing a common cultural identity (Talmon 1982, 173–212). Their support was based on the prevalent notion that the multicultural population of the Hapsburg Empire would exist only as long as the individual could be perceived as part of a national minority. The issue of a separate Jewish territory was clearly not of great significance.

Berdichevsky on Fahan

Berdichevsky's response to Fahan's book *Mehayei HaKaraim* (From the Karaite Lives) was published in 1908 in *HaOlam*, the organ of the Zionist movement (Berdichevsky 1960, 172–73). Berdichevsky had a particular aversion to the book, due to the way in which it endorsed "laboring in the present" by acknowledging and legitimating Jewish existence in the Diaspora. He commented that Fahan's patronizing tone toward the Karaites in this collection of stories was a form of self-glorification characteristic of Diaspora Jews, intended to distract them from the deep despair in which they were engulfed. The narrator, according to Berdichevsky,

> [is introduced] as a Rabbinite [Orthodox Jew] who supervises the Karaite temple and proceeds to condemn, condemn more than narrate, forgetting that we ourselves are not firmly situated, and that we ourselves are people of a Diaspora. . . . The types the narrator presents to us, with their miserable minds and experiences, may as well be affiliated to Rav Ashi . . . rather than to Anan [founding Karaite]. (Berdichevsky 1960, 173)

Berdichevsky indicted Fahan for setting up a false opposition between Rabbinite and Karaite Jews. Because he saw Jewish life in the Diaspora as quite undesirable, Berdichevsky believed that the Galician Jews had chosen to construct this fictional opposition as a means of displacement. Instead of facing their own bitter plight and admitting their own position of weakness, they projected their misery onto the Karaites' even more miserable predicament, thereby softening the harshness of their own fate. Elsewhere, in his article "Adama" (Territory), Berdichevsky alluded directly to supporters of Jewish autonomy in the Diaspora. Just as he regarded the literary and political output of Galician Jewry as flawed, he was critical of the Austro-Hungarian supporters of autonomy. He faulted them for having relinquished the territorial imperative that he thought was mandatory for establishing a national identity (Berdichevsky 1960, 62–63).

Berdichevsky's rather too conspicuous bias reveals, however, that Fahan and Fernhoff were actually proposing an alternative Zionist vision, one that included an acceptance of the Diaspora. As the leading voices of modern Hebrew literature at the time, Brenner and Berdichevsky were, it seems, prescriptive spokesmen for the canonical literary center, which itself represented a national community modeled largely on the modern sovereign nation and autonomous moral Subject. This fully rounded character was designed to arouse in its readers, themselves members of an "imagined" nation, feelings of identification based on universal attributes that presumably were shared by themselves and the character(s) portrayed.

In the historical context of early twentieth-century Hebrew culture, this notion of a minority as a national majority held pride of place. On the one hand, modern Hebrew literature was grappling with a self-image that reflected its own frailty (Miron 1987, 23–56). On the other hand, alongside the Zionist movement there evolved a flurry of cultural and literary activity that had a powerful imaginative, utopic dimension. For instance, the leading Hebrew literary journal, *HaShiloah,* was founded in 1896, one year before the establishment of the Zionist organization and the first Zionist congress in Basel. As mentioned earlier, the alternative Galician writers proposed was altogether more compatible than a focus on the misery of the Diaspora with the emergent viewpoint of the national Jewish minority in the Diaspora. This Jewish ethnic minority was busy fighting for its autonomy against the multinational backdrop of the Hapsburg Empire and staunchly opposed the Zionist demand for a sovereign, territorial nationalist entity (Talmon 1982, 173–77). The rift between local Galician writers and leading literary figures such as Brenner and his colleagues began to grow, and their political differences were finally manifested in aesthetic and poetic terms. The writers Brenner accused of having produced noncanonical, unaesthetic texts were in fact following the rules of an alternative aesthetic, which, under the historical circumstances of Hebrew literature at the beginning of the twentieth century, could be described as subversive, seeking as it did to undermine the hegemony of the emerging national culture.

Majority versus Minority and Fiction versus Documentation

From the outset, Brenner considered Galician Zionism to be provincial (Sadan 1967, 133). He perceived it as limited in Zionist conviction, as a consequence of the Galicians' constricted mental and spiritual abilities. Brenner also believed that the Galicians had little, if any, capacity for literary writing. And what little they had was flawed, for it shaped inadequate Jewish social structures (Brenner 1985a, 275–76; 1985, vol. 1, 251).

When Brenner addressed Fahan's *From the Karaite Lives*, he expressed rage at Fahan's artistic presumptuousness, that is, at his "very pretension of being artist." He did not deem Fahan's text worthy of being called literature and suggested that it should rather be relegated to newspaper publications and placed alongside journalistic correspondence. Brenner emphasized the problematic status of Fahan's book as a work of art and, in effect, worked to remove it from the canon of Hebrew literature. The main reason for exclusion lay in its apparently dubious generic affiliation, implied by the book's subtitle, *Types and Illustrations*:

> It may indeed have been inconsequential for our writer here to pen lengthy correspondence to "The World" about the way he sees life in the Karaite quarter, which was no doubt extremely interesting: laws of purity and profanity, sitting in the dark on the Sabbath, etc., etc.,—No! His subtitle, "Types and Illustrations" . . . And did not Zangwill describe the lives of children in the Ghetto, London Jews, so why shouldn't Reuven Fahan compose "Types and Illustrations" from lives of the Karaites? And lest you ask: where are the "Lives of Karaites"—do the Karaites live a secluded existence, an independent economic life, a life in which they construct spiritual categories of their own, a life which can determine its own value and significance? (Brenner 1985, vol. 3, 253)

Brenner thus delegitimated Fahan's canonical status, stipulating that in order for a text to be incorporated into the literary canon, it must portray a complete lifestyle experience, possessing a distinctiveness of its own. More aptly, Brenner's nationalist patterns of thinking called for a distinctive lifestyle whose particular attributes could readily be represented in universalist terms. Thus, we see here how the success or failure of the work to transform particular human traits into universal ones became the criterion through which Brenner distinguished among documentary representation, journalistic writing, and literary fictional representation.

The distinction between realistic fiction and documentation is often a matter of interpretation. As noted by Roland Barthes, realism is not a window looking out onto reality but the outcome of symbolic processes. Reading a text containing representations of objects that exist "out there" in the world as realistic fiction—in the case of Fahan's work, "types and illustrations"—basically amounts to interpreting the textual representation of other texts. Hence, the "realistic" effect is achieved primarily by identifying represented elements as familiar textual products, rather than as objects that actually exist in the world. In this sense, these elements are believed to possess universally omnipresent powers (Barthes 1970, 20–23, 122–28). Concerning the "types" indicated in Fahan's subtitle, Brenner, Berdichevsky, and M. M. Feitelson all specified that they had no "individual mental attributes" (Feitelson 1970, 156). What they meant, most likely, is that Fahan's characters do not have attributes that make it easy for us to perceive them as individuals in their own right. Yet "individuality" is by no means an isolated, one-time occurrence. Indeed, the individual stands in binary opposition to the collective, and as such is grounded on the representation of the human by and through an accepted universal criterion, rather than by forming particular identities. A critical interpretation based on Fahan's text therefore presumes the existence of a desirable extraliterary world juxtaposed to the alternative "reality" constructed within the literary text. Thus, the critical claim concerning the absence of individual characters in Fahan's text is based on a normative concept of reality that is diametrically opposed to the literary text. It is this normative concept that underlies Brenner's, Berdichevsky's, and Feitelson's canonical criticism and poses the individual character as a universal category, which is first and foremost universally human and only then ethnic or nationally specific (Feitelson 1970, 255). The primary function of this normative view of reality is to outline the future utopian dimension of national survival for members of the contemporary national community. This normative view advanced by the critic-interpreter does not care to represent reality as it is but rather seeks to construct a desirable version of reality; it thus plays a crucial role in constructing the imaginary national community (Anderson 1991).

Distinguishing between the fictional and the documentary or historical is synonymous with distinguishing between a truth claim and a fictional claim. Hence, the distinction between reading a text as fictional or reading it as documentary has nothing to do with the reader's degree of success or failure but rather with distinguishing among a range of different reading aesthetics, all of which may be applicable to the same text (Stierle 1980, 83–105). Documentary representation calls for truth validity, for it applies to representations that have a concrete status in time and space. In contrast, realistic or plausible fiction establishes generalizations that demand recognition as truth, a validity that may not be concretely valid but would ring conceivably true in a range of possible instances.

What determines whether or not a particular fictional character meets the required standards of realistic fiction? First and foremost is the appraisal of the critic-interpreter. Critical sensibilities concerning the extent to which a fictional character is universal or typically human will be shaped by a critical assessment of the text's target readership. When the critic-interpreter discerns a readership that is likely to perceive a character as "representative," he or she will accordingly introduce this character as a product of realistic fictional representation. But if the critic-interpreter is unable to discern whether or not a readership would identify a character as the overall generalization of a familiar "slice of life," he or she will not be able to site the said character as the product of realistic fictional representation. When the critic-interpreter decides that the readership is unlikely to attribute universal traits to the fictional character in question, he or she will thereby preclude the possibility of identifying the text as fiction. The critic-interpreter will therefore classify the text as nonfictional or documentary and identify its textual components and embodied characters accordingly.

The fictional/documentary opposition often proves to be an application of two possible critical strategies. Inability to adduce one option will promptly lead to application of the other. This dichotomy also pertains to the political implications that followed the critical appraisal of Galician literature: interpretations of literature as fiction were committed to national utopia and the rejection of the existence of the Diaspora in the present. For Brenner and Berdichevsky, standards of realistic fiction functioned as aesthetic guidelines in the formation of the national literary canon.

Fiction by Brenner and Berdichevsky

Brenner wrote prolifically during his sojourn in Galicia, where some of his works were also published. Alongside critical works and public debates, he also penned two of his more celebrated works there, "Shana Ahat" (One Year) and "Min HaMaytzar" (From Wretchedness). Both works adhere to literary standards authorized by Brenner himself. Brenner sought to create an effect of fictionality in a most radical mode. As Menachem Brinker (1990) has shown, he used the nonfictional illusion of autobiography to enhance the authority of his fictional writing. Brenner used what Brinker calls the "rhetoric of honesty" to mold personal data into fictional types. These types had the power to represent an era and a national community. Thus, although in his critical essays Brenner demanded a clear distinction between fiction and nonfiction, in his literature he liked to employ nonfictional illusions, and he thereby contributed to the transformation of documentary, autobiographical (i.e., minor) representation into universal (major) representation.

At the center of his Galician and other works, Brenner located a Subject, the young Jewish recluse, often featured in other Hebrew literary works written toward the end of the nineteenth century and early in the twentieth (Halkin 1958, 339–71; Bakun 1978). Most conspicuous examples of this character were Dr. Vynik, the protagonist of "HaTalush" (The Detached), by Y. D. Berkowitz (1904), and Michael, the principal figure in "Mahanaim" (Opposite Camps) (1900), by Berdichevsky. The biographies of the central characters in these texts represent, as it were, the collective biographies of the younger generation, who on the one hand renounced their parents' Orthodox way of life yet on the other were frustrated by the fact that Enlightenment values could not reconcile the unmistakable contradictions in their lives. Having experienced profound spiritual and mental crises, members of this generation returned to the fold of the national collective, more often than not as individuals taking comfort in their own inner worlds.

Such a process of individuation is undergone, for instance, by Berdichevsky's protagonist in "Menachem" and by other characters in such works as "HaZar" (The Foreigner) and "Mahanaim." This duplicitous process of negative universalization entails the characters' differentiation from configurations of social identity such as the family, the community, and the nation, at the same time that they accumulate great personal strength, grounded in the characters' withdrawal from the constraints of social identity and their increased resilience as individuals. The basic structure of character representation in Berdichevsky's fiction is a conflictual one that evolves into an oxymoronic situation.

In "Menachem," for example, the principal character's name is grounded in an oppositional allegory comprising light and darkness: he is "Menachem of the Meir [illuminating] Family," while "his forefathers went about in the dark, and his townspeople went about in the darkness" (Berdichevsky 1991, 19). Menachem renounced his life as a Jew among his own people and went to a foreign land to acquire knowledge, focusing on erudition and the sciences. His dependence on secular Enlightenment values was apparently rife with inner contradictions, including the radical elimination of Menachem's traditional Jewish past and the construction of a new lifestyle: "Everything he had had before was taken away and given to him anew . . . he lost everything yet he found everything . . . having rejected everything, he rebuilt everything by himself" (Berdichevsky 1991, 19). The central conflict in this narrative collapses when Menachem realizes that his quest is in vain, for wisdom and science will get him nowhere. The rational maskilic resolution gives way to a vitalistic one: "His soul is devoid of vital substance, his life depleted of the ability to live, his heart bears no love or kinship" (20). Menachem relinquishes all former social bonds and dispositions ("He has neither a people nor the need for a people, no parents or kinfolk, he cries out for love and the sorrow of love" [21]) and turns to the only possible resolution, a universality realizable only by way of the isolated individual:

At last he found everything by losing everything . . . his soul is now
steered by his head, for he is master of all his own thoughts and visions. All the riches in the whole world are now being kept for him,
for he has had none of this happiness yet, that is, he is master of
everything even as he has *not mastered a single corner.* (Berdichevsky
1991, 21; my emphasis)

In this way, Berdichevsky's texts construct autonomous ethical-
moral Subjects, fully "rounded" individuals who persuasively im-
press their readers as truly representative because of their universal
attributes, which are shared by characters and readers alike. Unlike
the documentary text, which bases its rapport with the reader on
unique, specific familial and tribal features that appear at given
moments in time and space, the fictional text establishes an affiliation on the basis of plausible universal attributes in a familiar historical situation. Hence, it is apt that the modern nationalists, who
perceived the concept of the nation to be vital and all-encompassing, placed the Hebrew individual at the center of the nation.
Thus, the national literature seeking canonization molded a hegemonic world picture authorized by its very ability to create com-
pelling forms of generalizing representation.

The canonical writers functioned on behalf of a "major literature" in the throes of a power struggle with the Galician "minor literature," which comprised marginal and secondary literary works
(Deleuze and Guattari 1986). Indeed, to bar the minor Galician
writers from the emergent national canon, Brenner bombarded
them with propositions that authorized the aesthetic standards of
the major literature. Trying by way of aesthetic statements to delegitimate the Galicians, Brenner masked his political interests
through aesthetic claims. Like other members of the major literature's critical coterie, he referred to Fahan's book, for example, as
an ethnographic documentary, a work comprised of elements that
may be significant in their own right but are ultimately lacking because they cannot be generalized. The book's shortcoming, in
Brenner's eyes, lay in its presumption to be a work of literary fiction. Brenner believed that Fahan's text lacked the universal features required to generate any empathy in its readers. More impor-

tant, Fahan's writing lacked the features required to help its audience construct a notion of modern nationalism.

Originality versus Collectivism in "Minor Literature"

Unlike Brenner's and Berdichevsky's commitment to individuals, minor Galician texts foregrounded collectivist discourse, primarily through the construction of characters. Feitelson (1970, 157) and Berdichevsky criticized the monotony of the Karaite characters in Fahan's book—their similarity to one another and the superficial differences among them. Unlike major literary texts, Fahan's minor texts specify private life experiences that are at the same time devoid of the individualist autonomy meant to represent the national community. Hence, noted Feitelson, "human being within the Karaite [community] is not well portrayed." He also pointed out that Fahan did not really portray individuals who were Karaites (as one would portray them in belletristic writing) but rather male and female Karaites (Feitelson 1970, 157).

A common manifestation of Galician cultural collectivism is the blurring of the private and public realms. Thus Brenner, in his critical diatribe on literary and polemical writing in Galicia, ridiculed the way in which Galician writer Gershon Bader failed to distinguish between his private affairs and the public issues he was supposed to be writing about (Brenner 1985a, 271). The minor text's collectivism is measured, among other things, by its tendency to obscure its own artistic origins. Unlike major literature, which seeks to highlight the originality of the literary text and the fact that it has been produced by an individual artist's imagination, minor literature introduces the text as the product of a collaborative effort. It was common in Galician cultural arts to obscure and blur the boundaries separating the original work, the professional artist, and proficient readers, who were themselves often writers (see Kleinman 1908).

Fahan's and Fernhoff's minor literature refuses to report how autonomous Subjectivity is acquired, and in this they denied the task of a major literature. This refusal on the level of the represented world embodies another refusal on the level of the mode of representation. Instead of appearing in an original and autonomous text that has explicitly artistic roots, the minor text adopts strategies that are contingent, as it were, on previous texts. Brenner was indignant about the fact that half the stories in Fernhoff's book were adaptations and translations, and that in the subtitle the author made no attempt to mark the texts as original. Elsewhere, Brenner criticized a calendar edited by Gershon Bader at Lemberg for incorporating the reprinted works of well-known authors (Brenner 1985a, 275). A text signed by Adondon (1908), apparently a pseudonym used by S. Y. Agnon in his youth (see Kressel 1968; compare Bakun 1982, 98–122) after he immigrated from Galicia to Eretz Israel, harshly criticized Fahan's *From the Karaite Lives,* stating that the book represented all that was deficient in Galician literature and that no one had been able to find in it "anything original, everything is always 'about something or other' that already exists" (Adondon 1908, 72). We are just one step away from more detailed claims against the poetics of minor literature, such as, for instance, Berdichevsky's critique of the narrator's rhetoric, whereby "he generally *informs rather than composes,* and when he does compose, he repeats the same tune over and over, till we know it from beginning to end" (Berdichevsky 1960, 273; my emphasis; see also Feitelson 1970, 256). Berdichevsky bemoaned the narrator's privileging of telling over showing; telling leads to indirect, unmediated speech and obscures the autonomic effect of the major Subject. The greatest degree of "telling" takes place when there is what Berdichevsky called a lapse from fictional narrative into documentary reporting, and from original utterances to imitation and simulation: "the narrator copies into the stories complete prayers from the Siddur; often completely forgetting that he is a narrator, he reads the inscriptions on the graves of the deceased heroes, row by row" (Berdichevsky 1960, 273).

The stories' predictable and schematic plots undermine the autonomy of the represented subjects. The canonical hegemonic Subject constructed by Berdichevsky and Brenner rejected the social context in which the Diaspora existed, and it is this total rejection that led to the establishment of the radical Zionist alternative option. But when rejection of the Diaspora is only partial, as in the

Galician texts, the alternative option proposed is not mandatory. Hence, compromise led to the collapse of the universalist grounding of the national Subject. In addition, the critical advocates for the majority literature could not come to terms with the lack of originality or autonomy of the subjects constructed in Galician literature and therefore did their best to exclude this literature from the canon of modern Hebrew literature.

Chapter 2

Nationalist Satire and Its Victims: The Politics of Majority and Minority in S. Y. Agnon's "With Our Young and Our Old"

Universalist Satire and Political Satire

There is no doubt that S. Y. Agnon's writing was institutionalized in Hebrew literature as a canonical fortress supporting Zionism and providing a major voice to its claims. In this sense, Agnon is the most prominent writer to realize the tradition of the universal national Subject, as it was formed and designed in the work of Brenner and Berdichevsky. Both writer-critics supported and encouraged Agnon's writing from its very beginning. It then developed concurrently with the aesthetic norms Brenner and Berdichevsky constructed and fostered, and finally it became no less than the major formative voice in modern Hebrew literature.

Agnon first published his satirical story "Bineareinu Ubizkeineinu" (With Our Young and Our Old) in the sixth volume of the literary journal *HaTekufah* (The Era), which appeared in Warsaw at the beginning of 1920. (Page references in the text are to this version.) It was a grand narrative project in which Agnon incorporated a broad spectrum of the everyday life of the Jews of Galicia at the beginning of the twentieth century. Later on, Agnon revised the story twice. A thorough revision was carried out before it was published in the three-volume version of his writings and a lesser one before its inclusion in the *Collected Works* (on the changes, see Halevi-Zweik 1968, 240–46).

At the heart of the story are the events surrounding the general elections to the parliament in Vienna, capital of the Austro-Hungarian Empire, that took place in Galicia in 1907. The Zionist groups in Galicia, among others, presented candidates who stood in these elections. In so doing, they opened a front for political clashes between

themselves and other sectors of Jewish public life in Galicia, notably
the assimilationists. The story, which centers on the character Hemdat, Agnon's alter ego, unfolds the tale of a pogrom that took place
in Pitcheritz near Shebush, which represents none other than
Buchach, where Agnon was born (see Brawer 1958; 1973; Livnat
1976). The pogrom against the Jews is presented in the satire as a moment of crisis for the Zionists of Galicia, testing the depth of their national faith and their level of commitment. The supporters of Dr.
Davidson, the failed Zionist candidate for Shebush, do try to save the
Jews of Pitcheritz from the attack, but it soon transpires that their intentions are not serious, and their dedicated nationalist statements
turn out to be worthless slogans. Instead of trying to do something for
the Jews, they choose the more lucrative alternative of a good meal
and spend most of their time organizing a Zionist ball. In contrast,
the one person who takes personal responsibility for the fate of the
Jews and suffers extended incarceration as a result of his actions is
Alexander, the Bundist (the Bund was a socialist Jewish party that was
founded in Russia in 1897 and opposed Zionism but supported Yiddish cultural autonomy), who is an activist of the self-defense network. The drastic opposition between the grand pronouncements of
the local Zionists and the stark fate of the proletarian Alexander
forms the axis of this satire, which describes the lives of the Zionists
in the Galician Diaspora as false and miserable.

Agnon's satire does not limit its critique and lashes out merci-
lessly at a broad array of characters, mainly the local Zionists. Agnon
even allows himself to point his barbs at real personalities of Galician
life of that time. Dr. Davidson is based on Dr. Natan Birnbaum, one
of the leading Zionists of Galicia in those days, while the real-life historical equivalent of Sebastian Montag is Stern, the mayor of Buchach
(Brawer 1958, 40).

The satire attacks its victims for a series of defects that cover a
broad spectrum of possibilities. Most of these defects are part of the
general tradition of satire. Among others, we discover in the story the
crook and the cunning trickster; the opportunist, who quickly adapts
to any new situation; and of course, bodily humor ranging from the
bearers of insatiable sexual lust to those enslaved to their bellies to
such an extent that they will forget any commitment. These are negative characteristics whose perverseness needs no secondary proof.

Agnon employs universalist moral criteria in an intensive manner and uses them to judge his victims and to condemn them out of hand.

A typical victim of this satiric approach is the character Daikseel ("fool enough" in Hebrew), president of the Jewish Students' Union, whose name implies his stupidity. In his speech at the Zionist ball (which takes place as an ironic ending to the pogrom plotline and the trips on the train between Shebush and Pitcheritz), he compares the ball (*neshef*) to life in the Diaspora (*galut*) and goes on to claim that just as "after the *neshef* a clear day will dawn, so the light of our dawn will come and our salvation will rise up soon, etc." (Agnon 1920, 92). The satiric critique of these bloated statements is exposed here in the double meaning of the word *neshef*: the original meaning of the word is "night"; to this is added its secondary meaning as "party," which totally contradicts the accepted interpretation of *galut*. The immediate satiric effect that is created is based on the speaker's linguistic ignorance. This may extenuate the satire on Daikseel by suggesting that the semantic confusion into which he falls is the result only of his ignorance of the Hebrew language and not of some basic flaw in his character. Agnon, however, combines his critique of Daikseel's basic foolishness with a specific critique of his political views.

This double meaning in the satiric voice leads to a blurring of its authority. The satiric mechanism, which proceeds by defining an objective yardstick of behavior and then judging a certain sector of human activity according to it, appears to mix two different criteria here. The first, which is more apparent, uncovers the faults of Jewish society in Galicia, especially of its Zionist activists, in the light of universal norms of any time and place. Thus, for example, Daikseel is clearly a negative character because he is a coward (hiding behind Hemdat's back when they run into a bunch of drunken thugs), heartless (when he denies his responsibility toward Peishi Sheindel, whom he has impregnated), and a charlatan who wishes to decide on questions relating to Hebrew grammar even though he has no knowledge whatsoever of the language in general and of the grammatical question under debate in particular. But the satiric linguistic mechanism also incorporates an element that questions its absolute authority, since the satiric critique is dependent to a great extent on the specific political perspective from which the events are presented. What may appear ridiculous and a source of mockery from the perspective of the total rejection of the Diaspora, and therefore also absurd in its comparison to a *neshef,* can be seen in a more lenient light from the perspective of a sympathetic Zionist political conception. Thus it can be said that "party" or "ball" as the secondary meaning of *neshef* is an acceptable definition of the Diaspora, viewed as a formative cultural experience in preparing the Zionists in the Diaspora for their future role. The linguistic irony that arises from Daikseel's words encompasses not only a generalized denunciation and mockery but also a specific political critique. Alongside the sense of disgust that his cowardliness, ignorance, and behavior toward Peishi Sheindel arouse in us, Daikseel's ridiculous speech offers traces of the specific ideological struggle in which Agnon's text is engaged. Agnon not only attacks Daikseel's idiocy but also condemns him as a supporter of a political, Zionist approach that takes a lenient stand as far as the rejection of Jewish existence in the Diaspora is concerned.

The Satire on the Zionist Conception of "Laboring for the Present"

"With Our Young and Our Old" was written from the viewpoint of a political, Zionist position that radically negated the Diaspora and embodied a view of Diaspora life as the main source of the deformation and degeneration of Jewish existence. As satire, it is a systematic attack on the more moderate Zionist stance that developed around this time in East European Zionism. As mentioned in chapter 1, against the total negation of all aspects of the Diaspora and the subordination of all Zionist resources toward "laboring for the future" (i.e., the elimination of the Diaspora and the building of the homeland in Palestine) there arose at this time a Zionist position that recognized the national importance of "laboring for the present" in the Diaspora and that rejected the future-oriented claim and saw the importance of carrying on a national Jewish existence in the Diaspora during a transitional period that might be quite long. At the Helsingfors Convention of Russian Zionists in December 1906, decisions were taken that supported the struggle for the rights of the Jews as a national minority and recognized the importance of laboring for the present in the Diaspora. Agnon's satire creates an equivalence between the

Diaspora (*golah*) and a party (*neshef*), making the Diaspora not only worthy but possibly even pleasurable. The satire is thus not only evidence of Daikseel's ignorance but also a mocking representation of a specific Zionist political position that somehow accepts the ongoing Jewish existence in the Diaspora. This view is rejected by Agnon's satiric text.

In choosing the option of laboring for the present as the object of his satiric attack, Agnon touches on one of the most hotly debated topics of early twentieth-century Zionism: the support for cultural activities, consciousness-raising, and national rights in the Diaspora versus the urgency of achieving a territorial concentration of the Jews in the land of Israel. The opening lines of the story, which describe the parting from Dr. Davidson (i.e., Dr. Natan Birnbaum, who lost the elections of 1907 in Galicia), already set the political context of the satire and its specific victims. The historical Dr. Birnbaum was the originator of the term *Zionism*, but later became one of Herzl's main opponents. He was one of the main supporters of the "laboring for the present" school of thought. In the complex process of ideological transformation that finally brought him to oppose Zionism altogether, during the very same years, around the turn of the century, Dr. Birnbaum supported the attainment of national autonomy for the Jews within the multinational Austro-Hungarian Empire (Doron 1988, 12). The growth of national consciousness among the Jews of Galicia developed through a process of conflict with, and influence from, other national minorities in the empire. In contrast to the Russian Jews, the Jews of Galicia were relatively successful in attaining civil rights. The installation of a new Austro-Hungarian government in 1906 and the hope that it brought for democratization aroused new political trends among the Zionists of Galicia that strengthened the supporters of laboring for the present, who saw a political future for the Jews also in the Diaspora.

In the Zionist conference of July 1906 in Kraków, there were clear voices demanding that a party be established that would aspire to "a political organization of the Austrian Jews in the context of the monarchy in order to uphold their national freedom and the development of the cultural, political and economic rights of the Jewish nation in Austria" (Gelber 1958, 526). Their opponents in the Zionist camp emphasized, as might be expected, that there could be no solution for the Jewish problem in the Diaspora. As might also be expected, there was widespread criticism of Zionist activity in the Diaspora from the assimilationist camp, and later this critique was turned against the moderate Zionists during the elections. In contrast to the Helsingfors Convention, however, which took similar decisions in support of the struggle for the rights of Jews as a national minority and the importance of laboring for the present in the Diaspora, the Kraków conference led to real results. In the general elections that took place in May 1907, the Zionists gained considerable political strength, and the trend toward support for national autonomy under the Zionist flag grew more powerful (Gelber 1958, 192–94, 522–28).

The clash between Agnon's textual approach and the social and political reality of Jewish society in Galicia at the beginning of the century is therefore a clash between rival political forces. Agnon's vitriolic disdain for the pompous and fictitious style of Zionist life in Galicia at the turn of the century is an expression of the struggle between different perceptions of Zionist theory and action.

Agnon, who published his story in 1920, was not a disinterested or objective critic. His use of satire to deal in such specific detail with social events that took place thirteen years earlier is connected to the fact that, at the time of writing, the alternative of the national minority had once again become a central topic in the Zionist political and cultural debate. In Galicia itself, the echoes of the First World War had not yet died down, carrying with them memories of the cruel fate of the Jews who, caught between the Poles and the Ukrainians, had fallen victim to disturbances and persecutions. The pogrom in Lvov in November 1918 almost completely halted Zionist political activities. The Zionists wanted to remain neutral in the national struggle for control of Galicia that broke out with the collapse of the Austro-Hungarian Empire. The members of the Galician delegation arrived at the peace conference in Paris together with Jewish and other delegations. Hoping for Polish support, they attempted to realize one of the main visions of this conference under the guidance of President Woodrow Wilson, which was to give a clear basis for the national rights of the many minority national groups spread around Europe. This hope for an existence as a national minority with full civil rights was, in the first years after the war, perceived as a real threat to a mainstream Zionist ideology that totally rejected the Diaspora.

Agnon as satirist fought the battle from a specific, particularist point of view. The perspective of the power struggles in which he was involved forces us to observe closely the manner in which he reacted to and took on those against whom he was pitted. Some of the literary mechanisms of "With Our Young and Our Old" become clearer if we place this text in the context of a satiric discourse of 1920, aimed against specific models of power and preoccupied with the concrete repercussions of the question of minority rights in Galicia at the beginning of the century.

The main thrust of literary studies of "With Our Young and Our Old" has been to emphasize the universalist aesthetic aspects of the satire. In his article on "With Our Young and Our Old," Gershon Shaked wrote: "The objects of the satire's critique do not yet give us the source of the work's comic power. They are just the author's raw material. The internal organization of this material is what makes it comic and also what gives it a deeper resonance" (1973, 73). The political context of the story (i.e., the critique of false Zionism and of laboring for the present) has not been ignored (Brawer 1958, 46; Knaany 1949, 164–90), but most readings of "With Our Young and Our Old" have neglected to examine the correlation between Agnon's political stance and the structure of his satire. In other words, most Agnon criticism presents Agnon as a writer for whom the artistic qualities of his work are totally severed from his political values. In such a reading, Agnon's specific political critique of Zionist activities in Galicia at the beginning of the century becomes merely a universalist critique, apparently based on a disinterested point of view; thus the critique gains increased legitimacy. But a study of the structure of the satire and its literary devices proves this disinterested universalism is not what it seems. The authority of the satirist is not a "natural" phenomenon, based on ahistorical and independent moral truths, but is in fact the result of a neatly structured framework that is chiefly arranged around political interests that were central to the Zionist politics of that period. Satire is not only a form of discourse that mirrors the objects in their exact historical context; it is also a discourse that informs and constructs this reality. Thus the satiric narrator and, likewise, the object or victim of the satiric attack are structured and defined according to the political interests that inform the processes of communication that the satire produces.

Even the ironic title of the story, which quotes both the words of Moses describing the children of Israel leaving Egypt (Exodus 10:9) and the famous poem by Y. L. Gordon describing the Jewish emigration for the United States, gives evidence of the manner in which Agnon produces the victims of his satire not just as objects of ridicule but as objects that obey political modes of thought that he condemns and attacks. The dual intertextual reference of the title mixes the return to the Promised Land and the emigration to America. The ironic representation of these implied meanings in such a conjunction is an attack on the passive acceptance of the futility of the Zionist dream (which demands an immediate fulfillment of the vision of the return to the land of Israel). Such acceptance is seen as equivalent to the emigration to the United States. Agnon's irony is aimed at the Zionist political option that questions the total rejection of the Diaspora, even as it also attacks the non-Zionist approach to the suffering of the Jews in the Diaspora. Further evidence of this ironic trend can be found in the fact that the house of Alexander, the most positive character in the story, is described in metaphoric terms also used to describe the land of Israel, and his detailed desire to emigrate there is also foregrounded. The story of the pogrom in Pitcheritz, too, is not merely inserted to show the empty jabbering of the Shebush Zionists. The satirist is far more intent on showing his victims' misguided political faith in the democratization of Austrian life under the auspices of its enlightened capital, Vienna.

Thus, Agnon's universalist satire has certain limits. Beneath the apparent universalism, Agnon also has produced another kind of satire. In contrast to totalizing criteria based on the principal image of the "decent and honorable man," Agnon's satire uses far more specific criteria, whose authority lies in the political meaning they took on at a particular moment in time. Agnon has undertaken, therefore, a double movement, going in two opposite directions. On the one hand, he wrote a universalist satire that can apply to any historical or political reality, and thus he appropriated an apparent air of neutrality, a seemingly universalist, ahistorical authority that does not need to refer to concrete historical detail to uphold its power. On the other hand, his satire exemplifies the opposite approach as well. In contrast to the apparently neutral, disinterested observer, who just points out those human faults that are common to all ages, Agnon is cast in the position of a politically involved observer who is aware of the issues, knows the participants well, and brings up their past misdeeds to discredit their present activities. Thus his satire is a blatantly political act that bears its own and his specific political motivations in a specific historical situation (Cohen 1970, 422–30). Regarding Mayor Stern, for example, Agnon wrote to David Zakay: "In my youth, he was close to putting me in jail because of a Zionist deed acted against the Poles of Moses' descent [i.e., Jews], but he changed his mind since he did not want me to become a martyr" (Agnon 1970, 608).

But by this splitting of the satirist's authority, Agnon's satire undermines its own credibility. Along with the criticism against those who put their hopes in the failing empire, the satire sets up a more subjective context in which Agnon, who appears in the story as the narrator in the person of the Hebrew writer Hemdat, questions his own identity in this political and cultural situation. The ridiculous adventures of the Zionists, like other elements of this narrative world, are presented from his perspective. The false climax of the story also appears mainly on the literary and journalistic level: if the Zionist ball is the false pinnacle of the story of the pogrom, then the unique personal profit that Hemdat gains from the situation is that his letter about the ball is published in the newspaper. Agnon thus thematizes the relationship between the writer and his nation: his possible and necessary national roles, the poetic options open to him, and those that he must reject.

The collective narrator exposes himself to the critical eye of the reader in the very first chapter of the book. He both expresses his belief in the principles of justice of the Austrian democracy and makes lame attempts to explain away Davidson's failure as the result of intrigues by the Head of the Citizens (the mayor). The impression that the narrator himself is caught in an unreal world of political naïveté is strengthened when he outlines the Zionists' fantasy that Adolf Stand, the head of the Zionists in the Austrian parliament, will raise the issue of the corruption in the elections in Shebush, and that this will rectify the situation.

The Narrator as Victim of the Satire

The narrator is often the butt of the satire, and this is made clear almost from the outset of the story. In many cases, there is no way of ascertaining whether the ironic effect is created by the narrator's self-conscious mocking or by a naive narrator directed by the author, who sacrifices him for the sake of the readers. In a relatively long section that appeared in the earliest version of the text, the satirist explains his position with regard to the act of storytelling and the story:

> Dear reader, I know very well that you will ask yourself what this author wanted in writing about these matters. Is he taking on the part of a minister that he recalls all the names that were inflicted by Mrs. Gold on Mrs. Silber, or perhaps like all storytellers he is telling something that never really happened at all.
>
> Here, I myself tell you that I am neither a minister nor the son of a minister. And thank God that my place among the authors is not there. But rather every day early in the morning when I am on my way to the synagogue to pray, I pass by the butcher's shop and I stand there for a while to listen to the people talk, the words of the people, like Rabbi Mendel Lipin, may he rest in peace, who copied the proverbs of Solomon to Ivri Taitsh, whose seat sat in the butcher's shop so that he could soak in the simple words that every Jew understands.
>
> This is a sign that I only want to find the truth, since I have not told you anything about the actions of Peishi Sheindel and the secrets of her heart, the look on her face and her inner thoughts, for how should I know the secrets of her heart and I have not met her nor have I spoken to her. Even should I speak to her I would not take away from that meeting things that were not hers. On the other hand I have gone on a bit about the deeds of people who at first glance might appear unimportant in your eyes, but if they do not matter to you, they matter a lot to the people of Shebush, and let us say no more on this matter. (Agnon 1920, 49)

What is this "matter" on which we should "say no more"? What is the thing that will be unimportant to the reader "at first glance" but that matters a lot to the people of Shebush? What is it that might also be of importance to the skeptical reader who is not directly linked to the intimate existence of Shebush (which is none other than Buchach and "Pitcheritz," which apparently is Monasteritz)? In other words: how does the author suggest that local material, of the kind that is abundantly present in the plotline of "With Our Young and Our Old," fills a meaningful function in a more general context?

To sharpen these questions, let us emphasize the clear contradictions between the poetics expressed in this section of the text and the narrative practice within which this text is placed. The declared intention in this section is to stick to the model of a storyteller/chronicler who blesses the Lord that he is not among professional authors. In contrast, the narrator takes on the identity of a recognized artist whose pen is committed to serving the national interest. Similarly, his statement of principle that he has not told anything of Peishi Sheindel's inner thoughts is contradicted by the fact that a few pages earlier he took the omniscient position and described how she, who had been "Alexander's fiancée, had started likening her betrothed to Daikseel" (Agnon 1920, 26).

These and many other contradictions show Agnon's narrator in this story to be one who commits himself to something and then does the opposite. His apparent naïveté does not fit in with the lucid criticism he levels against his people (93). His unrestricted admiration for the idiotic antics of Mr. Ani-VeAfsi-Od (literally, "Mr. I-don't-care-for-anybody-but-myself") is hard to square with his impressive wit. Yet, at the same time, his lack of credibility as a narrator does not mean a systematic and logical development of his limitations and oddities. In line with the tradition of Menippean satire, the character of the narrator has been constructed in a broad field of stylistic flexibility, in a great array of shifting positions, and, most important, in the constant tension between retaining and changing his identity as a writer. The narrator's characterization as an author is complicated by this and other declared poetical sections. This phenomenon, which is prevalent throughout Agnon's work, is given so many contradictory facets in this story that it is difficult to reach any clear critical summation about the character. The shifting distances between the narrator and his object, the constant emphasis on the changing of his positions, are elements that force readers to focus their attention on the more stable element in the story—the realistic victims in the political-social reality of Galicia at the turn of the century.

The emphasis on these two points of tension—the professional writer versus the chronicler and the inconsistency of the narrator in his approach to the poetic option of omniscience—encourages a reading of the story as a text that uses these contradictions to focus on the relationship between the author and the national collective within which he lives and works. The historical context of the elections in Galicia in May 1907, in which the Zionists also participated, and the pogrom in Pitcheritz, which instigated the attempt by Dr. Davidson's supporters to help the Jews there—along with the more alluring alternative of a good meal and the organization of a Zionist ball that finally overcame their intentions to help the Jews of Pitcheritz—all form the pretext for the satire, which describes the falseness and the misery of the lives of the Zionists in Galicia and in the Diaspora. Yet, beside the critique of those who pinned their false hopes on the Austro-Hungarian Empire is also, as already mentioned, a more subjective context in which Hemdat, the Jewish writer, examines his own identity in this political and cultural situation. The ridiculous adventures of the Zionists, as well as other elements of the narrative reality, are related from the perspective of Hemdat, the author. Agnon again thematizes the relationship between writer and nation in terms of the writer's national poetic options.

The withdrawal of Zionist activists Gold and Silber from their planned lecture on Jewish art and Jewish singing just because they cannot borrow the periodical *Öst und West* from Daikseel (Agnon 1920, 53) is reason enough for them to be mocked. At the same time, this episode exhibits a sensitivity to the blurring of the values of originality and creativity in a minority culture that is massively mobilized, without the necessary restraints, toward national causes and other collective aims. Hemdat himself is a young author at the beginning of his career, part of whose professional credentials are his achievements as a reporter. The overriding democratization of the world of arts and letters that is the outcome of this process tends to blur the hierarchical order inherent in professionalism. This cultural model that blurs the professional identity of the author can explain the dual characterization of Hemdat, the author, in the story. As narrator in his metapoetic statement, the satirist emphasizes the problematic function of the author in a national context. As a character in the story itself, Hemdat is split between two characters who cooperate with each other. One of these characters is the young Chachkes, who is the butt of the satire that focuses on his self-satisfaction with his literary success in having his poems published in the paper *HaMitzpeh* (Agnon 1920, 35). At the same time, the story integrates the perspective of the elder Agnon, credited in the story as being the author of "The Tale of Rabbi Gadiel, the Baby" and of "And the Rough Way Will Become Plain," who, in 1907, thirteen years before the publication of the first story and five years before the publication of the second, met Mr. Hoffman, the grandson of Kreindel Tcherni, and her great-grandchildren. This dual temporal perspective can explain the flexible and undetermined space of the narrator Hemdat, who functions both as the satirist and as the victim of the satire. Hemdat is also an author and, by ridiculing others and himself, integrates in the voice of the objective satirist a particularist element that is closer to the objects of his satire and more involved with them. The criteria that are employed by this satiric voice are at least partially corollaries of decisions taken in relation to a specific political and social situation, which is the topic of the satire. The satiric deformation develops in this case through a highly conscious selection process among the specific behavioral patterns of the reality that is being challenged.

In Ronald Paulson's terminology, we might say that any discussion of "With Our Young and Our Old" as a satire demands special attention to the elements of representation in the story: the world it presents and its value system no less than the attention given to the rhetorical means of the story (Paulson 1967). The use of absolute values such as "speak the truth" or "take responsibility for your actions" allows the satirist to condemn his victims without having to commit himself to a clear decision in a concrete situation where these absolute values might come into conflict with one another. The blurring of boundaries—between the representation of the narrator as a truly naive character and his representation as one who pretends to be naive but actually observes his surroundings from an ironic position—highlights a series of unresolved conflicts. This blurring between the ironic and the naive makes it difficult for the reader to determine the level of commitment of the satiric narrator to the judgmental positions he upholds. There is a constant tension between the judgment passed on others and the self-reflexive judgment of the satiric narrator. The reader is unable fully to determine the basic source of authority of the critique and thus cannot resolve the tension in the story between the universalist judgment, based on absolute values of an objective standard, and particularist judgments, based on values and interests that are political and subjective.

The Collectivist Discourse of a National Minority

The sensitivity in "With Our Young and Our Old" toward the object of its attack is the political sensitivity of a satirist who is involved in the specific dynamics of his contemporary Zionist politics. Agnon's satiric pronouncement presents its object as connected to certain interests and to certain political qualities. That the satire is aware of the unique qualities of the political and cultural phenomena it attacks is apparent from the fact that these are represented, in an aggressively negative manner, as the cultural discourse of a national minority group. When the narrator, Hemdat, emphasizes the tension surrounding the poetic convention of the author who can enter at will into the inner recesses of his characters, we see how Agnon struggles with the option of a minority national culture that often tends toward collectivist models of discourse.

Hemdat's poetic statement sets up a scale of judgment that criticizes the tendency to look at literature from a point of view that gives a collective value to all works. We have seen that Agnon attacked Galician literature for being the provincial literature of a national minority. This entails a systematic breaking of the mechanisms that arrange and define different levels of discourse and human experience in a given cultural field. Minority discourse, including the literary discourse of the minority culture, tends toward a collectivist presentation of its materials and positions. In general, it finds it difficult to accept the autonomy of private experiences, and its representations tend toward a blurring of the demarcation between the private/personal and the public/social. The drama of a private life will turn into a political drama one way or another. As discussed above, Gilles

Deleuze and Félix Guattari, in their book on Kafka (1986), pointed out this mechanism of almost total collectivization as one of the distinguishing features of what they call "minor literature," a literature that often finds itself in opposition to the literature of a dominant culture. Agnon activates his satiric movement from a double-edged sensitivity that includes both the universalist attack, based on values that are true for any time and place, and the specific assault aimed directly at behavioral patterns of those with a provincial mentality and the sense of inferiority of a national minority living in exile. Thus, the description of the Zionist relief delegation to Pitcheritz exposes the patterns of self-deception in the behavior of the delegation. Agnon adds to this a ridiculing description of the collectivist thought processes that excuse this weak behavior, and he structures this passage as a parody of a talmudic debate of Diaspora Jews, the sons of a national minority group:

> Since we wander around the streets in groups what are we and what is our strength? And if you should say: Thus can we see that the blood of the people of such-and-such street is more than the others; then it must be answered: Since the main part of our help is in the form of sitting around and doing nothing, this means that the action is not important, but rather just our presence in town, and it goes without saying that we need not wander around the streets in groups. (Agnon 1920, 28)

The mocking of the provincial collectivism of the Galician Jews is most apparent in the complex network of switched identities and character doublings that abound in this story. This is a traditional satiric device that aims to undermine the individualized characterizations of its victims. Yet, beyond this level, in this story the satire mocks the tendency toward collectivization, which blurs any kind of personal identity, that characterizes the discourse of a national minority. Thus, Mr. Levy is also called Cohen, Daikseel is paired with Vaikseel and Silber with Gold. Peppi Meller, who wears the clothes of a Hasid and does her hair up with side locks, is the object of veneration for Mundspiel, who immediately tries to imitate her imitative behavior. Silber and Gold are mocked when they are shown repeating, over and over again in their speeches, a tradition of national pairings that includes Moses and Aaron and, in their wake, Herzl and Nordau (35).

Also among the Zionists, distancing themselves from the fate of Alexander is excused by the vigorous and deformed development of an ideology of a national minority. At first they complain that he did not change his identity to that of a Gentile. Then they raise a localized argument as they expand their Galician provincial identities to such an extent that they may claim Alexander is "as a stranger in our land" (46). A whole section in the story is titled "In Arts and Letters," and it is devoted to developing this characterization of the minority culture as a culture of imitation and doubling, one that reaches a normative poetic definition that demands "that the artificial must seem to have life, and anything that lives must be made artificial" (44). The outstanding example of this norm is the works of the painter E. M. Lilien, one of the main contributors to the periodical *HaKeshet*, the Hebrew language journal of arts and letters published in Berlin, which is mentioned in the story.

The suspicious approach to the collectivist spirit of the national minority group is apparent also in the behavior of Hemdat. One example of this is Hemdat's falsely innocent statement attacking the liberty that authors take in entering the innermost being of their characters. Hemdat appears in this section as a naive local writer who tells only what his eyes have seen. But he also wonders at the intricate interrelationship that exists in the story between the spiritual and libidinal levels and the political level. For example, one of the criteria for the success or failure of the Zionist ball is the possibility of finding a mate there (92), and the descriptions of Dr. Davidson given by his supporters imply a strong erotic awareness in him and in his viewers (23, 28). Another libidinal theme, central to the satiric shock effect, is the relationship of Peishi Sheindel with Alexander, the Bundist, and her subsequent pregnancy by Daikseel. Yet, beyond all this, the satire is woven into a "national allegory" that marks private spiritual and especially libidinal experience as having meaning on the public and national level.

The trope of the national allegory is a typical form for members of a stronger culture observing a culture that sees itself as weak yet is perceived as being in basic opposition to the majority culture (Jameson 1986, 65–88). In consequence, the minority culture is seen by the members of the majority culture as having no compunctions in enlisting all possible resources in their struggle, whether spiritual or political, thus bringing about a blurring of the distinction between these fields. From the critical viewpoint of a sovereign Zionist identity that Agnon's satire offers toward the position of the national minority and the provincial "laboring for the present" carried on by the Galician Zionists, the latter's cultural practices are projected into the trope of a national allegory. Thus, for example, Agnon presents the episode of Daikseel's denying his sexual relations with Peishi as analogous to his public insincerity as a national politician. Agnon also uses this fusion of the erotic and the political to distinguish the positive hero of the story from the negative characters. Alexander, the heroic and brave character of the story, distinguishes clearly between his erotic interests and his political involvement, and thus he postpones his physical reckoning with Daikseel until after he has found respite from the antisemitic onslaught.

The gap between the symbol of masculine power in the story (Alexander, the Bundist, the only one who knows how to carry out the idea of self-defense) and Daikseel's cowardliness (he is more apprehensive of Alexander's revenge than of the physical danger of the mob), as well as the ridiculous airs of masculine behavior that Silber puts on when he tries to protect the honor of Mrs. Silber and invites Gold to a duel, clearly serve the scale of values of the political forces that appear in the story in such a way that there is a total correspondence between their political presence (especially that of the Head of the Citizens) and their implied sexuality. In the case of the mock duel between Silber and Gold, there is an echo of the conflict that came to symbolize the question of the relations between Jewish youths and the Austro-German etiquette of honor. Natan Birnbaum (Dr. Davidson of the story) was one of those who demanded that Jewish youngsters be "manly" and brave and not avoid dueling (Doron 1988, 43–44). An especially powerful example of the satiric attack on the mixing of the political and the libidinal appears in Hemdat's dream in his father's house (Agnon 1920, 76). The dream is a visual concoction of sexual fantasies built around the context of the struggle that took place in reality between Berish Stern, the head of the citizens of Buchach (the prototype for Sebastian Montag in the story), and Dr. Birnbaum (the prototype for Dr. Davidson). The fact that the main source of political and sexual power in the dream is attributed to

Rabbi Yosef de la Reina, who was a kabbalist, emphasizes the context of national (Zionist) salvation that arises from it.

Part of the attempt in the story to question the status of national minority discourse by means of an internal, particularist satire is concretized by drawing a logical connection that leads the Jew straight into the arms of the antisemite. A mechanism of doubling and identity switching is also used to present the Jew as a member of a minority group who is exposed to antisemitic violence. Pen Dovidzeni, Silber's consultant while he is preparing himself for the duel, tells Silber how the son of Count Pitzuwinski was cheated in his desire to marry a good Jewish girl by Alterl, who sent the count's son a Gentile maid who knew Yiddish dressed in Jewish clothes (Agnon 1920, 56–57). Pen Dovidzeni develops his argument by an association that contrasts Silber, the Jew, consulting him, the Gentile, with the dubious assistance given by Alterl, the Jew, to the count's son. The antisemitic conclusion of this analogous argumentation, which doubles the model of identity switching of the national minority, is presented in the story as a totally natural and clear conclusion for the Gentile:

> You are asking me, Mr. Pharmacist, what weapon to use against that bastard of yours, what's his name? Silber! Oh, sorry, Gold! I'll give you the following advice: take a shotgun. Pow! Pow! And your antagonist lies dead before you. One less Jew in this world. (57)

National Language and National Minority

In the Austro-Hungarian Empire, with its multiple national groupings, language became the main criterion for the identification of nationalism and especially for its continuity (Doron 1988, 62). Agnon re-creates the dark period of the language battles between Hebrew and Yiddish (one of whose climaxes was at the Tchernovitz Convention of 1908) and is loyal to the official Zionist position that preferred Hebrew over Yiddish. The lack of knowledge of Hebrew among the Galician Zionist group is vehemently attacked and is presented as a mark of shame, exposing the gulf that exists between their pretensions of developing Zionist culture and the impoverished reality. Thus, again, Agnon exposes the pretensions of the Galician Zionists and the falsity of the image they try to project. But the main focus of criticism is the attempt by the Zionists in Galicia to uphold a national existence in the linguistic reality of a national minority in the Diaspora. The main quality that characterizes this reality is one of deterritorialization, a linguistic reality that questions the existence of a natural connection between language and territory, a link that is characteristic of modern images of national identity. In his criticism, Agnon not only exposes the self-deception and small-mindedness of the Jews of Galicia but also attempts to uncover the specific cultural mechanism that allows them to continue within their minority national culture. Deleuze and Guattari have identified deterritorialization as a characteristic element of minor literature (1986, 16–27). The writer of a national minority group who wants to stake out a space of independent existence may often write in a language that questions the linkage between language and territory that is a basic image of modern nationalism. To achieve such a project, he or she may have to write in a language that is not the writer's own, or write in his or her own tongue but outside the writer's homeland, or write in a language that is different from that of the sovereign language. In Dov Sadan's words, the Zionist discourse in Galicia of those days was run "in the tradition of the assimilationists from time immemorial, in the language of the ruler, even if the ruler was only a minority group in the area, even if for most of the readers of the author the language they spoke at home and in the street and among themselves wasn't Polish but Yiddish, and the language of their culture wasn't Polish but Hebrew, and the language they were educated in wasn't Polish but German, and the language of the majority of the population surrounding them wasn't Polish but Ruthenian" (Sadan 1967, 135).

The tendency to question accepted models of linguistic usage was often a part of the cultural practices that emphasized the Diaspora Zionist attitude of laboring for the present rather than a Palestine-centered orientation. This approach was most prominent in Poland in the literary works of Eliezer Steinman and Z. Z. Weinberg and other writers who were involved with the periodical *Kolot,* which appeared in Warsaw in the early twenties and is discussed in the next chapter. In some of their statements, these writers acclaimed the special potential of the Jewish existence in the Diaspora and emphasized as an advantage the deterritorialization of the Hebrew language as against its territorialization in the cultural center in Eretz Israel (Steinman 1923, 117). This is apparent also in Agnon's story, where, for example, the ridiculous argument over the correct pronunciation of a syllable comes up in the political context of local Galician support for the concept of territorialism that stood behind the Uganda project in Herzl's days.

Hemdat's overexcited response to Dr. Davidson's demonstrative populism, when he would "talk to people even in jargon" (Agnon 1920, 23)—that is, in Yiddish—sharpens our consciousness of the problematic relationship between the politics of laboring for the present and the popular appeal to the masses. The ridiculing of the authors in the story is carried out through a process that presents them, each in his own way, as trying to realize this cultural logic of a deterritorialized minority literature. Thus the writer Gamliel Podhotzer Tintenfas solves the "Hebrew-Yiddish dilemma" (Agnon 1920, 33) by writing in Polish.

The general ignorance of the local Zionists when it comes to Hebrew literature is part of a pattern. But the absurdity that the satirist finds in the struggle to develop Hebrew literature in the provincial Diaspora, sunk in its state of national apathy and ignorance, is by and large presented as an attempt to foster an autonomous national minority culture in the Diaspora (55). This explains, for example, the total disdain that Gold and Silber show when they come to questions of national culture and literature. The direct result of this apathy is the vain exercise of presenting the argument between Yiddish literature and Hebrew literature, where each character in turn manages to present his opponent's position. The ridiculing of this cultural mode of a national minority does not, however, take place only through external means but also through extending its logic and absurdity to its most extreme limits. Thus, for example, the narrator says that during the reconciliation and withdrawal from the duel, "Gold took it upon himself to have Silber registered in the Golden Book" (82). This bilingual witticism that mixes Yiddish and Hebrew (in Yiddish: Gold asked to register Silver in the book of gold) represents a typical kind of nationalist activity, which exhibits a comic approach to language as a game, thus creating a kind of autonomous space that is not referential and therefore is also not territorialized in the national existence in the Diaspora. But the most extreme example in the story of this

mode of deterritorialization characteristic of the discourse of a minority is the hyperbolic description of Mr. Ani-VeAfsi-Od as one who
learned the language by memorizing the dictionary.

Hemdat's attempts to release Alexander by intervening with the
authorities are unsuccessful. The final passage of "With Our Young
and Our Old" is also a new beginning (typographically as well). The
train journey from Shebush to Pitcheritz and back to Shebush again
is the organizing pattern of the plot as well. This circular pattern is
broken, however, with the passage that starts, "One last drop of ink
stands on the edge of my pen" (94), and reconfirms the story's status
as a "diary of the author." Sitting in the railway carriage taking him to
Shebush, Hemdat is confronted with the policeman leading Alexander in chains, and he wonders: "Has chance decided to enact this
melodrama in front of me?" (94). The coolness and distance aroused
by this generic-theatrical description of the fate of the sacrificial victim of the Jewish self-defense organization is repeated also in Hemdat's attempt to express to Daikseel his authentic worry for Alexander's fate. Daikseel, who has been giving a speech, "has his arms full.
A bouquet of flowers had been raised in tribute to the speaker" (93).
Daikseel has received a thanksgiving offering in the form of flowers,
while the real sacrifice is Alexander, led in chains to prison. This
ironic opposition is brought to a climax when the handcuffs are described as part of a ceremonial sacrifice: "The cuffs were ancient and
full of rust and slightly reddish; apparently the policeman had tight-
ened them so hard around Alexander's wrists that they spilled his
blood on the handcuffs. But the flowers of Mr. Daikseel, my friend,
were fresh and new." But even before that, the narrator says, "Yes, my
friend, there is no full joy in the *galut* [meaning exile as well as Dias-
pora]!" (94) is Daikseel's answer, which closes the dialogic circle of
understanding, bringing together pathos and irony, the particular
and the universal, and suggests a new context of understanding in
which truly "there is no full joy in the *galut*."

Chapter 3

From Exile-without-Homeland to Homeland-without-Exile: Hebrew Fiction in Interwar Poland

Following the route of the majority's discourse and its taking control of the Hebrew culture arena during the first decades of the twentieth century necessitates a study of the development of literary writing in the Diaspora. In opposition to the strengthening of the voice of territorialization in Zionist literary discourse, other, constant literary voices continued to write Hebrew literature at a distance from national territory. Such minor voices were especially prominent in the Hebrew literary center in Poland; this cultural center was hurled into an extremely dramatic and conflictual situation between the two world wars.

Writing about Hebrew fiction in Poland between the wars entails examining an entity whose most prominent feature is void or nothingness. The twenty years that elapsed between Poland's independence in 1918 and its collapse in 1939 witnessed the decline of Hebrew literature there, a process portrayed in the harshest terms by its own readers and writers. In renewing the publication of *Luah Ahiasafin* (1923), Dr. Yehoshua (Osias) Thon wrote about the hopes aroused by the revival of the literary annual. In the same breath, however, he went on to stress that the publication lacked writers of stature, and he forecast the criticism it would receive in consequence. During the same period, Z. Z. Weinberg, one of the last Hebrew writers in Poland, described the desolate condition of Hebrew literature in that country, concluding with the somber proclamation that "the time has come for grave digging and burial" (Sternberg 1923, 242).

The broader causes of this decline have been widely considered. Overwhelmed by a sense of defeat, members of the interwar generation continually speculated about its causes. The unstable regime of post–World War I Poland subjected its Jewish citizens to physical and spiritual tribulations, persecutions, pogroms, and official restrictions such as Wladyslaw Grabski's tax laws and the anti-Jewish *numerus clausus,* applying to university admissions, that hastened the decline of the country's Jewish intelligentsia, who often opted for emigration, particularly to Palestine. In fact, during these years the Hebrew cultural center in Palestine grew and flourished, sometimes at the expense of Hebrew cultural centers in the Diaspora. The emergent center of Hebrew culture in Palestine now proved capable of offering an alternative that endangered the survival of the Hebrew center in Poland.

The golden age of Hebrew culture in Poland coincided with the early years of the twentieth century, which produced a profusion of eminent periodicals such as *HaTzefirah* (Dawn), *HaTzofeh* (The Observer), and *HaDor* (The Generation). Pre–World War I Warsaw attracted numerous Hebrew writers, including Y. L. Peretz, H. D. Nomberg, H. N. Bialik, Yaakov Fichman, David Frishman, Yaakov Steinberg, Zalman Shneor, Yaakov Cohen, and Baal Makhshavot (Miron 1987, 23–429; Shaked 1983, 249–50). Even after the devastation that befell the Jews during World War I, attempts were made to resuscitate Poland as a center of Hebrew culture. A not inconsiderable number of Hebrew writers, fleeing the Russian Revolution, settled in neighboring Poland. Leaving Moscow, Abraham Stiebel transferred his publishing house to Warsaw; prominent among Hebrew periodicals, *HaTekufah* (The Era) likewise moved to the Polish capital, where it was edited by David Frishman, Yaakov Cohen, and Fishel Lahover. The journal's editorial policy sought to elevate *HaTekufah* into the principal outlet for the works of leading Hebrew writers, whether in the Diaspora or in Palestine. But in this, *HaTekufah* was exceptional; in contrast, most of the Hebrew journals appearing in Warsaw were characterized by an awareness of the secondary place they occupied in relation to the Palestinian center. In spite of all efforts, Poland failed to regain its former position as a center of Hebrew culture.

The Russian Revolution also contributed to the decline of Hebrew culture in newly independent Poland. The enforced separation of Poland from the Hebrew-reading public in the Soviet Union gave a further boost to Yiddish culture and literature, to which many readers of Hebrew now turned. In the first edition of *BaDerekh* (On the Road), the Hebrew weekly that commenced publication in Warsaw in the early 1930s, Yitzhak Gruenbaum diagnosed "an important rule in our cultural life":

> The educated portion of the [Jewish] people, the Hebrew[-reading] portion, which in large part is likewise numbered among the educated portion, is incapable of supporting any cultural institution uniquely unto itself alone, neither a genuine theater in the spoken tongue nor a Hebrew press. This may be because it cannot resort to them exclusively, being both able and obliged to resort to the press in other languages, [and] to cultural institutions of other peoples. The Hebrew intellectual is unable, so to speak, to enter into exclusive communion with his press, [or] with his Hebrew literature, particularly in the Diaspora. In Palestine, such communion is facilitated by local conditions, and behold a strong foundation for the Hebrew press and for Hebrew literature is coming into being [there]. (Gruenbaum 1932; Hazan 1927)

Gruenbaum concluded that it was vitally important to increase the number of consumers of Hebrew culture, which should be extended to broader classes, to "ordinary readers" who read for pleasure. This broadening should be done even if it meant employing "simple Hebrew," a concession reflecting the powerful competition the waning Hebrew culture faced from its Yiddish and Polish rivals. Without doubt, Gruenbaum was also referring to the graduates of the Hebrew "Tarbut" school network in Poland, who failed for the most part to become consumers of Hebrew books or papers, and certainly not exclusively of Hebrew works published in Poland.

Reviewing an issue of *HaTekufah* in 1925, L. Eliav noted that, with the exception of Stiebel, Hebrew publishers in Poland had ceased to function. Three years later, the manager of Ever, Warsaw's Hebrew bookstore, pointed out the decline in purchases of Hebrew books in Poland, noting that his store was now the only one in the country devoted entirely to Hebrew books and papers (Zemer 1928). A few years later, A. Urinovsky wrote that, aside from a few textbooks, not a single Hebrew book had been published in Poland during the preceding year (Urinovsky 1932).

The dwindling number of Hebrew readers, particularly among the less elite classes, was reflected in the pitiful state of the Hebrew novel in Poland. A not inconsiderable portion of the novels published in Poland during this period were by Hebrew authors writing in Palestine, who, like Aaron Reuveny (1923), were forced by their precarious circumstances to fall back on the generosity of Warsaw's Stiebel publishing house. A humorous piece written at the time by Nachman Mifelev features a Hebrew writer who, having pursued a wearisome and hopeless courtship of the publishers, only to find that they prefer translations to original Hebrew manuscripts, concludes that his sole hope of a literary future lies in working as a translator (Mifelev 1928). Indeed, an examination of *HaTzefirah*, the veteran Hebrew daily that defied difficulties to continue its sporadic appearance throughout the interwar period, reveals that translations provided the bulk of its literary material.

The bleak state of Hebrew fiction in interwar Poland was attested by the critic Benzion Benshalom, who, after serving as a lecturer at the university of his native Kraków, reached Palestine in 1940. Three years later he wrote a summary of Hebrew literature in interwar Poland, focusing exclusively on poetry because, as he noted, "in the sphere of fiction, Hebrew literature in Poland in the period under discussion did not produce significant talents" (Benshalom 1943, 13).

In the long view that reaches up to the present day, one tends to gauge the achievements as well as the failures of the decaying Polish center against those of its emergent Hebrew Palestinian counterpart. It is important to recognize here that Zionist ideology has colored attitudes toward Hebrew literature, and a historiography that accepts Zionist teleology tends to overlook manifestations of cultural vitality in the Diaspora. The brutal eclipse of these manifestations, moreover, has led to their being portrayed as marginal to the creation of the cultural center in Palestine. Looking only at Hebrew fiction in Palestine, one cannot help but endorse Benshalom's assertion that its Polish counterpart was insignificant. A similar view can be found in the comprehensive "Al HaSipur HaIvri" (On the Hebrew Story), published in 1930 by the Palestinian critic Yaakov Rabinovitch ([1930] 1971, 63–76). Nonetheless, in our recollection of the terrible tragedy that befell Jewish culture in Poland, and in our awareness that its physical destruction was preceded by a progressive decline, we run the risk of overlooking its unique inner dynamism.

Redemption and Writing in a Conflictual Condition

This working hypothesis of an inner dynamism is best examined at the intersection of the spiritual complex delineated as "exile/homeland," which stands out among the themes explored by Hebrew fiction in interwar Poland. Indeed, the contrast between an increasingly impoverished Diaspora and the renascent homeland provided the spiritual focus for those who, while languishing in the Polish Diaspora, regarded themselves as citizens of the world of Hebrew culture.

A most characteristic example is Leib Hazan's *Geulah* (Redemption), one of the few Hebrew novels written in interwar Poland (Hazan 1930). It was published in Kovel in 1930, in the middle of the period under discussion. The book relates the story of a group of Jewish revolutionaries who dream of redemption in the form of a worker's uprising. Throughout, the novel depicts their revolutionary aspirations in analogy and, indeed, in genetic relation to Jewish religious hopes. Their Marxist conviction that the economic crisis that marked the early years of Polish independence would undermine a decaying capitalism and replace it with a new and just society is exhibited as a further expression of the traditional Jewish yearning for redemption.

In more specific terms, the novel's cast of characters features an apparent contrast between Reb Abraham Joseph, the simple Jewish beadle whose entire existence is given over to hopes of religious redemption, and his hard-working neighbor Hannah Leah, who dedicates her life to dreams of redemption arising from her revolutionary faith. Hannah Leah's home serves as a meeting place for the Jewish members of a revolutionary party. These revolutionaries are apparently adherents of the Bund, specifically of its left-wing faction, which strove for collaboration with the Komunistyczna Partia Polski (KPP, Polish Communist Party) while dismissing the Polska Partia Socjalistyczna (PPS, Polish Socialist Party) as reformist (Mendelsohn 1976, 196). When Hannah Leah's pretty younger sister, the pleasure-seeking Rivka, moves into the apartment, she intensifies the erotic pressures imbuing and confounding the activities of the revolutionaries. The group's political failure is highlighted by the revelation that Berish, the most enthusiastic and dogmatic of their number, is an informer who has betrayed his comrades to the police.

The book's intellectual code exposes the perilous delusion of Jews seeking to reform a society to which they do not belong. This is illustrated, in the story as in real life, by the antisemitism of the non-Jewish revolutionaries. On the personal plane, Rivka marries a factory owner, a representative of the opposing side. Rivka's triumph is contrasted with the setback Hannah Leah suffers in her romantic relations with Comrade Stach, who is more moderate than she in his political views. Personal and political themes again merge with the decline of revolutionary ferment, which leaves time for intimate concerns and permits Rivka's industrialist lover to marry her. Hannah Leah's emotional sacrifice in dedicating her entire life to revolutionary redemption is compounded by personal disaster, even though she narrowly escapes the trap laid by Berish, the negative protagonist; her suicide terminates a life of illusions, personal no less than political. After the disintegration of the revolutionary cell, the reader is left with the character of Stach, who discards his revolutionary illusions and leaves Poland.

In concrete terms, Stach's plan also represents the ideological solution proffered by the novel. In Gershon Shaked's historiographical study of modern Hebrew fiction, approached largely from the Zionist perspective, *Geulah* is presented as a novel whose literary structure reflects its author's Zionist ideas; it is described as a "Zionist ideological novel" (Shaked 1983, 286). Certain aspects of the story may allow Stach's ultimate decision to leave Poland to be depicted as a Zionist choice. Hazan's narrator, however, who is critical of ideology, signally refrains from an unambiguous affirmation to this effect. It is only in the standard context of accusations and imprecations directed against Stach by his adversaries on the Left that he is described as a "Zionist," an appellation that could be interpreted as derogatory, coming as it does from those who take a poor view of what they regard as Stach's constructivist deviations. Moreover, the precise national identity of the new society Stach hopes to establish "there in that distant land" is not specified; it could be interpreted as referring to the socialist colonies in Palestine, but Hazan leaves its specific identity open (Hazan 1930, 228).

The basic plot structure contrasts Jewish hopes of religious redemption, as expressed by the beadle, with the parallel aspirations of the Jewish revolutionaries; this contrast is highlighted in the dialogue between the old man and Stach, when the two examine the various paths to redemption. The beadle propounds the traditional Jewish doctrine of "I wait for the Lord, my soul does wait, and in his word do I hope" (Psalm 130:5), rejecting despair and seeing himself duty-bound to hope for succor even when the sword is at his throat. On this occasion, Stach presents his views in unequivocal terms, as he proclaims his universalist quest "to find happiness for myself and for the whole of humanity" (Hazan 1930, 228).

A resolution so ambiguous and open-ended in a work that, in all its other formal characteristics, is a *roman à thèse* clearly calls for thorough explanation. Defying our expectations of this genre, which typically presents a clear ideological position, the book takes us back to the contextual and thematic point of departure, with its emphasis on void and nothingness. The writing and publication of a Hebrew novel were relatively rare in interwar Poland, and this ultimately shaped *Geulah*'s literary structure. The open-ended plot, avoiding clear ideological definitions, can be largely explained by the broad range of cultural and social functions undertaken by Hebrew fiction in Poland. In contrast, any attempt on the part of Zionist historiography to fill the gaps left by the novel's failure to make an ideological choice is liable to overshadow the internal developments unique to the environment in which it was written. Like the few other Hebrew stories that appeared in Poland between the world wars, *Geulah* should be judged in light of the fact that most of the Hebrew writers still living in the country wrote and published little or nothing. The ideological ambiguity evident in *Geulah* can be interpreted as representing a reluctance to offer its readers a coherent ideological message. The literary ruse of an open ending may also reflect a kind of ambivalence toward the ideological task of representing and influencing reality by means of a literary text. It is noteworthy that, in literature as elsewhere, such an ideological task is generally performed by subjects who convert their particular view of the social or economic situation in which they find themselves into a total, overall portrayal that is presented as both self-evident and unavoidable (Eagleton 1979, 62–80). The common ideological pattern whereby a social vision is transformed into a coherent literary reality is, however, sometimes replaced by an ambivalent and critical attitude toward the real-life conditions and factors constituting and influencing that vision. As in other works written at the time in Poland, Hazan's novel makes extensive use of lacunae, inexplicable jumps, silences, and a refusal to make literary decisions, which together proffer a soberly critical message.

Hebrew writers in interwar Poland were confronted by cultural options in a state of tension that could lead to antagonism. In view of the rapid emergence of Hebrew culture in Palestine, the decision to continue writing Hebrew in the Polish center-in-decline entailed an evident paradox. The near automatic assertion of creative activity in Hebrew Zionist ideology made Hebrew writing in the Polish Diaspora an endeavor inclined to perceive itself as nothing more than a means or a preparation, subsidiary to authentic creativity in the Palestinian center. This tension found expression in the controversy aroused throughout the Zionist movement by the decisions of the Helsingfors Convention in 1906. Polish Zionists, as elsewhere, were divided between supporters of "laboring for the present" and disciples of "laboring for the future." On the political plane, the debate was reflected in the disagreements between the Et Livnot (time to build) faction, which held that the principal task of the Zionist movement was to organize mass emigration of Polish Jews to Palestine, and the Al HaMishmar (on watch) faction, headed by Yitzhak Gruenbaum, which argued that emigration to Palestine should be selective and that parallel efforts should be made to foster Jewish national existence in Poland and to cultivate the Zionist consciousness of the potential emigrants to Palestine (Mendelsohn 1976, 198). This was a late version of the turn-of-the-century conflict between laboring for the present and laboring for the future. Gruenbaum's strenuous activity within the Minorities Bloc, formed in the Polish Sejm (House of Deputies) during the early years of the country's independence, reflected his determination, as far as possible, to seek equal rights and a dignified existence for the Jews within the multinational patchwork of the Polish state.

Zionism's *shelilat hagolah* (disapproval and denial of the Diaspora) branded Hebrew cultural activity in Poland as secondary, thereby largely eroding the motivation of writers and, equally, readers to recognize Hebrew writings as effective ideological weapons. The double pressure exerted by a hostile environment and the absence of a steady audience led to a marked decline in Hebrew literature as a channel of communication. A paradoxical predicament arose, that of a literature composed in a language bearing a clear ideological label, and on behalf of a well-defined ethnic group, that effectively set itself the task of diminishing the numbers of its own readers. When the writer Z. Z. Weinberg left Poland and set out for Palestine, the ambivalent comments of his colleagues sharply reflected this inner tension (see, for example, Zohar 1934).

Given the historical situation of a stricken Diaspora and a blossoming Hebrew homeland, Hebrew writings were inevitably drawn to national themes. But efforts to produce ideological utterances capable of resolving, or at least moderating, the inner contradictions of the society within which they were generated became progressively more arduous and hopeless. In addition to the unequal battle that Hebrew literature was obliged to wage against popular Yiddish culture, with its broad appeal and its intensive backing by the Bund and others, in Poland the literature became the target of a kind of pincer movement by its Palestinian counterpart. First and foremost, the latter robbed it of readers and writers, who elected to express their Hebrew interests in their ideological homeland in Palestine rather than in what they perceived as an extremely precarious, temporary shelter. In addition, Palestine offered Hebrew writers and readers still residing in Poland an alternative form of literary creation and consumption that was far more attractive than Poland's product. Palestine's Hebrew presses and literature made persistent efforts to establish direct contact with the Hebrew-reading public in Poland. Whether on ideological grounds or due to a lack of high-quality material, the Hebrew press in Poland was likewise in the habit of reprinting material from its Palestinian counterparts or publishing the works of Hebrew writers living in Palestine. Matters were exacerbated by the inclination of Hebrew writers in Poland to publicize their works through Palestinian periodicals and publishing houses.

Journalistic Writing in a State of Crisis

The ideological and creative blind alley depicted here was perplexing for some of those Hebrew writers who wished to continue their creative activity in Poland. The inability to choose between emigrating to Palestine on the one hand and exchanging the dismal Polish Diaspora for European exile in another form on the other, as in Hazan's novel, had been preceded by a solution of a different kind, which achieved relative prominence in the Hebrew literature produced during the early years of Polish independence. Only a close scrutiny of the dynamics of Hebrew writing in Poland can reveal the significance of this intriguing phase, when Hebrew culture grappled with the sense of its own decline and with the inner contradictions threatening to destroy it. Along with a shared awareness of its own decay, Hebrew literature in post–World War I Poland developed an opposing frame of mind that endeavored to think in more positive, though nevertheless sober, terms. Alongside a bewailing of the prevalent disintegration and decay is evidence of literary and journalistic activity aimed at making the best of the situation.

Economic and political constraints, together with restrictions on immigration, severely limited the feasibility of finding a solution in Palestine. Consequently, one possible way of resolving the dilemma lay in attempting to preserve and reinforce the unique nature of the Diaspora, in contrast with the new homeland in Palestine and in spite of the latter's blossoming. In other words, the interwar Diaspora in Poland saw a striving to transform weakness into a measure of strength. This school was largely represented by the Warsaw periodical *Kolot* (Voices) and its moving spirit, Eliezer Steinman. Steinman reached Poland shortly after its liberation, remaining in the country for four years before his emigration to Palestine in 1924. "Here, in one of the cities of the exile," he wrote in the third volume of *Kolot*, "it is necessary to build a center of Hebrew culture, an electric power-station to distribute light. This center is the observant eye of the pulsing Hebrew heart, the voice heralding, in [all] lands, the existence and resurgence of our culture, the unifying telegraph" (Steinman 1923a, 117). Drawing an unusual distinction, Steinman in effect proposed a Hebrew version of S. M. Dubnov's autonomist views, differentiating between a cultural center in the Diaspora and its periphery, which, as he defined it, could be taken to include Palestine. In another issue of *Kolot*, Steinman criticized the cultural pretensions of the new Palestinian center while simultaneously conceding his own dependence on it: "Woe unto us from the construction and renewal of the Israeli center after the manner of existence of all the false centers of our society; and woe unto us from its total destruction" (Steinman 1923b, 204).

Steinman presented the Hebrew language as a kind of national ontology capable, on the linguistic plane at least, of offering a genuine alternative to the emerging Palestinian entity:

> We, who shall not despise the Diaspora, and shall not flatter the Hebrew language by dispatching it to be the [sole] heritage of the one hundred thousand strong Jewish community in the land of our forefathers, but shall, instead, aspire to see it flourishing in the mouths of seventeen million Children of Israel in all the [lands of] exile throughout the world; we who contemplate the whole existence by way of the twenty-two Hebrew letters, we shall uphold the tradition. (Steinman 1923c, 30–31)

The historical and conceptual analysis proposed by the historian Yitzhak (Fritz) Baer in *Galut* (Diaspora) illustrates clearly that as far back as the period of the Second Temple, when the Jewish state and the Temple were still in existence, the Diaspora was not regarded in purely negative terms, solely as a form of political enslavement; the Diaspora also played a positive role in teaching and propagating the true faith throughout the world (Baer 1980, 9–19). The sharp awareness of the physical and spiritual decay of the Polish Diaspora between the two world wars likewise produced an ephemeral blossoming in spite of the unfavorable conditions.

Steinman's proclamation was not an isolated occurrence, as is evident from the emergence, albeit limited, of daily papers such as *HaTzefirah* and *HaYom* (Today) and of periodicals such as *Kolot* and, later, *Zeramim* (Currents), *HaSolel* (The Trailblazer), and *Galim* (Waves), all of which aimed at providing platforms for discussion of the problems and dilemmas peculiar to Hebrew culture in Poland. This period also saw an upsurge of genres such as sketches and seminarrative essays, which achieved great prominence in Hebrew writing during the early years of Poland's independence. The wide disparities among prevalent historical codes, the pressures of an everyday reality that increasingly demanded literary expression, and the profound contradictions underlying Hebrew cultural activity in a renascent Poland combined to demolish coherent narrative structures. They were replaced by the feuilleton and the sketch, with their particular interpretations of the relationship between Diaspora and homeland.

A characteristic example is "Levado Nishar: Tsiyur" (Alone He Remained: A Sketch), by Nachman Mifelev (1921). It sings the praises of Yosef, the son of Hayim Reuven, and his obstinacy in clinging to the soil of his devastated Lithuanian township. After the death of the father, the rest of the family moves to America, where one of the brothers has already prospered. But Yosef, foreseeing a rosy future in Lithuania, stays on in the town to rebuild the family home destroyed during the war. In this story, the conflict between homeland and exile is removed from the Zionist context, with the Eastern European Diaspora legitimated by its own vitality and persistence. In Steinman's "BaNekhar" (In the Foreign Parts), published at about the same time, a similar set of oppositions is presented. The decadent "foreign land" is Belgium, depicted by the Jewish immigrants settled there instead of in their native Poland and in conflict with it. Poland, though it is a form of Diaspora, is the object of their yearnings and thus achieves the status of virtual homeland (Steinman 1922, 117–44).

In contrast with later texts, which highlight the hopelessness of Jewish existence in Poland, the travel notes published by Yakir Warshavsky in 1926 are a panegyric to Poland's landscapes, culture, and history. The writer's Jewish identity quickly comes to the fore through the imagery used to compare Poland's vistas and the landscape of Palestine. "Vavel!" Warshavsky exclaims while describing his tour of Kraków. "How uplifting is that name to the heart of any son of Poland, how it carries within it Poland's joys and sorrows! This mountain is linked with the course of Poland's history as Mount Zion is with that of the Jew. It penetrates the very depths of the people's soul, blending into it in a single amalgam." Referring to the Vistula, he writes, "This river is the heart's artery of this land, like the river Volga of Russia's soil, and the Jordan of the Land of Israel." But Warshavsky's ideological motivation emerges in full force when his tour of Jewish

Kraków leads him to exclaim over the mere fact of existence in a universal exile. In consequence, he does not feel himself to be a stranger in Kraków: "And I, a strange wayfarer, from a distant city, nevertheless am not alien in any way. I am among brothers, sensing myself linked and united with those about me, with those dispersed among the nations and states, and with all the generations which preceded me" (Warshavsky 1926).

Whereas Hazan's novel and its open-ended ideological conclusion reflect the instability of the historical situation it depicts, the stories published a decade earlier, just after World War I, present a clear ideological message whose unambiguous formulation was sometimes accomplished at the expense of balanced narrative development. The immediate need to publicize a specific viewpoint, which characterized Hebrew writing in Poland at the time, ultimately affected the literary structures that became prevalent. The want of literary talent and the decline of creative writing undermined standards of quality and compelled the dwindling ranks of Hebrew writers to assume dual roles, as polemicists and creators of belles lettres alike (Yakubovitz 1932). The pressure to produce an immediate ideological response was exemplified in the seminarrative pieces, characterized by intellectual shortcuts. In ever-increasing measure, narrative development was subjugated to the ideological positions the stories were expected to represent and exemplify. A critic referring to Yakir Warshavsky's *Maalot Umordot* (Ups and Downs), subtitled *Sipurim VeTsiyurim* (Stories and Sketches) and published in Warsaw in 1925, wrote that fortuity has a central role and described the transitions as overabrupt (Kahin 1927). Indeed, one of the more prominent pieces in the collection, "Yaldey HaVisla" (Children of the Vistula), illustrates the manner in which the Polish-Jewish conflict is handled, with the narrative mechanism secondary to the story's philosophical message. The piece stands out for its balanced development of the symbiosis between the two peoples. The crisis arising from the romantic relations between a Jewish youth and a Polish girl induces the former to commit suicide. Subsequently, however, the two sides make a marked effort to maintain their symbiotic relationship in mourning the calamity. Nevertheless, at the conclusion of the story, the narrative mechanism unexpectedly breaks down. In stark contradiction to what has hitherto transpired, the dead boy's father finds an exclusively Jewish solution that he is unable to share with his Polish friends. This denouement conveys the impression of serving to propagate a notion without foundation either in the characters portrayed or in the story's plot structure (Warshavsky 1925).

At about the same time, Warshavsky published, in serialized form, his story "Itim Hadashot" (New Times). The first installment, composed as an essay, describes the antisemitic ferment in Poland. Reb Yitzhak, known as Panie Itsheha, a standard Polish nickname for the Jewish stereotype, serves to demonstrate how antisemitism grants legitimacy to one, individual Jew who is acknowledged as being different from the other members of his race. This literary device highlights racist generalizations by focusing the plot on a character who proves the rule by constituting an apparent exception. The composition of the fragment restores the "deviant" example to the level of generalization by means of a sentence attributing overall historical significance to Reb Yitzhak's fears, as he senses that the upsurge of anti-Jewish discrimination will ultimately undermine the foundations of his own existence. The second installment expands this illustrative plot by depicting the sorrow of a father when his son decides to quit Poland and sets off to study in Switzerland. The father is anxious about the future in Poland, yet he grieves over his son's departure. As far as he is concerned, the central conflict is between continuing his existence in Poland and the fate of his son "in an alien land, seating himself to dine at the table of strangers." As all of Reb Yitzhak's children leave him and go their separate ways, he is left in his empty home to reflect over their aims. The younger generation exchanges one exile for another, with Zionism making its sole appearance in the form of orations by Zionist leaders; and even these are coupled with similar speeches by socialists (Warshavsky 1925–26).

In playing down the role of Zionism, Warshavsky shared Steinman's opinions, which were in turn influenced by David Frishman. Frishman was well known for his reservations about Zionism and his espousal of the aesthetic qualities of Hebrew literature. Leaving Moscow for Warsaw not long after the October Revolution, Frishman dedicated himself to editing and translation. He died in 1922, at the commencement of the era under discussion; right up to his death he continued to publish his series of biblical tales, *BaMidbar* (In the Desert) (1909–21). These stories exercised little influence on Hebrew fiction in Poland, but it is worth noting the ideological link between his interest in the desert wanderings of the children of Israel and his view that the Diaspora, far from being merely a preparation for emigration to Palestine, existed as an autonomous entity that shaped the Jewish people's culture and guiding principles. Frishman's story "HaMekoshesh" (The Wood Gatherer), composed in his characteristic biblical style, endows the exile in the desert with the status of a normative form of existence. The story traces the political and judicial institutionalization experienced by the children of Israel during their wanderings in the desert. To illustrate the powerful disciplinary aspect of biblical law at the time, it describes the stoning to death of a poor man who collected firewood on the Sabbath (Frishman 1921; Numbers 15:32–36).

An instructive illustration of a highly developed narrative solution, depicting an exile self-sufficient and unconnected with the homeland, is provided in the 1926 story "BeHararei Karpat" (In the Carpathian Mountains), by Reuven Fahan, whom I mentioned in chapter 1 as one of the outstanding figures in Galicia, which after the First World War was annexed to Poland. Set in a hamlet in Red Reissen in eastern Galicia, in the Carpathian Mountains, the narrative juxtaposes the "palace," the home of the local feudal landlord, and the nearby inn, inhabited by Yisrael the taverner. This contrast, heightened by the comment that the taverner's forefathers "came to Poland and Ukraine in freedom, a freedom that was not bequeathed to later generations" (Fahan 1969, 189), effectively sketches the lines of the conflict and the potential scope for its predictable resolution. The wanderings of a young family from Starona, a Carpathian mountain village, to the Ukrainian town that is the home of the young husband Rabbi Moshe Solotviner, are depicted in the story as enforced exile to a place of learning (following the traditional Jewish precept, quoted in the story: "Be exiled unto a place of learning"; 197). The story expresses this theme in concrete terms when the rabbi tells his bride that "the time has come to distance us from the table of your father and draw near to the table of our Father in Heaven. . . . Here, there is a laxity of learning, and that is a great sin. Let us then make preparations to journey to *our state!*" (197; italics mine). The traditional motif of Jews separated from their community unfolds here to a miraculous resolution, whereby the discovery of pearls provides the taverner's daughter with a dowry that rescues her from the threat of sexual conquest by the feudal lord. The supernatural elements of this story in effect emphasize and embellish the inner richness and validity of life in the Diaspora. The difficulties and crises endured collectively by the Jews on account of their national and religious identity are resolved here by means of miraculous connections and legendary characters. Matching the account of the rabbi's magical links with the Baal Shem Tov, the Ukrainian bandit Dobush is transformed into the rabbi's faithful servant and vows that he will never again harm a Jew.

To add further prominence to this modern imitation of Hasidic legend, Fahan relates the story of a blood libel, presented as an example of "one of those arduous times to which Israel is accustomed throughout the generations" (1969, 207). The corpse of a young maidservant, whom her master the priest murdered and flung at the door of the Jewish taverner in one of the villages, provides the standard pretext for expulsion of the Jews from the Carpathians to the Lvov community. Calling on his mystical gifts, Rabbi Moshe Solotviner invokes the spirit of the murdered girl, which unmasks the real murderer, thereby fending off the calamity that threatens his co-religionists. Here again, it is noteworthy that Fahan puts the rhetoric of his account to unusual use in depicting exile as a permanent condition, characterized by conflicts that are nevertheless capable of solution. When the Jews are ordered to be expelled, the narrator offers his interpretation: "Behold, another exile is added, from one land to another, on top of all the other exiles" (209). In this manner, the narrative progressively strips the concept of exile of its normal binary opposite, the land of Israel. To Rabbi Moshe Solotviner, the Ukraine is "our state" rather than "our homeland"; likewise, the story depicts expulsion from the Carpathians as the replacement of one land of exile by another. This is not exile from a homeland; rather, it is exile-without-homeland.

The rabbi's endeavors to refute the blood libel are analogous to the chronicle of his wanderings, from the house of his father-in-law in the Carpathian home and, from there, after years of service to his people, back to the region where he had lived previously with his father-in-law, in the nearby town of Solotvina. In essence, this journey represents the renewal of those spiritual and mystical links with the Carpathian landscape that had accompanied him throughout the course of his life. In terminating the exile the rabbi had undertaken for the purpose of study and his religious duties, Fahan's story is content with restoring him to his spiritual and mystical origins, which are linked to the Carpathian landscape. In a similar manner, the mystical event succeeds in abrogating the expulsion decree in the analogous subplot relating to his ethnic community. Admittedly, this is not exile from a perfect homeland, for, as already cited, the freedom of the taverner's forefathers has not been "bequeathed to later generations"; nevertheless, the homeland-exile opposition is transferred into Eastern Europe, where one polarity offers direct and vital contact with a land and its landscape. (Fahan sets his story in his native village of Starunia.) In this manner, exile becomes a prolonged and vital form of existence in which the absence of a homeland is soberly taken into account.

It is nevertheless noteworthy that this ideological pattern displays a singular sensitivity toward the Zionist option. When the omnipotent Dobush offers to lead his friend Rabbi Moshe Solotviner to Palestine, by way of hidden tunnels and caverns (according to a well-known folktale), the rabbi rejects the offer, "because he did not wish to employ venality for the purpose of holiness" (Fahan 1969, 207). In other words, the land of Israel is not a realistic option in the context of the exile, but even if Zionism is not a genuine way out, it does exercise a tangible hold on the drab, painstaking historical process. Though invoked to resolve conflicts and crises throughout the course of the story, mystical motivation is rejected outright in relation to the land of Israel. Taking a kabbalistic perspective, the rabbi refuses to countenance a temporary alliance with evil, not even for the sacred goal of redemption. Even at the furthest extremities of exile-without-homeland, messianic and mystical semantics are barred from trespassing into areas dominated by an antimessianic orientation.

Fahan's story, the narrative form of which draws largely on the fantasy of traditional Hasidic tales, may be regarded as a connecting link between the seminarrative genre so prevalent at the beginning of the interwar period and the novelistic forms that gained prominence halfway through it, around 1930. The early works of Steinman, Warshavsky, Mifelev, Yehoshua Heschel Yevin, and others were largely limited to sketches, feuilletons, essays, or longer works that avoided the ideological issues of their time (for example, Eliezer Steinman's novel *Esther Hayot* [1923]). In this they responded to the pressures that later found expression in Hazan's *Geulah*, which, like traditional romances and intrigue literature, relies on fortuity and coincidence to unmask the villain. To return to Hazan's novel, even when it traces a process of ideological disillusionment, manipulating the reader in relation to the "good guys" and the "bad guys," no fundamental change comes about. Stach's constructivism is a basic component of Hazan's novel. In direct, almost mechanical response to the dramatic events he experiences, the suicide of his lover and the disintegration of the revolutionary cell, he resolves to leave Poland. It should be recalled, however, that given the circumstances at the time of the novel's composition, the ideological foundations supporting the cast of characters are not sufficiently firm to lead them to an unambiguous adherence to Zionism.

But how does one move from the personal essay, the sketch, or even the longer story that patches its plot together by means of miracles to the larger narrative framework that would provide an ideological response to the pressures exerted by real life? Hazan encountered difficulties of composition that stemmed from the disparity between his desire for ideological expression within the broad framework of the realistic novel, which seeks to integrate the individual into his background, and the linguistic possibilities, in the spiritual and ideological sense of the term. An intriguing solution to Hazan's difficulties is to be found in Z. Z. Weinberg's *Bayit URehov: Shnot 1918–1926* (House and Street: The Years 1918–1926), published in 1931, at about the same time as Hazan's novel appeared. (Stiebel, whose later removal from Warsaw to Tel Aviv and Berlin reflected the disintegration of the Hebrew center in Poland, issued the book.) At the time, Weinberg was regarded as one of the most prominent Hebrew writers in Poland. Like Hazan, whose novel was also written halfway between the two world wars, Weinberg directed his attention, as the subtitle indicates, above all to the formative early years of Polish independence. The book traces the sufferings of the Jews of Poland as the country becomes a battlefield.

As in the fiction composed at the beginning of the interwar period, this novel, too, harshly relates the tribulations the Jews endured in the Polish Diaspora. These sufferings emerge with particular clarity in the funeral of the priest who had protected the Jews from their tormentors. During the early days of the war, he defended young Jews against the Russians who accused them of espionage. When the Germans invaded, he stood up to them, too, whereupon he was harassed and sent to a detention camp. When the Poles took the town, the priest again defended the Jews against their enemies and protested the restrictions to which they were subjected. When the Bolsheviks occupied the town, he defied them in solidarity with the rabbis. Finally, when the Poles returned and began mistreating the Jews, he threatened to give up his position as spiritual leader of the community if the Polish soldiers harmed the Jews. "Holy soul!" the narrator exclaims, addressing the dead priest:

> Hearken unto the throbbing of hearts and the flow of sentiments and the pulse of life aflame within the spirits of your mourners, and be an honest witness before God's throne, for them and for their vanities and for their battles and for their lunacies on this dismal soil, the unhappy soil of Poland, which is powerless to extend maternal wings, the wings of a homeland, over all those born upon it and seeking shelter in its shade. (Weinberg 1931, 141)

Insofar as the novel expresses problematic aspects of Jewish existence in Poland, it does not propose any direct solutions. Such issues are raised by the very fact of the story's being written in Hebrew, as well as by the historical circumstances of its composition and, above all, by its intense preoccupation with the basic principles underlying the reality it portrays. Moreover, these issues affected the book's structure, primarily in Weinberg's choice of a genre closely approximating a documentary chronicle. The narrator is presented as having personally experienced the events he relates, and this explains and is supported by the book's form. Moreover, its account of Jewish sufferings is presented as personal viewpoint through the narrator's name, Michael Sternberg, which is the pen name Weinberg used in the pieces he published in *Kolot* and other periodicals. The book's autobiographical form enables it to avoid any clear ideological solution. The plot's motifs and conflicts, which draw on the most highly charged of historical materials, are processed through the personal filter of the narrator, whose subjective viewpoint remains noncommittal and who does not offer overall solutions to the ideological issues posed by his experience.

It may have been this lack of ideological interpretation and commitment that led critics to produce opposing views of the novel. G. Elkes, in Poland, overlooked Weinberg's explicit references to Poland's cruel past and prospective behavior toward its Jewish citizens. His comments were characteristic of those who clung to a belief in exile-without-homeland. After recommending that the book be translated into Polish, he added that the book depicts "the grief of a faithful citizen of Poland, who sees his beloved country in its waywardness. The author is bound by thousands of bonds to the soil of Poland upon which his fathers and forefathers lived and died. . . . And the author believes in a fairer tomorrow, and that hatred of nation for nation shall not dishonor the state of Poland" (Elkes 1932, 24–25). In a review written in Palestine, Shmueli gave the novel an outright Zionist interpretation, depicting it as "denying the Diaspora" and the rootless and hopeless existence it offered the Jews. The Palestinian critic complained, however, about the book's quasi-documentary character, on which he blamed its failure to grasp the fateful and fundamental dimension of the events it portrays (Shmueli 1931, 13).

The narrator of *House and Street* depicts Jewish existence in a turbulent Poland, commencing with his arrival in Warsaw immediately after the country's independence and concluding with his return, at the end of the period of upheavals and pogroms, to his native village and the nearby provincial town. By opting for a narrative in chronicle form, presented by a narrator who claims to be nonfictional, Weinberg was free to depict Polish antisemitism in its naked form, not forced to weave it into a "closed" ideological plot. In this manner, he made use of the ramified tradition of the essay and the sketch, transforming them into the organizing principle for a long and unified work. The narrator-chronicler whose presence generates this stream of memoirs may liberate the seminarrative genres from the forced and artificial character they sometimes receive under the weight of their ideological message. At the time, Reuven Fahan was likewise drawn to the documentary form. In a letter to H. N. Bialik, he sought counsel about the composition and publication of a book that, drawing on his experience in an important political post, would present the annals of the Jewish community of eastern Galicia at a critical time, "when the world war ended, and the Ukrainians took over the government in that country. At that time, the Jewish community was perplexed by the complexity of events: it organized, defended itself, demanded national autonomy etc., etc." (Fahan 1969a, 261–62).

The Jews' hopes of acquiring full rights as Polish citizens, aroused by Józef Pilsudski, are dispelled in Weinberg's book, which describes the crude antisemitism of Pilsudski's soldiers. The context of personal testimony within which the ideological generalizations are presented, however, gives Weinberg's work a potent human dimension that banishes any examination of the generalizations in a broader historical perspective. This occurs through the ironic reaction to the Jewish hopes of integration into Polish society in view of the pogroms accompanying the victories of the Polish army. These hopes are re-examined in the light of fundamental categories drawn largely from the reconstructed consciousness of the characters taking part. The latter are presented in the story, however, not as though they are the choice of an author with a highly developed historical awareness but through their fortuitous encounters with the narrator, in a variety of bizarre ways. It is by this literary device that Weinberg examines the Zionist option. Reminiscent of the ambivalence evident in Hazan's novel, Weinberg, too, leaves the issue unclear: the narrator's young friend and neighbor, the enthusiastic Zionist Tzali Freiman, comes to tell him that he has been released from the Polish army and is "a free Jew who wishes to savor the taste of a homeland" (Weinberg 1931, 117). The war against the Germans and Russians had aroused the young Zionist to nationalist fervor, for "Poland, which was trampled under the foot of the Tzar, and torn by the hoofs of the Prussian, has been restored to life. I am a Zionist. The dream of renaissance is my dream! Poland's banner is my banner! . . . Let the Poles know a voice whispered to me that the Jews, too, are a nation. The Jew is linked to his homeland" (118). The brutal antisemitism that subjects the young man to humiliation and imprisonment has ultimately brought him, in his disillusionment, to seek discharge from the Polish army. Even here, however, there is no clear alternative to the much-disparaged Polish Diaspora. In addition, it should be recalled that, within the literary context created by Weinberg, the collapse of Jewish hopes of joining in Polish identity likewise casts a heavy shadow over the Zionist motivation of the naive volunteer.

Grotesque and Ambivalence

The ideological hesitation evident in Hazan's *Geulah* can be interpreted as reflecting the difficulty of presenting an unambiguous position and, equally, as an attempt to give a unique ideological form to the paradoxical and hopeless situation of Hebrew literature in Poland. In considering the Hebrew literature produced in Poland, the emphasis on void and nonexistence as a substantial and structural element proves to be an equally effective point of departure with regard to more conventional plot solutions, such as that proposed by Yehuda Warshaviak's *Orot Meofel* (Lights from Darkness), published in Warsaw in 1931. As noted at the conclusion of the book, it was composed in 1928–29, when the economic crisis sweeping the country produced an upsurge of economic antisemitism. Like Hazan's *Geulah* and Weinberg's *Bayit URehov*, Warshaviak's work portrays the final days of World War I, the liberation of Poland from Russian occupation, and the rebirth of its independence, all blending as the formative experience of an entire generation. All three books highlight the hopes of young Jews for a dignified existence in a sovereign Poland. Similarly, anticipation of an imminent workers' revolution, so prominent in the novels of Hazan and Warshaviak, in the final account represents Jewish hopes of national equality and the elimination of antisemitism under a future socialist regime.

In an interesting blend of the hero of the *Zeitsroman* and that of the *Bildungsroman*, Warshaviak's Margolin undergoes a progressive process of personal and ideological maturation. The process commences with a Jewish soldier's returning from the battlefields of the world war to seek his way in life and concludes with his finding shelter in Zionist ideals, which he then puts into practice. In delineating Margolin as a character typical of the generation of young Jews who grew to maturity in interwar Poland, Warshaviak leads him, step by step, along the arduous path to the Zionist solution. When Margolin returns from the war, his rootlessness induces him to seek asylum in the arms of a Polish waitress employed at a railway-station snack bar. In the early sections of the novel, Margolin displays an alienated reserve toward the Jewish world in which he is expected to find his place. His first encounter with Zionism, in his native town, leaves him totally indifferent; by contrast, heroic tales of the Polish Uprising of 1863 ignite his enthusiasm.

Margolin is invited to visit the estate of Czortinski, the duke's son, and his acceptance is presented as a symbolic act of alliance with the Polish elite, which he achieves by overcoming mental and cultural obstacles. Even if he displays ambivalence toward Polish aspirations for national redemption (as reflected in his response to the tale of Antosh, the disillusioned disciple of Pilsudski, who exacted private vengeance on the Germans), Margolin finds that his visit to the Czortinski estate leads him to outright rejection of the Zionist option and to temporary relief from the despondency he has experienced working at his father's flour mill—though there, too, he finds an ephemeral vitality in sexual relations with a Polish woman, Yasha, the younger daughter of his father's employee. The next and decisive phase of Margolin's personal and ideological development occurs as he begins to respond to the revolutionary ideas implanted in his mind by Czortinski. Margolin's sense of disgrace and guilt over his abuse of the trust placed in him by Yasha's father puts an end to his attempts to settle down in his parents' township, and he sets off for Warsaw, to his friend Czortinski, now a political activist. Hoping to find substance for his life and convinced that proletarian unity requires the Jews to take part in the revolution, Margolin is drawn into active work for the party (apparently the Polish Socialist Party). His political activity, however, progressively exposes him to contradictions and pressures arising from his Jewish origins. Along with his party colleagues, he joins the Socialist National Legion, formed by the party to defend the Polish homeland against the Bolsheviks. The internal contradictions experienced by the Polish revolutionaries, torn between their loyalties to their class and to their nation, pale when compared with the profound inner conflict Margolin experiences as a Jew. He soon finds himself involved in a national conflict that expands until his disillusionment leads him to question, "What is in all this for us?" His tragic encounter with Jewish victims of abuse by Polish soldiers who were intoxicated by their triumph over the Soviets leads him to make his choice: he abandons the Diaspora in favor of the Zionist solution.

In the novel's concluding paragraph, Warshaviak rejects the concept of cultivating and developing the Diaspora, a concept belonging to a school of thought that criticized the Zionists for regarding Palestine as their homeland. The novel is imbued with the general conviction that the Polish Diaspora holds few prospects. After the initial hopes the Polish government inspired in its Jewish citizens, disillusionment was now general. The physical confrontation with antisemitism and the legal enactment of economic restrictions had shown the vision of the early days of Polish independence to be totally illusory. During the early 1930s, those who hoped to benefit from the collapse of Palestinocentrism, to pursue the idea of exile-without-homeland, were vigorously attacked by writers such as the Hebrew poet Malkiel Lusternik (1933). Indeed, Warshaviak dedicated considerable efforts to a rapprochement with Polish culture, with which he hoped to construct a symbiotic relationship. For example, the two volumes of his *Meal Gdot HaVisla* (Over the Banks of the Vistula), published in Warsaw in 1929 and 1933, were printed with Polish assistance; they comprise essays on Polish authors and on Jews in Polish literature. Likewise, Warshaviak showered praise on one work for the mere fact of its cultural uniqueness as a Polish novel about Palestine (Warshaviak 1931a). In *Orot Meofel*, Warshaviak's fluctuating attitude toward the relationship between the Diaspora and the new homeland took a new tack. The hero's departure for Palestine is depicted as a total relinquishing of exile, toward which there is now no trace of any positive sentiment: "The train hastened to leave behind the expanses of the soil of exile, as though fleeing from them in disgust. . . . The eastern horizon began to don a bracing and invigorating light. The dawn began to break. Margolin pushed his hands out of the window, and along with his hands, his eyes were drawn forward" (Warshaviak 1931, 188).

But the emergence of this new polarity, representing a Zionism based on homeland-without-exile, was not accomplished without difficulty. In numerous and intriguing ways, Warshaviak's novel continues to depict the Diaspora, with its strength and promise, as the focus of a powerful attraction. In opting unequivocally for a *Zeitsroman* to trace the ideological development of a young Jew in interwar Poland, Warshaviak highlighted the weaker points of his chronicle of the personal and ideological turnabout that led Margolin to Zionism. One reviewer expressed his dissatisfaction with the superficiality, fortuity, and emptiness characterizing Margolin and his path to Zionism

(Goldberg 1931). The turn at the end of the novel is explained, inter alia, by the mysterious illumination of a crucifix, leading Margolin to perceive the current historical situation as a renewed crucifixion of Jesus the Jew, who is required yet again to oil the wheels of historical change in the Gentile world. This mystical event underlines the leit-motiv of darkness and light that makes its first appearance in the novel's title and, after numerous repetitions and variations, returns in the final lines, where the light is represented as a metaphor for Zion-ist hope brightening the gloom of exile. This systematic develop-ment, which stresses the antagonism between Diaspora and home-land by associating it allegorically with the contrast between darkness and light, helps create the final effect of spurning exile in favor of the hope for a new homeland.

But alongside these motifs the novel develops an analogous story line whose grotesque configuration highlights the existential predica-ment of Poland's Jews. When the duke's daughter complains that the Jews, for all their sharpness of wit, find difficulty in drawing a distinc-tion between humor and reality, Margolin responds, "For us, a light-hearted jest has often been transformed into a cruel and merciless re-ality: the Jew dreads them both" (Warshaviak 1931, 95). His reply con-stitutes a link in a grotesque series that foreshadows his encounter, toward the end of the novel, with the demented laughter of the Jew-ish *halutzah* (Zionist pioneer woman) who has fallen victim to the cruel abuse of Polish soldiers.

Margolin's disillusionment with his former revolutionary ideals is further emphasized when the enthusiastic slogans lauding the vision of universal revolution punctuate the insane mouthing of the *ha-lutzah*, now deranged after the rape. The Zionist solution, however, meant to resolve or at least to draw sharp distinctions among the poles of the grotesque, the comic, and the nightmarish, is not char-acterized adequately to place it on an existential, personal, or social par with the pressures that, according to the novel, exile exerts on the Jews. One nevertheless cannot help being impressed by the rhetoric of the grotesque, whereby the novel displays the complexity and am-bivalence of its ideological perception of the interplay of exile and homeland. Czortinski, the Gentile, recalls how his Jewish artist friend Leibovitz showed him a painting of a Jew with his mouth open wide with laughter; Czortinski himself was struck by what he perceived as the subject's tragic expression. Czortinski elaborates the anecdote into an allegory illustrating the contrast between the Jews, with their candid eyes that reflect their genuine feelings, and the Gentiles, whose artful eyes conceal their inner mood. Margolin's turn to Zionism, depicted as his return to Jewish authenticity, is part of his effort to contend with manifestations of the grotesque. Early in the novel, Margolin is impressed by the Gentile workman, whose behavior blurs the distinction between the sublime and the ridiculous. Toward the end of the novel, this grotesque confusion of feelings is revived by the horrifying spectacle of the Pole Marginski, the venerable member of the workers' party, who, in time of war, emerges as a hysterical nationalist; his absurd laughter reminds Czortinski of the grotesque portrait painted by his friend Leibovitz. These changing responses further emphasize the personal and ideological metamorphosis Margolin has undergone: in the first case, when he is caught upon the horns of his grotesque dilemma, it is the solemn and sublime side that predominates; now, as he approaches the realization that there is no future for Jewish life in Poland, horror and disgust gain the upper hand. Czortinski's analogy between Marginski and Leibovitz's portrait also highlights the profoundly tragic element of this conclusion.

The novel's recourse to the grotesque, with the inner conflict characterizing it, is a symptom of the sharp ideological ambivalence that the grotesque leaves unresolved. The disparity between the questions the novel poses and the answers it provides emphasizes the fact that it is, in many ways, torn between the stark ideological conviction that there is nothing more to expect from a despicable Diaspora and the feeling that, for all its pathological contradictions, the Diaspora still retains its vital energy. As in the works of Hazan and Weinberg, this novel's ideological ambivalence repeatedly illustrates the intellectual division and confusion of its audience. The grotesque pattern of Warshaviak's novel and the contradictions so characteristic of it left it open to a variety of interpretations, in Poland and elsewhere. These inner conflicts and divisions detract from the integrity of the novel; its aesthetic flaws, indeed, drew harsh criticism (Goldberg 1933, 38–39).

In this connection, it should be reiterated that, in flagrant contrast with the thin trickle of literary creativity seeking to convey a coherent ideological utterance, there stretched an expanse of emptiness and nothingness in the Hebrew literature of interwar Poland. Warshaviak's work is perhaps the most striking example of an attempt to revive Hebrew literature at a time when the potential, whether collective, in relation to the audience, or individual, with regard to the talent available, was limited. He and others were the targets for the repeated criticism that, at a time of cultural decline, positions of unwarranted importance were occupied by all kinds of honor seekers and "graphomaniacs" who should properly be relegated to a marginal literary status (Riv 1936; Warshaviak 1936, 15).

As depicted in the novel, Margolin's anguished path of disillusionment stretches from a Diaspora with no longings for the Zionist homeland to a sense of homeland reinforced by disgust toward the Polish Diaspora. In his concluding Zionist address, delivered at the town assembly hall, he encapsulates his ideological message within his life's story. In other words, through the biographical format that provides the novel's structural framework, Warshaviak characterized Jewish life in the Diaspora, with its illusory hopes, revolutionary and otherwise, as being adrift in a world of legends. Margolin's Zionist phase is thus depicted as a response to the traditions of exile-without-homeland. In similar fashion, Warshaviak depicts Margolin's wonder at the patience and the submission to nature he detects in a homespun Polish peasant. Resembling the admiration for the simple Poles that can be found in Warshaviak's earlier stories (for example, "Bli Emunah" [Without Faith], which traces the fundamental religious doubts of a farmer's son; Warshaviak 1928, 5–27), this feeling enables Margolin, at an earlier stage of his development, to formulate his criticism of the Zionists' endeavors. His comments sound like a minor variation on the theme of exile-without-homeland, whose advocates voiced their criticisms of the Palestinian "Diaspora":

> You are too frantic and urgent, your garrulity overflows the deeds and enterprises; and who knows whether even the men of the Land of Israel have succeeded in extricating themselves from this Diaspora destiny, as Benyamin the coachman describes it: no matter how much a Jew hastens, he will always be late, and he will hasten nevertheless, even though he knows full well that he will be late, he will be late. (Warshaviak 1931, 81)

Margolin's view that "this Diaspora destiny" overshadows Zionist endeavors in Palestine, which are presented in the novel in a sober context, similarly disparages the attitudes still characteristic of the Hebrew center in Poland.

Literature of a Tribe or Literature of a People?

Admittedly, at this advanced stage, the Polish center no longer voiced pretentious declarations after the manner of Steinman's radical views from the early 1920s. A residue of the ideal of exile-without-homeland was still evident, however, in the heroic effort to maintain *BaDerekh* as a Hebrew weekly in Poland during the 1930s. The desire to preserve an organ of Hebrew cultural activity separate and distinct from the periodicals published by the Zionist pioneer movements, such as *HeAtid* (The Future), was supported by the demand that the Hebrew press in the Diaspora should serve as a common platform, with Hebrew providing a basic, common denominator adequate for expressing all the nationalist factions in Poland. An awareness of the cruel fate in store for Hebrew culture in Poland evoked repeated calls to close ranks, to downplay disagreements, and to endeavor to defend every Hebrew outpost—in this case, *BaDerekh* (Urinovsky 1932a; see Werses 1989).

A further echo of the survival of the concept of exile-without-homeland is found in G. Goldberg's review of Warshaviak's novel. In spite of his awareness of the work's flaws, the reviewer commended its author equally for exploring the life of the Polish people and for the mere act of writing and publishing a book "in the neglected field of our [Hebrew] literature in Poland" (Goldberg 1931). In a lecture published in Lvov in 1933, Simon Rawidowicz reiterated these notions: "Just as the Diaspora needs the Land of Israel, the Land of Israel needs the Diaspora" (Rawidowicz 1933). On a similar note, Rawidowicz responded enthusiastically to Asher Barash's harsh criticism of the contemptuous attitude toward the Diaspora displayed by the Palestinian center (Rawidowicz 1931). Barash, one of the leading Hebrew writers in Palestine, had voiced his criticism in a controversial lecture titled "Sifrut Shel Shevet O Sifrut Shel Am?" (Literature of a Tribe or Literature of a People?). Endorsing views similar to those expressed by Rawidowicz in *HaOlam* (The World), the organ of the World Zionist Organization, Barash criticized Hebrew literature in Palestine for its dismissal of Diaspora literature and for its tribalism, thereby questioning both the cultural roots and the significance of Palestinian Hebrew literature. Barash elaborated the concept of a legitimate and vital Diaspora existing side by side with a predominant metropolitan homeland and urged Hebrew literature in Palestine to grant a share in its own development to the Hebrew Diaspora (Barash 1931; Rawidowicz 1930).

In response, the prominent critic Yaakov Rabinovitch, residing in Palestine, affirmed that he was not concerned about the emergence of a tribe in Palestine; on the contrary, he hoped for such a development. He believed that adherence to Hebrew had constituted a force for salvation throughout Jewish history. At this time, it would also save the Diaspora from perdition and ultimately foster Palestinian culture to achieve the breadth and depth it deserved (Rabinovitch 1931). Writing in Palestine in 1931, Rabinovitch advocated a view astoundingly similar to the national ontology attributed to the Hebrew language by Steinman and his colleagues during the immediate postwar period. By contrast, it was the Warsaw periodical *HaTzefirah* that now proceeded to publish an article condemning Rabinovitch for his conviction that the Hebrew language alone could offer salvation both to the Diaspora and to the homeland (Zeligman 1931). Three years later, Lusternik, writing in another Warsaw periodical, *Reshit* (Beginning), attacked the Palestinian center for referring to itself under the demeaning term *tribe.* By his reproof, he showed himself to be more Jewish Palestinian than the Jewish Palestinians (Lusternik 1934).

Desperation Became Evident

With the passage of the years, a growing sense of dread and desperation became evident. The Nazis' rise to power in Germany in 1933 incited Polish antisemitism to frenzy. In a programmatic article titled "Yahadut Polin Heikhan?" (Whither Polish Jewry?), Leib Hazan wrote that Palestine was now the only lifeline, whereas in Poland "a chasm has opened up at the feet of the rising generation of an entire people!" (Hazan 1935). Gone was the ideological ambivalence of Hebrew literature; but concurrently, the literature itself was on the wane. What had still been feasible in 1930—the preservation, in literature at least, of a measure of uncertainty, complexity, and sobriety—became anachronistic in 1935 with the death of Pilsudski, who, notwithstanding the bitter disappointments he had inflicted on Poland's Jews, was still regarded as a ray of light in the terrifying gloom prevailing all around (as is exemplified in his eulogy by Meizel in 1935). Pilsudski's demise signaled the onset of a new and savage phase of persecution, which reached its peak in 1936–37 (Melzer 1982, 39–162).

In the sphere of literary genres, the most striking illustration of the change was the disappearance of the Hebrew novel, a literary form that could have attempted to contend with the wealth of material provided by everyday reality and the ideological pressures it generated. As the Zionist interpretation of Jewish existence in Poland grew more somber and unambiguous, the short story and the novella progressively replaced the novel. As the arena of struggle narrowed and its prospects grew dimmer, there was a return to the shorter and pithier forms prevalent in Hebrew fiction in Poland in the period immediately after the First World War. It is interesting that this is the precise reverse of the trend evident during the same period in Palestinian Hebrew literature. In the controversy that unfolded in Palestine at that time with regard to desirable literary genres, there were critical demands for more short stories, rather than novels. Yaakov Fichman, for example, saw the novel as capable of responding to variegated materials by conveying a clear ideological message (a novel about life in the kibbutz, a novel about the war years), in contrast with the greater flexibility of the novella. Like Rabinovitch some years before, Fichman recognized the genuine national-ideological need fulfilled by the wealth of novels, even as he simultaneously looked forward to the development of the novella (Fichman 1938; Rabinovitch [1930] 1971, 63–76).

This opposing emphasis highlights the contrast between the Polish center-in-decline and its flourishing Palestinian counterpart. It also points to the particular relation of dependence between the Polish center and its counterpart in Palestine. The fear evinced by Barash that the Palestinian center might become merely "tribal" amounts to a recognition that this relation of dependence was mutual. While the Hebrew center in Poland was obviously dependent on Eretz Israel, it is equally possible to discern the latter's need for the Diaspora's special contribution to its development. Now this pattern of mutual complementarity between the two cultural-territorial systems was actualized to some degree in the distribution of narrative genres. The short story and the novella, much vaunted literary goals for leading critics in Eretz Israel, were the principal narrative genres practiced during the last years of the Hebrew center in Poland. Conversely, the Hebrew realistic-ideological novel, which had virtually disappeared in Poland, was already prominent in Eretz Israel.

As Hebrew fiction in Poland progressively fell silent, it threw off all hope of survival in the Polish Diaspora. "Av Antishemi" (Antisemitic Father), written by Warshaviak in the anecdotal manner of Gershon Shofman's stories, portrays antisemitism as a natural phenomenon, indestructible and unaffected by environment or history. The antisemite, identified on the train solely by his movements and facial expressions, is depicted as relentless in his hatred of Jews. His display of tender feeling, brought on by the sight of his son's reflection through the sunlit carriage window, is an ironic device designed to bring out the deep-rootedness of the man's ill will toward Jews (Warshaviak 1935, 115–18; Shaked 1983, 270).

At the same time, Hebrew fiction in Poland showed a growing inclination toward the Palestinian homeland. *Sefer HaShanah LeYehudei Polanyah* (The Polish Jewish Yearbook), published by the Miflat publishing house in 1938, contains a story by Mifelev, significantly titled "Hu Lo Yireh Et HaAretz" (He Will Not See the Land) (Mifelev 1938, 200–14). Miflat set itself the sober objective of printing one or two Hebrew books per year and distributing a few hundred copies, as its "effort to maintain the outpost and the line," even though "the people of the Land of Israel may perhaps not understand the matter" (Zilberpfennig 1938, 356). At the beginning of the volume, its editorial board pointed out that the yearbook was being published "at a difficult period for Polish Jewry, at a time of increasingly aggressive anti-Semitism, at a time when despair is gaining control of the Jewish streets, during a time of spiritual and material decline of Polish Jewry" (6).

Mifelev's story describes the growth and expansion of Polish Zionism during the interwar period. The process is depicted in contrast with the progressive eclipse of Zvi Green, an old-fashioned Hebrew teacher and one of the earliest active Zionists. His want of political gifts and absence of leadership qualities, which lead to his decline, highlight the changed nature of Zionist work and the new attributes required for its pursuit. The fact that he finds his place in cultural activity emphasizes the futile nature of "laboring for the present." It gradually emerges that Green serves Mifelev as a satiric butt and an allegory for the Hebrew endeavor in Poland. Green's deteriorating economic status, in contrast to his persistence in cultural work, particularly in aspects lacking any real significance, is part of a broad canvas that also includes barbed criticism of the deceit implicit in the aid Polish Zionists receive from Palestine. The story reaches its climax when Green realizes that, precisely because of his naive Zionist integrity, he will not be able to fulfill his dream of emigrating to Palestine. Unlike those who, in spite of their indifference to the Zionist ideal, manage to find underhanded ways of acquiring immigration certificates, Green is condemned to remain in Poland, robbed of the reward he deserves for his efforts.

The new homeland in Palestine was now in the process of shaking off the Zionist Diaspora with its outmoded values. Caught between the efforts of the Polish government to solve its "Jewish Problem" by encouraging emigration to Palestine and the restrictions on immigration to that country imposed by the British mandatory authorities, Poland's Jews experienced a sense of entrapment that contributed to a decline in the Zionist parties. This process was hastened by the campaign mounted in the late 1930s by the Bund, which launched scathing attacks on what it depicted as a community of shared interests and policies between the Zionists and the Polish antisemites and their view of Poland's Jews as second-class citizens (Melzer 1982, 140–63, 196). In this atmosphere, the hopelessness of Green's personal predicament reflects the cruel triumph of homeland-without-exile. Mifelev's satiric allegory, whose form stresses its unambiguous ideological message, illustrates the great distance traversed by Hebrew fiction in Poland: from the seminarrative genres, whose ideas clashed with the pattern of their narrative mechanism, by way of the dialectical attempt to develop ideological utterances, through the realistic novel of ideas that conveys its statement in an ambiguous form, to the satire that colors its heroes in ideological hues of an untempered harshness. In an expanding void of literary creativity, a certain lassitude informed the ideological and poetical structures of Hebrew fiction as it endeavored to extract whatever was possible from a hopeless predicament.

Abandoned in the Diaspora

This tangled mass of tensions, manifestations of strength and weakness, whether conscious or not, was ultimately torn apart in the most vile and brutal manner imaginable. Like so many Hebrew writers in Poland, the tireless disciples of laboring for the present, who had sought to preserve a proud and vital Diaspora, ultimately fell victim to the alliance of domestic Polish antisemitism and German Nazi invaders. But during those final years before World War II, the stubborn defenders of the residual shreds did not shut their eyes to the imminent disaster. As the hour of decision approached, Hebrew literature in Poland, exhibiting an unflinching sobriety, expressed and recorded the conviction that the Palestinian homeland would soon be alone, left without the Polish Diaspora. Nevertheless, names such as *BaDerekh* (On the Road) (1932–37), *Reshit* (Beginning) (1933), and *Tishrei* (the first month in the Hebrew calendar) (1938), chosen as titles for periodicals, underline the waning optimism that characterized Hebrew culture in Poland. In 1937, some two years before the calamity, when the Hebrew periodical *Tehumim* (Spheres) was launched, its editors wrote that "at a time of terrible desolation and prolonged drying up of sources, as in our times, the mere preservation of a platform of Hebrew expression in the Diaspora is a desirable and favorable purpose."

Toward the end of the interwar epoch, the Hebrew poet Ber Pomerantz, who died in the Second World War, published a powerful literary essay in which he depicted the tribulations and lingering resentments that accompanied the agonizingly complex transition from exile-without-homeland to homeland-without-exile:

> The horror of the situation even exceeds its disgrace. The disgrace cries: Silence! The horror demands: Raise your voice, and hark. . . .
> The exile remains, doubly orphaned. Somewhere in the world,

there may be such a father who requests his children's permission to leave the house for a moment, promising to bring them bread, and goes out and abandons the children in their place of concealment for all eternity. If there is somewhere in the world such a father, he could be a fitting model for the Hebrew writers and poets. Our good mentors and fine friends, one by one, abandoned us in the Diaspora and closeted themselves somewhere in Tel Aviv. And even though they have yet to succeed in creating a center, in the singular, they have already created forums, in the plural, and undertake to influence the Diaspora from afar, from beyond the seas. (Pomerantz 1934, 38)

Chapter 4

Territoriality and Otherness in Hebrew
Fiction of the War of Independence

Israeliness and the Literary Canon

The violent struggle leading to the foundation of the State of Israel
brought about great changes in the discourse of most of Hebrew literature. Political sovereignty over the territory dramatically changed
the rules of the cultural game and the practice of Hebrew literature.
The literature written during the times of the struggle for independence and the times of war put enormous effort into the constitution
and the formation of Israeli identity; the identity thus created then
became an accepted given, which is active in the Israeli public discourse to this very day.

The question of "Israeliness," of Israeli identity, is an ongoing,
contested issue in Israeli discourse. While some deny the existence of
an essential Israeli cultural identity, others proclaim that the Israelis
are in the midst of an Israeli cultural renaissance. I argue, however,
that Israeliness is best understood as an ongoing process of the construction of subjectivity, and that those who participate in the debate
simultaneously participate in its construction.

The Israeliness that is now being forged is part of an ongoing narrative. The beginnings of that narrative are located in Jewish history.
To many Israelis, Israeliness represents the culmination of that narrative. In the disputes over Israeli identity, we encounter such questions as: Where in that narrative do we now stand? Where should we
be? How do we define its stages? What impediments await us? Are we
still in the first stages of the transformation of the Jewish entity into a
modern national unit? Or are we in the midst of the Zionist era, the
era of national liberation? Or, as some would argue, have we already
entered a new era, one that is witnessing the emergence of a post-
Zionist "Israeli" identity?

For nearly all Israelis, the crucial moment in the development of Israeliness was the establishment of the state. At one extreme are those who see the State of Israel as the culmination of Jewish history. To these people, Israel, as a Jewish state, must be constituted culturally and politically in a manner that is consistent with the Jewish cultural tradition and historical heritage. At the other extreme are those who view Israel not as a Jewish state but as the state of all its citizens, Jews and Palestinian Arabs alike. According to this group, the character of Israel should be defined by its citizens and not, for example, by Jews, past and present, living outside Israel. To both groups, however, the relationship between Israeli Jews and the Palestinian Other has a significant impact on the current definition of Israeliness.

Whether one defines Israel as a Jewish state or an Israeli state has significant political implications. Thus, to take one example, one who views Israel as a Jewish state, the state of the Jewish people, would consider the ongoing immigration of Jews from abroad to be a priority. This position is reflected in the massive mobilization of resources to meet the needs of the new wave of Russian and Ethiopian immigrants. Given the state's limited resources, however, and the disparity in the allocation of these resources between Israeli Jews and Israeli Palestinians, the impact of this mobilization is particularly felt by Israeli Palestinians. Those who argue that Israel is a state of all its citizens could very well argue that this immigration policy conflicts with the needs of a significant portion of its citizens.

To take a different example, the growing participation of Israeli Palestinians in certain areas of Israeli cultural life has a recognizable impact on the character of Israeli identity. To those who view Israel as a Jewish state, this impact may appear negative, whereas those who view Israel as a state of all its citizens likely will view it positively. These are but two examples of various political and cultural factors affecting the elusive boundaries of Israeliness.

In the ongoing debate over Israeliness, people often turn to literature in search of cultural models. Some of these models are drawn from the ancient past, while others are taken from the recent past. In this chapter, I discuss the models of Israeliness that emerged in Hebrew fiction from the period of the 1948 war. My point of departure is literary works that have conventionally been viewed as either marginal to or outside the canon of Israeli Hebrew literature. In light of these works, I then discuss works that have been seen as central to this canon. Such an analysis of what has traditionally been marginalized or expelled from the canon of Hebrew fiction helps us identify the borders of Israeliness as they have been defined in works of fiction and in the process of canonization itself.

Let me emphasize that in speaking of the canon, we are dealing neither with a fixed entity nor with an essence but with a dynamic *process.* Within this process, texts that have been excluded from the Hebrew canon serve as indicators of the limits imposed by the dominant groups within Israeli culture at a given point in time. I examine the doubly marginalized or excluded, those Others who were marginalized or excluded in texts that were themselves marginalized or excluded from the Israeli literary canon. Specifically, I focus on the depiction of the Palestinian Arab as Other in the writings of the so-called Canaanite movement, which was for several years an influential but noncanonical source of cultural models of Israeliness.

The Canaanite Movement

At the height of the struggle for Israel's independence, when the Zionist vision was being dramatically and enthusiastically realized, a literary and ideological countermovement emerged. Led by the poet and intellectual Yonatan Ratosh, the movement positioned itself in sharp opposition to official Zionist culture. This small, secular, anti-Zionist group emerged when Ratosh, after parting company with the right-wing Zionist Revisionist Party at the end of the thirties, established in 1939 the Committee for the Formation of the Hebrew Youth. From the beginning of the forties, Ratosh and his followers came to be known as Canaanites. The name, given to the group by its enemies, was a reflection of their belief that a new Hebrew nation, separate and distinct from the historical Jewish people, had come into being in the modern land of Israel (Eretz Israel), the contemporary analogue of the biblical land of Canaan. The historical, cultural, and national outlook of this group was that all those who lived within the borders of Eretz Israel were exclusively Hebrews, a claim based on territoriality.

The Canaanites wished to sever all links between the new national Hebrew culture in Eretz Israel and the historical, cultural, and spiritual heritage of Jewish life in the Diaspora (Shavit 1987). According to the Canaanites, a classical Hebrew nation and its civilization had existed in ancient Canaan. This nation and its civilization were to serve as the foundation for a new Hebrew identity, not only for those dwelling in the land of Israel but also for all the residents of the Middle East, the "Semitic space," or Eretz Kedem in Canaanite terminology. The Canaanites thus rejected the basic Zionist claim that the Jews were a territorial people expelled from their homeland, whose goal was to return to their homeland and build the Third Temple. To the Canaanites, the identity of the Jews was based not on national existence but on the existence of a religious congregation, with no real connection to the country or its past. Thus, in the view of the Canaanites, even the Holocaust was an event that had happened not to the Hebrew nation but to another people, the Jews.

Denying any ties to Jewish historical memory and denying any links between the Jews as a group and Eretz Israel, the Canaanites made the concept of territory the primary component of their own national identity. Rejecting the cultural heritage of Diaspora Jewry, they developed a concept of culture defined solely by the geographical boundaries of the land of Israel. To them, the true basis for a Hebrew, Eretz Israeli identity was the collective sentiment of nativeness. Whereas the Zionist narrative was grounded in the historical experience of the Jewish people, the Canaanite narrative revolved around territory, the culture that emerged in that territory, and the nation that dwelled in it. In their political essay writing, as well as in their literary writing, they tried to secure a nativist local writing that rejected the characteristics of Hebrew literature as a literature of the Diaspora. Unlike, for example, Hebrew literature written in Poland, which was torn between the diasporic pole and the desire to emigrate Hebrew literature to Palestine, Canaanite literature sought to invent itself as a local, nativist literary practice, independent from the commitment to Jewish life in the Diaspora—not even as a stage on the way to immigration to Palestine.

The revolutionary views of the Canaanites extended far beyond the small circle of their movement. Their strong "sense of a Hebrew homeland" permeated the thinking of many of the Eretz Israeli youth in the forties. So extensive was this influence that, in the fifties, the Israeli educational authorities became anxious over what they considered to be the Canaanites' dangerous effect on Israeli youth.

While its impact on the Israeli political system remained marginal, the Canaanite movement emerged as a significant cultural phenomenon, and several artists and writers were identified with it (Evron 1984). One artist, the sculptor Itzhak Danzinger, created a new kind of Israeli sculpting style from a fusion of modern and ancient Near Eastern cultures. Moreover, writers such as Binyamin Tammuz, Amos Keynan, and Aharon Amir, through their fiction and poetry, were part of an effort to create a new concept of a Hebrew nation, or in Benedict Anderson's terms, a Hebrew "imagined community" (Anderson 1991).

The cultural and political stance assumed by this extreme, marginal, anti-Zionist Canaanite group in the young Israeli culture diverged sharply from that of the dominant Labor-Zionist movement. Canaanite fiction protested against the norms of the Zionist Hebrew literary canon of the forties and fifties. Moreover, Canaanite fiction parodied the "positive" characters of canonical fiction, such as the warrior, the hero, and the moralist, and was alienated from the kind of commitment to Hebrew language that was rooted in the Jewish tradition. Using a very simple vocabulary and syntax and language charged with so-called pagan allusions, Canaanite fiction, with its flat and cynical characters, challenged the dominant Zionist canon (Gertz 1986, 214–31).

Canaanite writers were actually challenging the exclusive, Jewish-ethnic boundaries of the canon. Thus Ratosh, for example, contrasted the developing "Hebrew literature" to what he called "Jewish literature of a territorial nation, . . . the literature of a religious community" (Ratosh 1982, 37–41).

The Contradictory Representation of the Other

The Canaanites clearly repudiated the Jewish dimension of the emerging Israeli identity. In fact, their total negation of the Diaspora and their rejection of any linkage with Jewish history represented an anti-Jewish, anti-Zionist definition of the new Israeliness. Whereas the

Zionists linked the Israeli nation to the historical career of the Jewish people, the Canaanites defined the new Hebrew nationality in terms of a "territorial cultural society that is open to any person without race or religious difference" (Shavit 1987, chap. 6).

Given this definition, one might expect that the Palestinian, the Other, would be perceived by the Canaanites as equal to other Hebrews in the Middle East. Indeed, it seems reasonable to expect that the Canaanite anti-Jewish perspective would yield a new, inclusive representation of the non-Jewish Other. A careful reading of Canaanite fiction of the forties and fifties, however, reveals a different, more complex picture. In this critical area of Israeli identity, the borders of which are signified by the Palestinian Other, one finds conflicting modes of Canaanite representation.

A typical example of this conflict is found in "The New Morning," a story by Aharon Amir that was published in *Aleph*, the Canaanite publication, at the end of the War of Independence (Amir 1949). On one level, the story condemns the deportation of Palestinian residents from the new Israeli state. Gavriel, a Jew, tries to use his connections in the Israeli establishment to prevent the expulsion of Abu Hussein, his Muslim friend, from his land. Abu Hussein has been designated as a "Present Absentee," an oxymoronic euphemism coined by the Israeli authorities to refer to those Palestinians who, after fleeing or being expelled during the 1948 war, were prohibited from returning. Even those who did return discovered they had lost their rights over their property. But Gavriel's efforts are in vain. The Israelis are insensitive to the suffering of the Palestinians, the "sons of their homeland. Sons of their mountain. Sons of these mountains and this village and this land" (Amir 1949, 4). When the fighting ends, the Israelis gather the villagers who are returning to their homes and send them back to the Jordanian border from which they came. And then, at the end of the story, and independent of the villagers' deeds and of the fact that they fulfilled the expulsion order, they are shot.

In the basic thematic structure of the story, the cynical, powerful, cruel Zionist Jew is contrasted with the persecuted, powerless, and innocent Palestinian. Gavriel, the uprooted Jew of Diaspora extraction, sides with the rooted Palestinian and considers it his moral right to continue cultivating his land. The text is not consistent, however. Over and over the reader is confronted with another voice, one that cannot be easily reconciled with the voice of the narrator. Here and there, sometimes in the margins and sometimes at the center of the narrative, one finds suggestions of an alternative reading. For example, Abu Hussein, a Palestinian father, who is analogous to Abraham sacrificing his son Isaac, is depicted as being full of compassion. But this is balanced by the narrator's comment that this is probably the first time in many years that the father has embraced his son.

Similarly, while the narrator portrays the innocent deportees positively, this depiction is offset by the use of such negative terms as *murderers*, *evil people*, and *crooks*. Moreover, even the positive image of the Palestinian Other is projected indirectly, through the harsh criticism of the deporting Zionists rather than through a direct representation of their inherent positive qualities. Thus, the negative portrayals of the Other balance the passages that serve to evoke empathy in the reader with that suffering Other.

Moreover, Canaanite narrative is not devoid of stereotypical negative depictions of the Other. In Shraga Gafni's story "Praise the Lord" (1950, 9–12), the description of the Israeli conquest evokes a strong identification with the sufferings of the conquered. Through the voice of the narrator, our sympathy for a Palestinian child is aroused. The child hears the rumors about the Jews' cruelty. Like the other villagers, he hopes foreign soldiers will help defeat them. His mind is filled with heroic fantasies of fights with the Jews. But hopes and fantasies alike disappear when the Jews conquer the village and gain control over the villagers. The narrator then details the Jews' unjustified and pointless cruelty. The narrator shows his sympathy with the Palestinian villagers, yet he depicts them stereotypically and negatively; the child, for example, is likened to a trapped animal. The contradiction between the positive and the negative portrayals of the Palestinian Other becomes more intense as the narrative progresses. The Palestinians are shown to be sycophants, trying to gain the Jews' sympathy by chanting anti-British slogans.

The Territorial Solution

How can we explain this tension, this seeming contradiction in Canaanite discourse, manifested as an oscillation between compassion and contempt for the persecuted refugee? To answer this, we must contextualize the internal mechanism for representing the Other in Canaanite literature.

Despite their anti-Zionist positions, the Canaanites necessarily wrote from the position of conquerors. As part of Zionist society, in an asymmetrical power relationship, the Canaanites were thus confronted by the basic cognitive and psychological dissonance of a self that is struggling to remain unified. The discourse of the strong is always trapped in an ambivalent situation between "its appearance as original and authoritative and its articulation as repetition and difference" (Bhabha 1994, 107). The question is how to maintain an authoritative representation. There are two possibilities: either repetition of the specific representation of the Subject or its re-representation in a different manner. Consequently, the powerful Subject, when it represents the Other, is caught between two poles. On the one hand is the Subject's self-image as a powerful, hegemonic self, seeking to control the Other by repetition, which assimilates it and makes it the same as the Subject. But on the other hand, the dominant subject is anxious to maintain the differences between them, so as to maintain authority and control.

Within these asymmetrical power relations, the subordinated Other is represented through various figures of speech, presented as "true representations" (Spivak 1986, 226). Situating the Other in an inferior position, these figures of speech are employed so as to depict universal and objective truths. This figurative apparatus describing the Other marks the continuous struggle of the self to reconcile two opposing tendencies. On the one hand, the self, seeking to secure its unity, masks the gap between itself and the Other. This has the effect of creating an "improved" Other, an Other who is similar to the self and thus less ominous. On the other hand, this masking mechanism preserves the permanent difference between the improved Other and the powerful self, thereby ensuring the Other's subordinated, dominated position.

The powerful self, however, can never thoroughly eradicate the anxiety evoked by the threat that the Other poses to its own stable identity. Thus the fetishistic, simplistic, stereotypical representation of the Other reveals the obsessive anxiety of the representing self as well as the subjugation of the represented Other. Depicted as a fixed reality that is different from the self and thus visible, the Other is known in advance and amenable to control.

This stereotypical, repetitive representation serves to control or repress the anxiety that the Other will undermine the self's original authority. The Canaanite anxiety is especially acute. Like the Zionists, they are in an asymmetrical power relationship with the Palestinian Other. But in contrast to the Zionists, the Canaanites have severed their connection to the historical past, which provides the link to the nation's authoritative origins. All Israeli characters in these stories exist and move without reference to their historical past. Instead, their identity is grounded spatially and territorially. Elements of landscape and even human beings are represented essentially as spatial objects. In the Canaanite stories, roots, whether of plants, beasts, or human beings, are an exclusively territorial phenomenon.

Thus, in the Canaanite narrative, territorial space substitutes for an original, unbroken authority derived from historical continuity. Through an enhancing repetitive reconstruction of movements on the territory, the Canaanite writers seek to compensate for the insecurity resulting from their rejection of historical continuity. Their protest against the expulsion of the rooted Palestinians notwithstanding, the Canaanites, lacking their own sense of historical continuity, experience the Palestinian Other as a threat. In response, they reduce the identity of the Other to simplified and stereotypical spatial and territorial representations. Through this kind of stereotyping, the Subject is able to express its basic ambivalence toward the Other. Although sympathetic and hostile at the same time, it simultaneously denies or represses the hostile feelings.

The spatial, synchronic narrative reinforces the truth of this representation of the Other. The result is a reductionist, essentialist stereotyping of the Other. This "unchanging abstraction," to use Edward Said's phrase (1978, 7–8), produces a narrative that suppresses the historical context and the conditions that made possible this particular image of the Palestinian Other. In other words, the Canaanites' radical territorialization of national identity erases the historical context of asymmetrical power relationships. At the same time, this process enables the Canaanites to repress the fact that they are stereotyping.

"The Battle of Fort Williams"

As we have seen, the conflicting thematic representation of the Palestinian Other is reflected in the formal structure of the Canaanite plots. In Aharon Amir's "New Morning," we encounter a purportedly linear, narrative account of the deportation of the Palestinian Arabs. But here, too, the structure of the story is actually controlled by spatial rather than temporal motifs. The narrative is divided into five units, each containing one or two scenes. The narrative transmissions between the units, however, are not explicit. For example, the first unit depicts Gavriel's efforts to prevent Abu Hussein's expulsion, whereas the second unit already depicts the act of deportation. The movement to the last unit, in which the Palestinians are murdered, is also unexplained. Their murder itself is left seemingly unmotivated, since, as far as the reader knows, they obeyed the army's orders. The closing phrase—"and a new morning will rise at the edge of the East"—may allude to the words of *HaTikvah*, the Israeli national anthem, or to a number of other Zionist songs. The allusion ironically uncovers the price the local inhabitants pay for the dawning of a new Zionist morning. This results in an elliptical structure in which every scene is depicted as a repetition of a basic spatial paradigm. This repetition serves to undercut temporal continuity. When historical time is shrunk into the temporary present and there is no representation of historical movement, the Other is no longer depicted as the product of a *process*, which can be interpreted in different ways. Spatial representation minimizes the threat to the coherency and authority of the representer's viewpoint.

In "HaKrav Al Mivtzar Williams" (The Battle of Fort Williams), a story by Shraga Gafni (1950), the Canaanite protest against Zionism is conveyed through imagery that systematically displaces the territorial arena of the battlefields of the War of Independence. The plot consists of the seventeen minutes spent waiting for the attack of an Israeli unit on an Egyptian outpost. Danny, the commander, sees the people lying motionless, like "hewn stones sown along the slope." Most of the soldiers will be killed, regardless of the attack's success. The cruel fate awaiting them should they be defeated is represented as a cynical parody of the conventional representation of the dead— the "comrades," in the period's jargon—which is supposed to grant them final grace by a dignified burial. Danny also reflects on his own death, and he does so through a mock eulogy written by his sergeant, Yossi, which parodies the florid rhetoric of the time and exposes its inanity. In addition, the eulogized warrior is depicted as one who has already fought "in every major campaign ever fought anywhere in the world," which includes a mixture of Jewish wars and other people's wars, but with no hierarchy to testify to any identification with Jewish history. The history relevant to Danny and Yossi has nothing to do with the Jewish past. It is a private history based on street battles in their neighborhood and on adventure books they used to read. Gafni further foregrounds the displacement by describing Danny's devotion to adventure books through a terminology traditionally used to describe Jewish study of the Bible. The battles with the Egyptians as adults pale in contrast with a childhood battle twelve years before. The perspective of childhood war games erases the perspective of the national war of the Israelis against the Egyptians. From the Zionist perspective, the Negev is grounded in a historical heritage and a historical continuity, whereas the Canaanite view links the territory to children's war games, historical tales of exotic peoples, and stories of the Wild West. The Zionist narrative links the War of Independence to Jewish, and therefore Zionist, history, while the Canaanite narrative severs these ties. In the words of Yonatan Ratosh, "The Hebrew War of Independence is as much a struggle over the past as it is a struggle over the formation of the present and the vision of the future" (1982, 41).

But there is a price for this representation of the Other in the Canaanite counterdiscourse. The detachment from Jewish history, while undermining the Zionist claim to authority, results in inconsistent depictions of power relationships. In the fabricated analogy to the American Wild West in "The Battle of Fort Williams," the Israeli Sabra is identified alternately as a warrior fighting on the side of the American colonists and as a Comanche Indian fighter. Whether the story positions the Arabs as Indians or as cowboys, it is motivated directly by the Canaanite reduction to mere territory. The meaning of this option of role reversal is the deconstruction of the national binarism of Jews versus Arabs. (Binyamin Tammuz uses a similar structure in "Sabon" [Soap]; see Tammuz 1950a.) The representation of this territory is devoid of any dimension of historical continuity with a national meaning. The Arabs' positioning first as Indians and then as cowboys erases the historical dimension of their identity.

In the final analysis, all identities are reduced to spatial relations, which are merely repeated over time. These relations are materialized in one specific territory (in this case, that of the childhood neighborhood or the outpost in the Negev) on which both sides fight at a specific point in time. For example: "It's too bad," said Danny, the commander, "that these Egyptians aren't Indians, and that the Negev is not the Wild West" (Gafni [1950] 1994, 257). In other words, the historical context of the war is displaced. This Canaanite protest by displacement is achieved by entwining actual territory with the repression of historical memory. The final effect is as if Danny orders his soldiers to accomplish their territorial mission in such a way that, immediately after it ends, it will also be repressed and forgotten. The territorial accomplishment is not to have any role in the development of a continuous historical identity. When Danny gives his soldiers a Zionist pep talk, Yossi deflates it by shouting, "You're talking like one of the eulogies I make up.̇ . . . Let's take that enemy position, and forget it" (Gafni [1950] 1994, 257).

Minority Discourse versus Majority Discourse

The party that is subjected to moral judgment in the Canaanite narrative is a localized, stereotyped object rather than a morally responsible, autonomous being who has a history. In Gafni's story "Praise the Lord," the behavior of the Jewish conquerors is condemned, but this criticism is accompanied by the revelation that one of the Palestinian prisoners was involved in the cruel murder of Jews. The critical perspective on the behavior of the Jews resumes when they are described as guilty of a massacre of Palestinian Arabs. Yet this is followed by the criticism of a Jewish soldier for not killing a Palestinian boy. One explanation of this inconsistency argues that, from the Canaanite point of view, the Palestinian Arabs deserve their fate. As the story implies, instead of allying themselves with the native population, whether Hebrew or Palestinian, they joined forces with "foreigners," such as Arabs from other countries in the region and the English (Gertz 1986, 220). But this political analysis alone cannot explain the fragmented moral vision. While criticizing Jewish cruelty against Palestinians, Canaanite literature also praises the Jewish warrior who takes part in the war against the Arabs without moral qualms, feelings of shame, or any reflection on the meaning of his acts (Keynan 1949, 2).

This amoral Canaanite attitude conflicts with the underlying assumptions of the Zionist Israeli canon of that time. As opposed to the canonical "major literature," the Canaanites created "minor literature." In a manner typical of national major literature, the Israeli literary canon from the period of the War of Independence was "directed toward the production of an autonomous ethical identity for the subject," who represents the nation as a whole (Lloyd 1987, 19–21). This nativist literature follows, surprisingly, in the steps of diasporic literature, such as that written in Poland, and it adopts strategies of minor literature, acting as if written from the positioning of a national minority.

Unlike "minor" Canaanite fiction, the "major" canonical works of the forties and fifties speak in a universalist voice, representing themselves as "autonomous," that is, "both self-contained and original," seeing themselves as engaged in the "recreation at a higher level of the original identity of the race" (Lloyd 1987, 19). Minor literature, in contrast, as reflected in the Canaanite contempt for moral doubts and qualms, tends "to undermine the priority given to a distinctive individual voice in canonical criticism" (23).

In sharp contrast to the Canaanite group, the Israeli canon of the time is exemplified by the fiction of S. Yizhar, who has been praised for his great sensitivity to the Palestinian Other. In two of his stories, "The Prisoner" (1969, 107–28) and "The Story of Hirbet Hizah" (1962, 328–34), Yizhar represents Palestinians as victims of the war. In "The Prisoner," the protagonist-narrator follows an Israeli platoon that takes an Arab shepherd as a prisoner of war. Although the shepherd poses no danger to anyone and carries no important information, the Israeli soldiers engage in acts of excessive cruelty. The narrator, assigned to accompany the prisoner to another camp, experiences inner conflict and is torn between his obligation to follow orders and the voice of his conscience telling him to release the prisoner. Just before the end of the story, he justifies disobeying orders and releasing the prisoner by emphasizing his common humanity with the Arab. But at the very end, he does not release the prisoner. There is a very short interval in which the narrative suppresses the universalist motif of shared humanity. Momentarily disregarding his doubts and his inner conflict, the narrator, again focusing on space, begins to describe the beautiful landscape. But he soon resumes his inner struggle and again employs a universalist analogy based on "some waiting woman." Unable to resolve his inner conflict, he cannot bring himself to release the prisoner. But despite this, the Other is still represented as sharing a common humanity with the Jewish Subject.

In "The Prisoner," the representation of the Other is also stereotypical; he is under the domination of the Jewish narrator, and the story employs a universalist characterization of the Other derived from the Israeli Jewish perspective. Moreover, the Israeli asks, "Who knows what else there may be even more universal, which the setting sun is going to leave here, among us, without end?" (Yizhar 1969, 128). In "Hirbet Hizah," however, Yizhar's representation of the Palestinian Other is far more extreme. This story depicts the deportation of women and children from an Arab village at the end of the War of Independence. It is clear that for the narrator-protagonist, the deportation signifies the Israeli rejection of Jewish values, which, ironically, are then adopted by the Palestinians. The Palestinians own the future and now have God on their side. At the end of the story, God descends into the valley in order to determine, as in the case of Sodom, "whether they have acted altogether according to the outcry that has come to me" (Genesis 18:21; Gertz 1983a, 77). In Yizhar's stories, the biblical setting, infused with Jewish historical memories, contrasts with the Wild West setting in Gafni's "Battle of Fort Williams." Moreover, Yizhar, while sharply critical of the behavior of the Israeli Jew, never abandons the commitment to the historical continuity of the Jewish Israeli Subject. Ironically, it is the Palestinian refugees, rather than the Israeli Jews, who are the bearers of Jewish values. Thus, although the Israeli Jew fails to live up to Jewish moral standards, the chain of Jewish tradition is not broken. Yizhar replaces the failed Israeli Jew with Palestinian refugees, who thus become the new Jews.

This Jewish commitment to universal, humanistic values is reflected in many other canonical stories of the period. Even when the Israeli warriors (called Hebrews, as in Canaanite writings) reject, with anger and contempt, the Jewish Diaspora mentality, they do so in the context of a dialogue on the problem of Jewish values. This kind of dialogue, found in "In the Line," a story by Natan Shaham, one of the canonical Israeli authors (Shaham 1949, 51–52), differs significantly from the total alienation from Jewish identity one finds in a story such as "The Battle of Fort Williams." In contrast to Canaanite fiction, which surrenders the historical dimension in favor of the spatial, Yizhar's stories and those of other canonical authors continue to emphasize the Jewish historical dimension.

The contradiction between the attitude of canonical writers to the historical dimension and that of the Canaanites is visible in the opposing ways in which they represent the Other. Negating the unbroken continuity of Jewish history, Canaanite writers simultaneously negate the history of the Palestinian Other. Accordingly, while accusing the Zionists of subordinating the native Hebrew to Jewish tradition for their own nefarious purposes, the Canaanites also criticize Pan-Arabism as the creation of a foreign, imperialist interest in the region. Abandoning historical continuity in an effort to create a new identity, the Canaanites eliminate historical memory as well. Thus, Canaanite ideology espouses a plan to force Hebrew culture on the Arabs by drawing out from the Arabs the real Hebrew hidden within.

In conventional interpretations, Canaanism is depicted as the radical culmination of the Zionist negation of the Diaspora and the Zionist effort to normalize Jewish existence. But the Canaanite perspective of the Other renders this interpretation problematic, because the Canaanites developed a discourse that shares characteristics with exilic discourse. In rejecting the past and insisting on transforming the present into the sole determinant of Hebrew identity, the Canaanites elevated the present to the level of an absolute (Kurzweil 1971, 278). They thereby mirrored, albeit unknowingly, the position of those Zionists at the beginning of the century who believed, as we have seen, in the long-term survival of the Diaspora, advocating "laboring for the present." This position was connected to a conception of the Jews as a national minority in the Diaspora, with their own Hebrew culture.

Like Canaanite literature, much of the Hebrew literature created by the advocates of laboring for the present—for example, that created in Poland between the two world wars—subverted the mainstream Zionist literary canon. But this was subversion directed against the utopian Zionist conception of time. In contrast to the cultural and literary practice of a national minority literature, which acknowledges the limits of its power, and thus unlike the example of Poland, the Canaanites were part of an emerging sovereign state. Consequently, theirs was a situation of false consciousness, of those who hold minority attitudes in a reality in which they are the powerful majority. On the one hand, like the relatively powerless national minority in the Diaspora, the Canaanites were committed to a territorial vision. On the other hand, as part of the hegemonic group in Palestine, they tended to legitimate the uncontrolled use of power in an effort to enhance what they perceived to be their own weak position.

It seems, therefore, that the specific nexus of territory, history, and narrative within Zionist discourse made a genuine confrontation with the Palestinian Arab Other more likely than in the noncanonical Canaanite literature, or at the very least did not preclude its existence. Zionist literature always privileged a historical perspective over a spatial and merely territorial one. Thus, although, like Canaanite literature, Zionist literature occasionally denied the full humanity of the Palestinian Other, it never totally repudiated the link of Palestinian Arabs with their own historical past.

The Zionists could and did oppose the Other as an enemy and deferred responding to the Other's claim to civil rights and territory. Nevertheless, the Zionist commitment to a national historical past makes it harder for it to deny the national history of the Other. For better or worse, both Jews and Palestinians have a common history in Palestine. For better or worse, both participate in the same narrative and are, therefore, subject to the same criteria of judgment.

By reducing the Other to a spatial dimension alone, the Canaanites rendered it a convenient object for manipulation. It is far easier to deny claims to authority that are grounded exclusively in space and territory than it is to deny temporal, historical claims. Thus the Canaanites, and their heirs in contemporary Israel who deny historical continuity and define the collective identity of the Other according to territorial connections, consider it legitimate to transform and to do violence to that collective identity in order to preserve their own unified sense of self. Zionists have used history many times to justify repressing the history of the Palestinian Other, but it is never a totally successful repression. A conqueror and a victor who abandons his own historical continuity may escape conducting a dialogue with the subordinated Other, but a conqueror and a victor who has responsibility to historical continuity, albeit an egocentric one, is finally more exposed to the challenge with which the legitimate demands of the Other confront him. The Zionist "repressed" has more options of return to consciousness than the Canaanite "repressed."

Chapter 5

The Other Will Arrive Tomorrow:
Natan Shaham's They Will Arrive Tomorrow

At the beginning of the fifties, the Camery Theater of Tel Aviv produced Natan Shaham's play *Hem Yagyu Mahar* (They Will Arrive Tomorrow). (See the synopsis and a translated passage in the appendixes to this chapter.) Shaham was one of a group of young Hebrew playwrights and authors who began writing in the forties and who wrote about military actions, war, and life in wartime, before and during the War of Independence of 1948. The group was dubbed "the Palmach Writers" both because they were members of the armed opposition to the British and fought in the war and because they belonged to a generation and a general worldview so termed after the underground forces, the Palmach (a Hebrew acronym for "striking forces"). Shaham himself served during the war as a press officer on the Southern Front, and the play is based on his (fictionalized) experiences there. Moshe Shamir's *He Walked through the Fields* and Yigal Mosensohn's *In the Wilderness of the Negev*, plays written in the same period, depict similarly realistic situations. At the time, they provoked a good deal of public interest, especially among the fighters themselves, who were not always flattered by their stage image.

They Will Arrive Tomorrow (1949b) was based on a story called "They Were Seven" (1949a), published by Shaham in March 1948, and was adapted for the theater at the end of 1949, soon after the cease-fire. Its first performance was on February 1, 1950. The play is set in the later stages of the war, at the end of 1948, and revolves around a fighting unit that has failed in its attempts to capture an enemy emplacement. The unit takes up its position on a nearby ridge and awaits reinforcements. It appears that there are seven land mines on the ridge, laid at some time by the Israeli forces themselves, but there is no way now to ascertain their exact location. The soldiers are struck with fear and react by discarding all disciplinary restraints. Meanwhile, the local command is beset by conflict over how to handle the situation. On one side is Jonah, the commander. On the other is Abi, his deputy. In the middle is Noga, the wireless operator, who is Jonah's girlfriend and Abi's sister. One question at stake is how to deal with the soldiers in the unit, who refuse to move anywhere on the ridge. Does the commanding officer, in order to set a personal example for his men, have the right to endanger his own life? But the real conflict lies in whether or not the unit will conceal their knowledge of the mines from the approaching reinforcements. Not to tell them would mean letting the reinforcements die in their stead; to tell them would mean paralyzing them in the same way that the first unit has become paralyzed.

When the play opened, it provoked a good deal of criticism among the public. Among other things, it was hotly objected that commanders in the nascent Israeli army would have had either a copy of the map of the mined area they were occupying (the original of which has been destroyed) or some technical means for detecting where the mines were located. Primarily, however, the play was grasped as representing officers and soldiers as individuals who were helpless in the face of a threatening reality and unable to do anything but await their fates.

Discussions of Shaham's play reveal the persistent duality that characterized most of the critical responses. On the one hand, its reading as a typical, prominent participant in the literature of the struggle for independence aroused the expected reactions among the Israeli readership: Shaham's play was perceived as a central representation of Israeliness in the midst of a struggle with the Arabs, even as it constituted itself as their opposition. Critics at the time were enthusiastic over the originality of the play and the attempt to present an unvarnished view of the Palmach fighters (although they distinguished between artistic and technical-documentary truth). On the other hand, there were repeated signs of discomfiture and perplexity over the moral and conceptual lessons to be drawn from the play. The critics were unable to point to a clear-cut message or moral concept, and this led to the charge that the play lacked focus and asked more questions than it answered. One of the more notable critics of the play, the founder of the Palmach, Yitzhak Sadeh, asked:

"Why of all possible war situations did he choose precisely this one?"—since the play is based on the opposite of the logic that underlies the struggle of a people for their freedom. Instead of showing the willingness of soldiers to sacrifice themselves for the collective good, Shaham "pushed us into one corner of the battlefield, precisely into that corner where death has no logic, where death is fortuitous; contrary to a situation of action either active (attack) or passive (defense), such death is neither rewarding, useful or logical" (Sadeh 1950). Instead of emphasizing the affinity and bonds of loyalty between one soldier and another, "we have before us people in a different situation: each wants his comrade to fail, to be killed" (Zilbertal 1950). Zilbertal and Sadeh were the first to propose the existentialist interpretation of the play, which later became central (Ofrat 1975, 37–47; Gur 1982, 29–43). Nevertheless, Yitzhak Sadeh and Yigal Alon, both revered commanders of the Palmach, insisted that Shaham had the right to distort known military reality. As Sadeh said, the question was not a technical one: it was irrelevant whether or not a Palmach commander "knows that aside from sophisticated instruments of detection there are numerous other means for detecting the presence of mines and clearing a secure path between them" (Sadeh 1950). And Alon wrote that "Nathan Shaham has the right and full authority to relate life on the battlefield the way he has in this play" (Malkin 1950).

The discomfiture of the critics arose from the fact that Shaham was not expressing a pacifist point of view, even though some critics made such a claim (Hurvitz 1950), and that ideologically he agreed that the national war was a just one. In their opinion, if Shaham held such views, he should have done what other writers holding this conceptual approach did: he should have made it clear that the war was a collective phenomenon of solidarity. To their great disappointment, however, Shaham emphasized the exact opposite—that of hostility between soldiers on the same side.

The critics dealt with their discomfort by claiming that the play was immature, or that the plot was too dense, or that there was no balanced catharsis, or that there was an incongruity between the nature of the characters and the elevated register of their dialogue (Keisari 1950; Naiman 1950; Zilbertal 1950). Criticizing the confusion and the inner contradictions in the play, however, merely served to conceal

the fact that the critics did not know how to digest, describe, and cat-
alog the gap between what everyone assumed to be the accepted ideology of the writer and his generation and the aberrant conclusions
of the play. The characters, according to Binyamin Tammuz, "instead
of revealing their independence of character, their intellectual bag-
gage and their personal aspirations—are dragged into a whirlpool
that benumbs them and makes them into a collective mishmash
whose reactions are a function of the utter confusion into which the
author has hurled them" (Tammuz 1950). But above all, the critics
expressed amazement that, even with all the soul-searching and profound disapproval of the reality, not a single ray of hope emerged;
there was no positive solution. In this spirit, Yitzhak Sadeh expressed
his own hope that in the future, plays written by members of this generation "will emerge from the cul-de-sac into which this play has entered and light up our stages brightly" (1950).

The prevalent interpretation viewed the play as reflecting the disintegration of humanist values, unable to survive the cruel reality of
the war with the Arabs. Accordingly, it would appear that when prevailing conditions become extremely difficult—and choosing a minefield as a setting is extreme—the fighter-characters lose their moral
rectitude. Their education and values are portrayed as not strong
enough to withstand the test of an extreme reality. This interpretative
position was to remain prominent in later criticism and scholarship.

Y. Hirshberg, a critic at *Kol Haam* (The Voice of the People), the
organ of the Communist Party—a man who had offered the interpretation of the War of Independence as a war of liberty aimed not
against the Arabs but "against imperialism, which oppresses both peoples, and against its servants within the Arab ranks, who betrayed
their people" (1950)—criticized vehemently the grotesque interpretation given by the director to the Arab stepping on the mine:

> As for the direction, one cannot but comment on one element
> which poses danger to the audience, this is the scene of the Arab
> stepping on the mine, even though Shaham's realism is immaculate
> it is proper to undo this scene which makes the audience laugh as
> the commander calls the Arab. We are living in times of chauvinis-
> tic feelings and we should be very careful in everything, lest the play
> or the literary work will be misunderstood. (Hirshberg 1950; see
> also Sadeh 1950)

There would appear to be a thematic contradiction in the play. On the one hand, we have an extreme situation in which a unit finds itself in a minefield without being able to locate the mines. On the other hand, the play uses the minefield allegorically, as a representation of the situation that will exist after the war. More than a few critics referred to the words of Alex, the unit's intelligence officer, who claimed the mines planted during the war were liable to explode in the period of calm that would follow the war:

> In the first stage of reforming the universe, I would suggest that human beings think always of the worst possibility liable to spring from their actions, and then, perhaps, they will understand that they have to behave as if the mines under their feet were not only on this ridge but everywhere else in the world, in the fish market, in the office, in the lovers' embrace. (Shaham 1949b, 23)

Most of these critics interpreted the original staging of the play as a representation of an extreme situation in which the collective "I" was weak. This reading presupposes a humanist, liberal stance. Accordingly, killing or injuring others is, in fact, a violation of the norm. In the play, the violation of this norm is related primarily to the death of the elderly Arab prisoner of war, who is used as a guinea pig and made to run across the minefield. Institutional backing for a humanist interpretation of the play was provided by the censorship, which demanded that the scene in which the Arab is killed be deleted (Kisilev 1950). As stated in the playwright's comment in the program, the censored sequence does not appear in the synopsis included in the program. It does appear, though, in the book version of the play (Shaham 1949b, 42).

It is also possible, however, to read the play by reversing this logic and, consequently, resolving the contradiction. One can read *They Will Arrive Tomorrow* not only as a warning that hegemonic images— sacrificing the individual for the benefit of the collective, moral rectitude, solidarity, and so forth—will not stand the test or as an indication of their limits. One can also claim that the play attempts to show that this same immoral behavior, this same disintegration, is an integral part of the constitution of the national Israeli identity.

In such a reading, one is not talking about a perversion or aberration but about a central component in the constitution of national identity. Using an extreme situation is not a valid way of drawing the moral limits of the "I," that is, showing that moral rectitude is upheld as long as it is feasible but that when it becomes difficult and one stands face to face with death, knowing that "the death of your friend is your redemption" (Shaham 1949b, 38), one falters, preferring that one's friend die rather than oneself—or that one is ready to play Russian roulette with an Arab prisoner. It can be assumed, rather, that the use of an extreme situation allows for the possibility that a certain cultural mold was configured during the war and preserved afterward.

The accepted reading of the play entails a full affirmation of the hegemony of Israeli identity because it accepts it as an unquestioned given, only afterward examining its bounds as a moral identity. In contrast, the reading that identifies the process of disintegration of the collective as an immanent component of its identity does not accept the identity as a complete and unquestioned given. It points to it, rather, as a product of a cultural construction. The collective "I," the national "I," is thus grasped as a construction that is basically flawed. Its establishment through the justification of the sacrifice of the individual for the benefit of the collective requires accepting this behavior as moral. Other kinds of behavior too, however, such as wanton cruelty and torture, which are generally seen as immoral and inhuman, become moral by dint of their inclusion in this construction of a national Subject.

The essential mechanism with which the war culture, during the period of the struggle for national independence, confirmed the need to make sacrifices was the figure of the living dead (Hever 1986). This metaphor was designed to approve individual death by conferring on it a national, collective significance. It had a central place in the poetry of the period, especially in the influential poetry of Natan Alterman. This figure of speech, prosopopoeia, gives the poet the voices of those unable to speak. In his 1947 poem "The Silver Tray," which might be called the anthem of the War of Independence, Alterman describes two allegorical figures, a young man and young woman, who are the silver tray on which the Jewish state is being presented to the people. The presentation takes place at an impressive ceremony at whose climax it becomes clear that "the two stood silently and there is no sign if they are living or have been shot" (Alterman 1962).

This is also Shaham's point of departure. In the words of Jonah, the commander: "But the body will soon get what's coming to it, a mine or a bullet. . . . Here everything is present and absent at the same time. We too do not exist anymore. He awaits us outside like a loving, patient woman" (Shaham 1949b, 57). What Shaham has uncovered is the mechanism for the construction of the national Subject, sustained by the physical death of the individual. Individual death is, of course, final and incontrovertible; but the death of the individual who has sacrificed his or her life for the people is endowed with spiritual survival in the collective memory of the nation. In his story "In the Line," which, like "They Were Seven," was included in his collected stories, *Lazy Are the Gods* (1949, 49–61), Shaham describes the interiorization of death by the fighters in the struggle to break the siege of Jerusalem. They cope with their fears of death in war by turning it into an integral part of life. Death in life, like life in death, becomes a natural component of war culture. In this way, a cultural mechanism is created whose essence is the creation of forms for coping with fear by diminishing its power. Shaham exposes this mechanism in the play when Abi defines his generation as that "which turned its adventurousness into boldness, and its c*hutzpah* into pioneering" (Shaham 1949b, 51).

In *They Will Arrive Tomorrow*, the existence of the living dead is a point of departure. Living with the knowledge of almost certain and ever-present death (the hidden mines) transforms the people on the ridge into the living dead, those whose lives are threatened by certain, concrete death; therefore, they are dead-in-life. Yet, while the play employs this basic assumption in representing the reality of war, it proposes to investigate the next stage. Its primary interest is in the "day after" the war. What, it asks—as a kind of response to the then-popular song "The Palmachnik Is Searching for Tomorrow" (written by the "official" songwriter of the period, Haim Hefer)—will be the character of those who "will arrive tomorrow"? In the argument between Alex and Abi regarding their life after the war, Abi says that after the war he would like to do things that will be the direct outcome of what he has learned during the war. And when he defines those things as "something which is not naive and not selfish" (49), he also defines the basic components—being aware of the price of the national mission and being committed to the collective—of the living dead.

In his introduction to the play, Shaham explicitly defines the sharp change that has taken place in the situation:

> The time—the end of winter 1948. The War of Independence, which until now has had the character of a communications system, is acquiring the coloration of a war of conquest. Jewish soldiers are conquering villages and enemy emplacements for the first time, settling down in them and repulsing counterattacks. (6)

Shaham studies the cultural changes that occurred in the period after the second truce of the war (at the beginning of October 1948). What are the changes that will occur in the Subject of the Israeli fighter when the historical conditions change, and with them the images of strength and weakness that nurtured the construction of the Israeli Subject? In the new situation of a minefield, all the conventional notions of courage are completely overturned. When the soldier Shlomo Reich refuses to return to his barracks because he is frightened of the mines, Jonah, the commander, makes fun of him, asking: "So what if there are mines? Suppose that we are attacking. You run, take up a position and cover your comrades, attack. . . . The fate of the war depends on whether or not you run, run!" And when the soldier answers, "Now . . . there's . . . no battle" (15), he elucidates the question of what the character of the national Subject will be when the necessity of constructing it as victim—as a member of a nation on the defensive, battling for its national independence—lessens, and in its place comes a Subject based on an image of national might. What will that Subject's nature be when, on the one hand, the battles end and part of its efforts must now be directed, as in the play, to the defense of what has been conquered, while on the other hand, the psychological mechanism of the living dead continues to operate?

In Shaham's perceptive formulation, one thing is clear: the haziness between the world of the living and the world of the dead will continue to exist actively in the Israeli's consciousness. In his introduction to *Lazy Are the Gods*, he formulated his thoughts very clearly:

> The war is not yet over but there are no more battles. We will once again go out to pluck youthfulness and beauty on the fields of death, and the flowers of blood will be trampled underfoot by flocks of sheep. We will step on mines, not in fright but in amazement.

We are still alive and now we have to venerate life enthusiastically
just as we have until now venerated death. (1949, 16)

The land remains a testimony to battles and to the dead, as well as to
the psychological mechanism that made it possible to cope with the
fears of war. The mines are an allegory for the dangers that will remain after the battles are over, and for the need to stabilize and preserve what exists. Consequently, Shaham sees the land "as the death
mask of my great friend who died, large and mighty, and all the features of his character are scattered across the land" (16).

The construction of the living dead is founded on a clearly visible
system of oppositions—between attacked and attackers, Arabs and
Jews, our territory and their territory—whereas the question of the
cost of individual death is obscured. The national, normative Subject
of the living dead is formulated by blurring the figurative borders between the dead and the living: the death of the individual is incorporated into a broad network of signifiers. But this blurring is brought
into the foreground of its representation against a background, frequently unnoticed, of permanent and fixed oppositions. The positioning of the national Subject is thus signified through a series of oppositions, and as long as these oppositions are clear, the individual
death has a national, collective meaning. Furthermore, it follows that
from the collectivist function of the victim, his identity is determined
by a collective principle. That is, his identity is made up of those elements that suit the collective needs of the nation: he must be Jewish,
and manliness is preferable.

Therefore, that the victim is Jewish or, for example, that he is seen
as part of a hierarchical military system of soldier versus officer appears as a natural fact, taken for granted, intended to fill the collectivist function of establishing his identity. But when the clearly visible
structure of oppositions is undermined, the construction mechanism
of the national Subject collapses. Jonah, who is witness to such a
process of collapse, begins to make declarations designed to preserve
the collective authority. After the battle at the end of the play (which
the unit wins by chance), Jonah makes sure that the burial of the dead
is anonymous, so that it will not be possible to identify those who were
killed by the mines (Shaham 1949b, 72–73). Thus the dead all remain
members of the collective. In contrast to Abi, he disputes the legiti-

macy of individual guilt for acts committed during a war; and in his efforts to preserve military discipline, he attempts to reaffirm the collective, which disposes of individual responsibility:

> I am not I and you are not you. You can ignore me, you can hate me, you can belittle me. For you I am—responsibility. I am authority. I am the Jewish people. I am its destiny and you are obliged to listen to me as if you were listening to your own conscience. (28–29)

Nevertheless, none of this serves to stop the collapse of those clearly visible oppositions on which the entire structure has rested.

The play takes place in a new historical situation, neither war nor peace but an interlude in the battle. The previous, accepted balance of power has been undermined, and as a result, ordinary distinctions begin to blur. First, the dichotomy between "our" forces and those of the enemy completely disintegrates. From the minute your own comrade dies after stepping on a mine and thereby diminishes the likelihood of your death, his death, by redeeming you, has also turned him into the most concrete of your enemies. As Abi says to himself:

> The person one would, in the heat of the battle, sacrifice oneself for, and, covered in one's own blood, extricate from under enemy fire. One would be happy to see this other person die, and be released from the last mine. (20)

The same is true of territory. The territory is, on one hand, "ours." It was an enemy emplacement and has been conquered by the Israeli army. On the other hand, it is mined, and so constitutes a threat to our forces. It is true that we are in official control of the territory, but to no small extent, the territory controls us. The setting of the play contributes to this destabilization by locating the events in a ruined Arab house. The enemy is, then, both external and internal, both spatial (there is an enemy whose territory is outside of mine, but there is also an enemy within the same territory) and subjective (the enemy is alien, and the enemy is my friend and comrade in arms).

When the existential situation of living in a minefield threatens each individual separately, the hierarchy between officers and men becomes blurred. One of the central conflicts in the play is over whether an officer should endanger his own life to provide an example for his men, all of whom are afraid of the mines. The "economy" of the characters is organized in such a way that the family circle cuts through the army circle. Jonah, the commander, is in love with Noga, who is the sister of his deputy, Abi; and Noga disobeys Jonah's command and endangers her own life to tell Boaz, a soldier from the reinforcements and her former lover, about the mines. In doing so, Noga disrupts the hierarchical system of commander and commanded. The significance of the event is twofold: military and erotic. The ranking of the private (erotic) and public (military-social) realms is reversed. In this way, the subordination of the private to the public—usually a component of the living-dead mechanism—is violated: instead of subordinating the private to the public, Noga subordinates the public to the private. Noga wants to tell Boaz about the danger because she does not love him anymore, and she is afraid that the guilt of not telling him will haunt her forever (90).

The mechanism of the living dead is now confronted by a new system of threatening Others. The moment the binary oppositions collapse, the moment an entire series of dichotomies are confounded and a system assumed to be stable disintegrates, alternative binary oppositions evolve: the Jew becomes the enemy of the Jew, whereas the Arab is conceived of in erotic terms, analogous to the erotic way in which the woman is perceived. After Abi brings about the death of the elderly Arab prisoner, he says to his sister: "Did you see how the old man looked at me, with such love. It wasn't very pleasant" (42). Alex, who gives the command to kill the Arab prisoners, confesses that the main reason he did so was because "they saw even our fear" (40). The Arab appears to the Jewish soldiers as one who returns their gaze, that is, one who has his own subjectivity, which undermines the regular opposition between "us" and the "Others." Alex dwells upon this moment in terms that reveal the erotic component: "I've never seen such a brave Arab. He never took his eyes off me. Also, he has such a manly face, handsome" (40).

The army command disintegrates in the same way. The very act of commanding is grasped in the play as a performance, a kind of play within a play:

> *Abi*: At your command, my conscience.
> *Jonah*: Go to sleep and get up in the morning with calmer nerves.
> *Abi*: At your command, Captain Authority.

Jonah: Don't play with me. This isn't a theater. Be a man.
    Abi: What's that, a profession? (30; see also 85, 88)

While the oppositions are disintegrating, and with them the sustaining metaphor of the living dead, what had previously been natural and implicitly understood, and therefore concealed, now becomes eminently visible: the individual death of the soldier sacrificing his life for the nation is not that of just any person but of one of ours, that is, a Jew, whose death acquires a consoling significance within the collective. In the wake of the disintegration, it becomes clear that when the death is defined as the death of the "I," it is also a death that is positioned in opposition to the death of the national Other. That is, what is visible to the eye during the process of disintegration is that the mechanism of the living dead, which transforms the private dead man into a national living man, is a mechanism exclusively for Jews. The dead man is chosen from the dead: he is the preferable, Jewish dead man, endowed with the status of national victim. The Jewish dead man is constituted by the fact that he is not an Arab; what creates the "I" is the Arab Other. The undermining of the national Subject brings into view the essential ambivalence that characterizes the relations of power and control obtaining between the "I" and the Other. The disintegration of the national Subject brings to the fore the internal tensions and, in fact, the disintegration of fixed representations—the stereotypes of the Other.

The duality becomes increasingly clear: on the one hand, a desire to identify with the Other and have him identify with the "I," and on the other hand, the fear of being equal to the Other, a condition that is liable to undermine the "I's" control over him. The result is an ambivalent representation that combines fear with pleasure or defense with control (Bhabha 1994, 66–84). The Arab and the woman in the play are therefore both threatening and desirable at once. Jonah is the commander of the unit opposed to the Arab enemy; but Jonah and Noga carry on a relationship that is both military and erotic, at the end of which Noga is seriously injured by a mine. This creates an analogy between her and the Arab who is killed by a mine. In his confrontation with Noga, Jonah excludes her from the collective by returning her to function as the classic woman: "This is not a place for girls" (Shaham 1949b, 31). Jonah's and Noga's names add yet another element to the relationship between them: in Hebrew, their names form an anagram—they contain the same letters in a different order.

From the moment the oppositions are undermined, the general outlines become blurred, and the function of individual death must be examined anew. The identity of the individual dead man no longer makes him an automatic candidate for the mechanism that will turn him into a national living person. With this disintegration, additional Others are suggested as candidates for the negative definition of the "I": on the stage appears the woman, and with her the Arab and even some of the other Jews. From now on, death allows these Others to become legitimate candidates on behalf of the war and the people. Like the national "I," the Other also disintegrates, but this process culminates in physical disintegration. Death awaits everybody, but those marching toward death are no longer fighters representing a collective but a subjectivity breaking down into its physical components. The Jews either get killed or are mutilated; the Arab disintegrates into metonymic disconnected parts:

> *Jonah:* Well, feel better now? Now let's get onto business. Have you
>   interrogated those wogs?
> *Alex:* Yes, we were still out in the field, for classification.
> *Jonah:* Get anything out of them?
> *Alex:* Yes.
> *Jonah:* What?
> *Alex:* Blood.
> *Jonah:* Anything else?
> *Alex:* Teeth. (39)

An example of the functioning of this mechanism can be seen in how Abi treats the Jewish soldier Shlomo Reich, which is the same way he treated the old Arab. In both cases he takes the man over the minefield, and in both cases his conscience bothers him but he regards his actions as a practical necessity (Shaham 1949b, 43; Shaham 1957, 85). Even when the cultural and historical fields change, the mechanism continues to operate and to examine individual deaths in national categories. But because the hegemonic hierarchies have disinte-

grated, the process by which all the Others participate in the constitution of the national Subject is more conspicuous—each with his or
her own potential. In the new situation in which the hegemonic Subject has been undermined, the accepted, "natural" significance of the
"I" no longer excludes the Others from participating in the creation
of the national Subject. They are no longer concealed in order to create the effect of a universal, national "I," nor do they function only as
those who have been pushed to the margins by the central "I." The
words *comrade* and *enemy* have lost their fixed meanings, the death of
one soldier being the redemption of another.

The play illustrates just how the collective "I" constitutes itself, by
making itself distinct from the Other. As a result, dependence on the
Other is essential. The collective "I" in the play is put into a situation
that is not only extreme but examines its own structure "against the
grain." In the very heart of the national canon, the war leads to disintegration. In the process of this disintegration, Shaham shows that,
structurally, the enemy of the national Subject, the Other, was always
within. Until now, in the course of the war, the enemy was marked
primarily as an Arab, who had to be fought and killed. Now, in the new
situation, living in the midst of a minefield, the need for the Other
still exists, but its identity has undergone a change. Even under the
circumstances of relative calm, the Other is needed. Even now, the "I"
needs an inferior and oppressed Other in order to reveal himself as
superior and preferable. But the minefield has shattered the principles of classification and existing hierarchical relations, and new relations have not yet been determined. As a result, the Other can be an
Arab or a Jew, sane or insane, a man or a woman, or a combination of
these—as in Abi's description of how the soldiers looked erotically at
his feet when he crossed the minefield, comparing their glances to
those of "an impassioned virgin" (Shaham 1949b, 21). When Jonah
realizes that Alex gave the order to kill the Arab, he is furious:

> Anyway, who told you I mean to let them go on living? All I meant
> was that it would be a pity to finish off two wogs when we're in a hole
> like this. It'd be a waste. A waste: you understand? Two men, that
> means two mines. That's how it's going to be. Now there are six
> mines: after that there'll be only four. (40)

Jonah substitutes exchange value for human value: to locate the mines. But exchange value means that this function can be fulfilled by Jews as well as by Arabs; thus, through such a substitution in the Jewish domain as well, the critique of Jewish subjectivity reaches its climax.

In the argument between Jonah and Abi as to whether an officer should knowingly endanger his life in order to provide a personal example for his frightened men, the hierarchical relationship between officer and soldier is examined anew. Abi focuses on the existential point of departure of endangered human beings in general:

> There are six mines. Six people will get it. You won't be able to arrange for the mines to blow up people who don't do you any good. I understand you very well. You would like to see those killed who, in your opinion, are superfluous in this world. But it can't be done. Perhaps in battle you have to take special care of officers because they are like the head on a body and only unusual people can live without someone to head them. But here, in the minefield, it's every man for himself. You can't save us for the good of the world anymore than you can save a good locksmith or a good singer. Here we are like ordinary people awaiting their fate. (26–27)

Abi is capable of taking up positions that seem to contradict the humanist perspective. On the one hand, he is an unequivocal defender of moral rectitude (24). On the other hand, he will also condone acts of cruelty that have been committed out of necessity (44). At the end of the play, it turns out that Buma, the commander of the reinforcements, knew all along about the mines, even as the first unit attempted to withhold that information from him. Although this appears to censure Jonah and emphasize the worthlessness of his plan to withhold information from the reinforcements (Gur 1982, 36), in fact, the opposite is true. Instead of reinforcing Abi's humane position—to tell the truth whatever the price—it would appear that the practical option is the stronger: because for Buma, too, preserving the collective, even by closing one eye and keeping silent, not a natural, self-understood commitment to truth and absolute sincerity, turns out to be the preferred option. Holding back the information about the mines is also an effort to hold back the knowledge of the existence of death in life as a collective phenomenon.

This is Abi's demand to let each of them "be a hero of his own desire" (Shaham 1949b, 62), that is, to make fear into a private, and not a collective, issue.

Shaham focuses on the way in which the national Subject is constructed in the majority, canonical discourse. He has examined this through the metaphor of the living dead, which generally excludes the Other from the discussion. He has turned the Other into a function that can be fulfilled by various elements. Since the function of the Other is to constitute the "I" as a national Subject, that is, as a member of the living dead (either dead with a live national existence or alive as a person who has interiorized death and is dead within life), this function can be filled by anyone who threatens the "I" at any given moment. He or she can turn the "I" into a living-dead person regardless of whether or not he or she is the "I's" national enemy. In a situation of deterioration, this role can be filled by a woman, a friend, or an Arab. The process of disintegration Shaham has described is not an aberrant situation in which a stable and humanist Subject finds himself. It is, rather, a context in which the internal structure of the national Subject has been exposed in a critically profound manner.

APPENDIX A: Natan Shaham, *They Will Arrive Tomorrow,* **a play in three acts (four scenes); from the program notes, February 1, 1950**

The time is the end of winter, 1948. Jewish units, enraged by loss and suffering, start their spearhead attacks, intent on conquest. The war for independence, which up to that period seemed to have been a battle for communication lines, begins to acquire the characteristics of total war. Jewish soldiers take over Arab villages, conquer emplacements in enemy territory, fortify themselves there and heroically endure bitter and cruel counterattacks.

A Jewish unit that has gone out to conquer an enemy emplacement fails. Instead of returning to its base, this unit takes up its position on a hill, hoping for the arrival of reinforcements to rescue it or help seize its original objective.

The play opens shortly after the staff of this unit has set itself up in an Arab building that is to serve as its headquarters. The other members of the unit, numbering forty-one men, fortify themselves in a deserted British camp, spread out over the hill.

Synopsis of the Play

Act One
Scene One—Evening
   Jonah, the company commander, and Alex, the intelligence officer, discuss the defense of the hill. The situation is very serious. The hill has been mined at some previous date, but there is no way to detect the seven mines that lie waiting to explode when stepped on. The sapper who placed the mines was killed and the map destroyed.
   As Jonah and Alex talk, a soldier who has been hiding in the next room appears. By hiding, he has avoided crossing the stretch of hill to where the platoon is situated. Jonah commands him to rejoin his platoon. The soldier refuses hysterically. Abi, second in command, persuades him to go by going with him. When he returns, Jonah reprimands Abi for endangering himself without permission. Abi leaves on a reconnaissance tour.

Scene Two—The next morning
   Abi and Noga, his sister (a wireless operator), discuss their home. Alex returns from his tour, announcing that his men refuse to climb the hill. Jonah sends for the disobedient soldiers, as he fears such conduct will jeopardize the entire unit. No technical method of detecting the mines is available.
   Alex returns with one Arab prisoner. The prisoner attempts to escape and is killed by a mine.

Act Two—Half an hour later
   Noga reprimands Abi for his cruelty. Abi proves to her the logic of his conduct. At breakfast, a discussion evolves in which relations among the men are clarified; Alex goes out on a job.
   News arrives of a reinforcement unit due to reach them the next morning. Jonah suggests not telling the newcomers about the mines, as there is no escape from the situation anyway. Their ignorance will

be paradise compared to the hell his people have been living in. Abi disagrees: "Let the men be heroes out of choice," he says. Neither does he believe that this plot will remain secret for long.

On one of his tours, Alex is killed by a mine. Abi is badly shaken. In a harsh argument between him and Jonah, he reprimands Jonah for never setting an example himself to the men of whom he expects the bravery of walking in a minefield. Jonah believes his first duty is to preserve the C.O., even if this means the loss of his personal prestige.

Act Three—That night

The reinforcement unit under Buma's command has arrived. Two of the new men are killed and secretly buried by Jonah's soldiers. Abi returns from helping the newcomers. Noga hears that Boaz, her former lover, is among the new men, and she wants to go out to warn him. When Abi refuses to let her go, she admits that she must do this as she no longer loves Boaz. She is in love with Jonah. She leaves. Abi discusses Jonah's bravery with Uri, the latter's driver. Noga steps on a mine. When Jonah runs out to her aid, Abi tells him that "he has no right to endanger the C.O." Jonah shows Abi the withdrawal orders, in which it is specified that the command is now to be placed in Buma's hands. Noga dies from her wounds. Buma, the new C.O., orders the unit to retreat and leave nothing behind. "Leave nothing behind . . . ," says Abi thinking out loud of the lives the hill has taken. "Nothing besides the seventh mine," blurts out Buma, who has known about the mines all along.

APPENDIX B: Excerpt from Natan Shaham, *They'll Be Here Tomorrow* (1957, 27–31). The following is a slightly revised version of the original translation.

Jonah: Well, feel better now? Now let's get down to business. Have you interrogated those wogs? [The word used in the original is *arabushim*, which is no more complimentary.]

Alex: Yes, while we were still out in the field, for classification.

Jonah: Get anything out of them?

Alex: Yes.

Jonah: What?

Alex: Blood.

Jonah: Anything else?

Alex: Teeth.

Jonah: What sort of joke is that? Did they say anything?

Alex: Not a word.

Jonah: What's the problem?

Alex: The old one is just a stupid old fool: he doesn't know anything.

Jonah: And the young one?

Alex: Stubborn as a mule. You won't get anything out of him.

Jonah: *(incredulously)* What d'you mean?

Alex: If an Arab doesn't start talking after one kick in the face, he won't talk at all, and there's no use giving him the works, I don't want to open a butcher's shop here. Anyway, what more can he tell me than I've already seen for myself? There's at least a platoon posted on every ridge. They've got wise to the driving-in-a-wedge idea, and they've decided to strangle us. Serves us right, too. It's about time we stopped planning on the assumption that they're complete nitwits. Any force that tries to break through in order to re-establish contact with us will have to be at least a company strong. We've got to weigh up whether it's worthwhile wasting another company here.

Jonah: That's a decision which will have to be taken elsewhere. By the way, what have you done with your two pigeons?

Alex: What could I do with them? Would you like to have to feed them? I gave orders to finish them off.

Jonah: *(shouting)* You idiot! *(Calms down)* Sorry; that was stupid. Has it been done yet?

Alex: Not yet. I handed them over to Gideon.

Jonah: *(goes over to window and calls out)* Gideon, send those two over here at once. You come too.

Abi: Oh come on! Why finish them off? Let the wogs go on stinking. What harm can it do us? A few rations of bully beef?

Alex: Don't make me out to be a murderer, for God's sake! You know damn well that in situations like this one can't afford to have any passengers. First, because we haven't enough food for them. Second, because they've seen too much. They've even seen our fear. Third, if you fell into their hands, they'd make mincemeat out of you. I know that isn't a proper reason; but it'll help you carry out the rotten job that's got to be done of sending them express to kingdom come. . . . All right, if you want to be obstinate about it, have it your own way. But remember, I've warned you. You know, that young fellow's a right lad: I've never seen an Arab as tough as that. You should have seen the look he gave me. Good looking bastard, too.

Jonah: *(contemptuously)* Hell's bells! For once in your life you see an Arab act like a man, and you'd let him have your sister. Anyway, who told you I mean to let them go on living? All I meant was that it would be a pity to finish off two wogs when we're in a hole like this. It'd be a waste. A waste: you understand? Two men, that means two mines. That's how it's going to be. Now there are six mines: after that there'll be only four.

(Gideon appears in doorway.)

Gideon: Here they are. What d'you want 'em for, anyway?

Abi: How d'you propose to do it?

Jonah: Very simply. We'll just let them do a bit of running up and down our sports ground out there until they find their mines. Gideon, get the young one outside. Give him some parade-ground drill.

(Gideon stands in the doorway and shouts commands to the Arab. Abi and Alex stand at the window. Alex immediately returns to his place. Noga does not move.)

Gideon: *(with back to audience)* Ruh hunak! Ta'al hon! Yallah, yallah, ruh hunak! Kaman marra. [Arabic: Go over there. Come here. Move it! Go on, over there! Again!] That's it, and again: it won't hurt him. Ruh, ya ibn al-kalb. Leish btistanna? [Get a move on, you son of a dog! What are you waiting for?] Why's he standing still, the stinking carcass? Does he think we're playing games? Give him one! No, you fool, not a bullet: hit him with the butt of your rifle. That's better. Ruh, ya ibn sharmuta! [Get going, you son of a whore!] If he doesn't get a move on, fetch him another one with your rifle butt. Hey, careful there! You'll kill him that way, and what good will that do? Look how the poor bastard's bleeding! Get a move on there, will you! Doesn't want to, eh? Well, we'll soon make him want to.

(*shouting*) Hey, look out, he's running off! Where are your eyes, blast you! Go on, let him have it, shoot him! *(Several shots nearby)* You missed him. He's just shamming dead. Give him a burst. No, stop wasting so much ammunition. Give him single shots. Call yourself a marksman? Look he's getting up. Ah, that's got him. Stop: he's as dead as a sheep by now. The bastard thought he'd get away, did he? Good looking bastard, wasn't he though?

Jonah: You've simply killed a human being.

Abi: It won't work that way. You've got to use different methods. Get him to go of his own accord. Watch me make the old fellow do it. Here, give me some bread. *(Alex passes him a hunk of bread. An old Arab, dirty and disheveled, appears in the doorway. Abi goes up to him.)* Khud lak. [Take this.] *(The old man takes the bread and starts gnawing at it hungrily. He is full of wonderment and alarm, but his mistrust soon disappears, and he blinks his gratitude with watery eyes. He seizes Abi's hand and attempts to kiss it, but Abi snatches it away.)* Off you go, you son of a whore! Take this.

Old Arab: *(sobbing)* Ya ibni, ya ibni, ana baheeb el-yahud. Ana baheeb el-yahud ktir. [My son, I love the Jews. I love the Jews very much.]

Jonah: He loves the Jews very much, does he? Trash, that's what they are, not men.

Abi: Ruh ya'ammi, u-jibli shwaiyet khashabat. [Go on, uncle, fetch me a little wood.] If he gathers enough firewood he's sure to find his mine. *(The Old Arab goes out.)* It really is a shame. However, he hasn't much longer to live anyway.

Old Arab: *(turning back)* Min sha'nak, ya ibni, kull ma baddak. [For you, my son, (I'll do) whatever you like.]

(Old Arab goes out; they wait tense with expectation. Then Old Arab returns with a bundle of wood.)

Abi: Kaman, kaman. [More, more.] *(Old Arab goes out again.)* He mustn't come back again, he mustn't: I can't stand it. If he comes back again, we're finished. I've had enough. Did you see the way he looked at me? *(Noga looks at Abi.)* What d'you want of me? What's the matter?

Noga: *(expressionless)* Nothing.

Abi: Oh, damn it all. *(breaking)* Curse those mines. *(A heavy explosion)*

Jonah: *(looks outside, returns, and says quietly)* Five mines.

(Curtain)

Chapter 6

Minority Discourse of a National Majority: Israeli Fiction of the Early Sixties

Yehoshua, Oz, and Kahana-Carmon

By the end of the fifties and the beginning of the sixties, a new generation had appeared on the literary stage: Israeli writers who started on their artistic way after the founding of the State of Israel. In Hebrew poetry and in Hebrew fiction, a rich literary corpus emerged and crystallized into a literary type called *Dor HaMedina*, "literature of the generation of the state." Amos Oz, A. B. Yehoshua, Amalia Kahana-Carmon, Yitzhak Orpaz, Yeshayahu Koren, and others formed in their writings a literary canon that quickly became the "classics" of Israeli literature. But a closer look at the dynamics of this development reveals extremely complex and conflictual aspects that undermine the homogeneous appearance of this "major Israeli literature."

In September 1970, several weeks after the end of the War of Attrition at the Suez Canal, the critic Mordechai Shalev published an article titled "The Arabs as a Literary Solution" (Shalev 1970). The article deals primarily with A. B. Yehoshua's 1963 story "Facing the Forests" (1975), one of the most significant works of Israeli literature to appear in the period preceding the 1967 war. Referring to the story's main characters, Shalev writes: "The way the student's problem is transformed into the Arab's problem is illegitimate, androgynous, irreconcilable" (1970). For Shalev, the central issue in the story is the rebellion of the son against his father figures—chiefly his own biological father and the old forest supervisor. In the story, this rebellion extends further, encompassing the student's ancestors and, indeed, his whole Jewish past. "Crude and clumsy literary stitching glosses over the effort to convert the personal predicament of the student, struggling to preserve his youth, into the tragedy of the Arab whose village has been destroyed and tongue cut out" (Shalev 1970). He goes on:

> One cannot, of course, deny the existence of a moral plane as regards the Arab. But the feeling of guilt over the Arab is nourished first and foremost by a feeling of self-guilt at a life which has lost its vitality, a life left without the validation of content and fulfillment. Against the background of such an existence, the Arab's life is conceived as overflowing with vital strength and primary content, and the real question preoccupying A. B. Yehoshua is not who has wronged whom ("We or they, what differences does it make?"), but whose life is worth more.

Shalev suggests that "Facing the Forests" be seen as a discourse wherein a relation of moral judgment is recast as a relation of power. The structural flaw in the story, according to this view, is its use of the political story line as a vehicle for the presentation of a libidinal, Oedipal pattern. Shalev proposes that we consider the course of action in the story from the perspective of power relations. But does this interpretation contribute toward a resolution of the blatant structural cleavage at the heart of the story? Will this power-oriented account of the story help bridge the gap between the political and ethical narrative of Jewish-Arab relations and the inner, spiritual narrative of the individual Jew?

Yehoshua's story belongs to a literary canon that came into being within the context of the majority culture in Israel. But if we examine its poetics, it becomes clear that Yehoshua in essence develops his tale from the viewpoint of a national minority. "Facing the Forests" was written in the language of the majority and by an author belonging to the culture of the majority in the State of Israel; yet its rhetoric bears the clear stamp of minority discourse, and its stance toward the majority culture is that of a minority in internal opposition to it. Shalev and others have found in this story its Jewish heritage: in settling his Oedipal accounts, both personal and collective, with his Jewish forebears, the Israeli Sabra in the story looks for support to the figure of the Arab.

It has often been argued that the founding of the State of Israel and the consolidation of its national sovereignty were themselves dynamically bound up with a rebellion against a Jewish Zionist tradition stemming from the legacy of an oppressed minority. As the hallmarks of a minority ideology persisted even while the new configuration of a Jewish majority in its own sovereign state was taking shape, profound tensions arose almost of necessity (Shaked 1988). Still, a clarification of the relationships among the forces at work in the literary discourse through ideological stances such as the above is likely to reveal far-reaching poetic strategies functioning in Yehoshua's text and in others like it.

Discussions of the relation between majority and minority are frequently characterized by a particular kind of semantic camouflage. Cultural categories of this sort are typically couched in quantitative terms that pull a euphemistic veil over the real nature of majority–minority relations: that the issue is one of power, not quantity. The powerful majority controls the political apparatus of government and expects it to serve them; the powerless minority is branded as inferior by its very nationality. And even the most enlightened democracy, with the most deeply ingrained respect for minority rights, cannot undo the essential inferiority and weakness of being a minority. The cultural and literary aspects of this situation provide an important cognitive perspective of the political forces at work in the confrontation between minority and majority. A central tool in this political confrontation is that of literary canonization. The authority that accumulates around a particular canon is a dramatic manifestation of its power. The works that compose this canon are officially promulgated by the establishment; they can count on an automatic endorsement, or at least on legitimation, from prestigious literary criticism; and of course, they dominate our high school and university curricula.

In this chapter, Yehoshua's "Facing the Forests" serves to exemplify one of the options available to national minority fiction in the Israeli culture of the mid-sixties. Three other options are then presented through further stories from the same period: "Nomads and Viper," by Amos Oz; "Heart of Summer, Heart of Light," by Amalia Kahana-Carmon; and several works by Shimon Ballas. The works of Yehoshua, Oz, and Kahana-Carmon, as the last decades of the twentieth century demonstrate, have assumed (along with their authors) a central position in Israeli culture (see, for example, Shaked 1970;

Gertz 1980; Sadan-Lowenstein 1981; Gertz 1983; Gertz 1983a; Hertzig 1983; Rattok 1986). As such, they can serve as privileged exemplars of the ideological and literary options presented below. And yet, despite their canonical status, these stories reflect the ambivalence of the cultural situation: in them, an empowered majority acts as befits the weakness of a minority, yet the stories themselves are masterworks of the majority canon.

The protagonist of "Facing the Forests," the fire warden who ends up fanning a forest fire, is both an exemplary allegorical representative of the national condition and a misfit, a marginal character existing on the fringes of Israeli society and academic life. The warden or watcher is an intellectual who is alienated from any direct sense of class or group interests—but he is equally alienated from the intellectual community, which ejects him to the solitude of the forest. Yet we must not forget that he is also his friends' emissary, charged and indeed compelled by them to accept the job of fire watcher in the forest (Yehoshua 1975, 358–59). This dual status of nonrepresentative representative becomes plausible when examined from the perspective of "minority literature," which seeks to invest everything with collective value. At issue is a systematic violation of the cultural mechanisms that regulate and discriminate among the various domains of human discourse and experience. Minority literature is usually, as stated above, reluctant to grant the individual any personal autonomy and refuses to distinguish the personal from the public. In various ways, it tends to recast every drama of personal life as a political drama.

Minority consciousness cannot be fully accounted for as a separate entity or by means of some ethnic label. Rather, it must be viewed as a type of political position (Kaplan 1990, 357–68), that is, in terms of the power relations obtaining between the minority group and the hegemony of the majority. That is why Shalev's reading, in foregrounding the Oedipal dimension in the story and the power relations it displays while backgrounding the student's personal crisis of conscience, leads us to view this text as seeking to legitimate an oppositional minority stance. What might seem a structural defect in a narrative belonging to majority culture, where a clear distinction is maintained between the personal and the public, can be reinterpreted as a fusion or a joint exploitation of both these spheres in the construction of a "national allegory." Such a literary solution is characteristic of the oppositional culture of a minority or an oppressed social group (Jameson 1986), which mobilizes in its cause all available resources, whether political, spiritual, or other.

As mentioned, one characteristic of a minor literature, according to Deleuze and Guattari, is that it stands in permanent opposition to the literature of a dominant majority (Deleuze and Guattari 1986). An additional factor they single out in the oppositional literary stance of the minority is the undermining of the natural link between language and territory. This link, as in Herder's formulation, is paradigmatic of the modern conception of nationhood: "Denn jedes Volk ist Volk; es hat seine Nationalbildung wie seine Sprache" (For every people is a people; it has its own national image, its own language) (Herder 1879, 106). The national minority author, by contrast, writes in a language that is not his own, or writes in his own language outside his homeland, or writes in a language that is not the dominant one. Deterritorialization, in effect, is part of a more general process in which language is destabilized.

To clarify the role played by the relationship between language and territory in the structure of "Facing the Forests," it must be stressed, first of all, that the plot itself is presented as a hermeneutic process involving a textual and linguistic critique. We see this first in the craving of the "word-weary" student (Yehoshua 1975, 357) for a solitude that will enable him to pursue his research. For the student, textual interpretation proceeds simultaneously with anticipation of fire: "For a week he crawls from line to line over the difficult text. After every sentence he raises his head to look at the forest. He is still awaiting a fire" (368–69). His taking control of the forest is explicitly presented as continuous and, in fact, coterminous with his taking control of the text (374). Accordingly, the forest fire at the end of the story can be interpreted as an act of aggressive deterritorialization of modern Hebrew, the political and ideological vehicle of the new nation-state. It is an act that contests the power, legitimacy, and authority (Kubayanda 1990, 246–51) obtained by the majority culture through its use of the territory's "natural" language. Such an undermining of the natural tie between language and territory is part of a political struggle—realized here, significantly, at the hands of a historian delving into documents written in Latin, the preterritorial, universal tongue that preceded the rise of the modern European national languages (Anderson 1991, 67–82). How fitting this interpretation is for the student, who says of himself: "Trees have taken the place of words for me, forests the place of books. . . . I am still awaiting a conflagration" (Yehoshua 1975, 382).

And indeed, among the reasons presented in the story in justification of the student's need to distance himself from the city and give himself over to a life of solitude is the explicit remark that "he just needs to strengthen his willpower" (358). This linking of a striving for power and a need "to renew his acquaintance with words" (358) illuminates the power implications of the linguistic deterritorialization carried out in the story. For the isolation he achieves is best stated in terms of communication: his instructions are communicated to him only in writing (362), and here, too, he carries out his linguistic critique, "drawing" his pen like a sword (Yehoshua uses the Hebrew verb *sholef*) and making "a few stylistic corrections" (363). His attempt to open up a less-mediated form of communication by initiating a telephone conversation ends in disappointment and a deepened sense of disconnection (363–64). So his longing is directed elsewhere, at other voices once heard on this same land: "What interests him in particular is the village buried beneath the trees. That is to say, it hasn't always been as silent here" (370). He searches the forest for "words no longer in use" (370).

Thus, "Facing the Forests" tells the story of the land rising up against those who control it—"the earth casting off her shackles" (388), as the narrator puts it in describing the forest fire. Such deterritorialization is typical and enables the discourse of the powerless outsider, who strives to exploit to the utmost this very marginality. The old Arab in the story is, for the watcher, both an object of identification and a substitute father figure. At the same time, however, once the Arab has done his part, the watcher has little compunction in discarding him. The watcher thus lives his identity as member of a national minority through a constant negation of any integrated form or positive definition of national life. Nor does Yehoshua have any prescription to propose for bringing together the separate worlds and discourses of the conqueror and the conquered (the old Arab's tongue has been cut out). There is no real collaboration, no hope for a shared life, no moral sensitivity to a wrong to be set right. On the contrary, the Arab fulfills, to use Mordechai Shalev's term, a "spiritual function" of the protagonist (1970). And so, once the Arab has made his contribution to the Jew's sense of minority identity, the Jew abandons him to the law. The Jew represents the potential for near-total exploitation of a minority situated, as if in principle, on the margins of any framework it might ever wish to approach or become part of.

The old Arab is not presented in the story as a member of an actual minority one might join or identify with. In fact, his function in the story is to enable Yehoshua's text to embody an even further marginalization of minority consciousness. Even the revelation hinted at in the story, the summons "to an encounter at the margins of the forest," is presented as yet another stage in the process of deterritorialization:

> But when he plunges out of the forest and arrives at its end, whether it be at night or at noon or in the early dawn, he finds nothing but a yellow waste, a strange valley, a kind of cursed dream. And he will stand there for a long time, facing the empty treeless silence and feeling that the encounter is happening, is taking place successfully even if wordlessly. (Yehoshua 1975, 384)

This is a particularly sharp portrayal of the vicious circle that repeatedly denies any possibility of territorializing discourse: like the attempt to hold a wordless dialogue with the tongueless Arab, this quest takes place on the margins of the forest, itself the embodiment of remoteness and marginality. Only here, in a place devoid of recent planting, can the Jewish student carry out a languageless encounter with the landscape and the territory.

The story ends in desolation and destruction. And yet, if we examine it from the viewpoint of minority discourse, we can see a number of positive elements. The student is left with two positive mementos of his exploits in the forests, each a realization of the goal of disconnecting language from external reality and, in particular, from landscape and territory. One is the schematic map of the ruined village that he draws so that it should not be forgotten, even signing his own name to it in advance (378–79)—a map that he points to "without a word" in the presence of his aging mistress when she comes for a visit (381). The other is his vivid and unfading memory of certain passages from the Latin documents he has been studying as part of his research on the Crusades from an universalist perspective. As he puts it: "The solitude had proved a success. True, his notes have been burned along with the books, but if anyone thinks he does not re-member—he does" (392). His historical research, too, though de-stroyed and never brought to fruition, finds a substitute in the form of his interrogation by the police: "A veritable research is being com-piled before his eyes" (390).

This critique of the connection between language and territory informs the student's response to his friends' suggestions and to the old forest supervisor's words at the beginning of the story. The stu-dent scarcely believes that there are any forests in Israel; though large-scale reforestation was a central symbol of the reclaiming of the land of Israel by Zionism, he denies the existence of the forests as the signified of this important cultural sign (358, 360). His critique of discourse, begun in stammering confusion, culminates in the vio-lence of the forest conflagration. In contrast to his earlier reluctance to enter into communication with the mute Arab about the past his-tory of the site—he "pretends not to understand" (385)—now, with the forest ablaze, the Arab "speaks to him out of the fire" (387). And in pointed contrast to the Arab's newfound power of "speech," the forest supervisor, the representative of sovereign authority, is pre-sented at the end of the story "as though he . . . had lost his speech, as though he understood nothing" (391).

The watcher's efforts extend even to helping the firemen docu-ment, in language of their own, the deterritorialization of language that he himself has effected (390). An important intermediate stage in this process occurs near the end of his term. The watcher "has lost all hope of fire. Fire has no hold over this forest. He can therefore af-ford to be among the trees, not facing them" (384). Resigned to the unlikelihood of a conflagration, he will now try to bring about a dis-connection between the language and the territory through alterna-tive means: he seats the Arab's little daughter in his fire watcher's chair instead of himself, delighted that "it has taken her no more than a minute to learn the Hebrew word for 'fire'" (384). And the ef-forts he devotes, early in his stay, to translating his Latin text into sim-ple mnemonic rhymes (369) prove successful as well: at the end of the story, as he had hoped, the words have truly blended in his mind and not dispersed in the surrounding silence.

The unremitting process of negation on the part of the minority finds further expression in the watcher's effort to create, as an intermediate stage en route to the final destruction, his own independent realm, the sovereign and unsubjugated kingdom of a national minority. The forest fire thus also marks the end of this private empire. When buzzing hordes of visitors invade his solitude, drowning out "the thin cry of the weary soil . . . consumed by the teeth of the young roots," the watcher is portrayed as "a dethroned king" (375). Earlier, the pine trees are described as appearing to him like "a company of new recruits awaiting their commander" (370), and the watcher "goes forth into the kingdom." Relieving the thirst of the visiting hikers with a sense of noblesse oblige, his is described majestically as "giving water to the nation" (372). When they light campfires, he is struck with a sense of "civic alarm"; then, "toward evening, he goes down to make a tour of his kingdom" (372). And yet, the founding of this empire is only a provisional stage in realizing the oppositional stance of the minority. When he and the Arab make common cause as arsonists, the forest becomes "their kingdom, theirs alone" (383).

Amos Oz's story "Nomads and Viper" has assumed an eminence similar to that of "Facing the Forests" in Hebrew literary criticism and in Israeli culture (Oz 1965; I quote in part from the English translation [Oz 1980] of the revised version of the story). It, too, appeared a few years before the 1967 war, and like Yehoshua's story, it brings to bear a variety of strategies that help mark it with the stamp of a national minority literature.

The narrator in Oz's story, after originally rejecting the young kibbutz hotheads' plan to respond with violence to the nomads' suspected thefts from the kibbutz, ultimately changes his mind. An attempt to come to grips with this change of heart will bring us close to the gist of the story. The narrator justifies his initial objection to retaliation on two counts: "First the use of brute force would dishonor the kibbutz. Second, nothing really serious had happened so far. A little pilfering was not pillage or rape or murder" (Oz 1965, 39). These are characteristic arguments of a ruling majority, content to entrust the punishment of lawbreakers to the proper authorities. Immediately thereafter, however, we also learn his reasons for enlisting with the vigilantes: "Etkin responded to the rudeness by depriving both Rami and me of the right to speak, and began to explain his position all over again. Rami and the other younger men glanced around in agreement. In the midst of Etkin's harangue they got up and exited the room with an expression of disgust, leaving Etkin to pour out his verbiage to four veteran kibbutz members. After a moment's indecision, I too walked out after them. True, I did not share their views, but I had been wrongly deprived of my right to speak" (39). In other words, the ethical prohibition against revenge is swept away here in the Oedipal act of rebellion of sons against their fathers (personified by the kibbutz veteran Etkin).

In contradistinction to Yehoshua, however, whose whole story consistently conveys the discourse of the majority as national minority, Oz vacillates between different points of view. On the one hand, the story presents the viewpoint of a majority standing apart from the minority and prepared to concede to it a measure of autonomous existence. In creating a frame of reference common to himself and the internal reader, rhetorically present in the text, the narrator confesses himself unable to fathom the ways of the minority—"inscrutable to the likes of you" (Oz 1965, 25). On the other hand, the narrator is presented as an accomplice in the act of vengeance against the Bedouins, seeking thereby (despite the uncertainty as to the thieves' identity) to attain psychological compensation or catharsis (39–40).

Apart from explicit criticisms of the minority, there is no doubt that it is the narrator's unreliability and the inconsistency of his status (both witness and omniscient) that constitute the principal means for undermining the minority position. Even the power of the authorities is portrayed ambivalently: it is the military, after all, who had permitted the Bedouins to go north—"A whole population, men, women, and children, could not simply be abandoned to the horrors of starvation" (25)—and yet the police are ineffectual in responding to the kibbutzniks' complaints of thievery (28–29). The struggle between the kibbutz and the nomads takes place outside the competence of the authorities. All the police can do is to convene a meeting between representatives of the tribe and the kibbutz. Thus, the officials themselves encourage the tribal leadership on both sides to act as surrogates for the central authorities (28).

The power that the nomads hold over the kibbutzniks demonstrates how the minority carries on its struggle with the majority through acts of linguistic deterritorialization. Like the ancient keen-ing of the Arab's daughter in "Facing the Forests" (Yehoshua 1975, 386), Oz describes the chanting of the nomads at night and the ca-dence of the drums that "beat a rhythm to your sleep" (Oz 1965, 26–27). The meeting between the representatives of the tribe and the kibbutz is also presented as a two-way act of deterritorialization. Each side speaks in the other's language: the Bedouin elder in Hebrew, Etkin in Arabic.

The story mocks the attempt to create a joint discourse of major-ity and minority by highlighting the anachronistic position of the gen-eration of the kibbutz founding fathers. Like the fire watcher's own fa-ther in "Facing the Forests," who seeks in vain to befriend the old Arab and his daughter with his few words of bad Arabic (Yehoshua 1975, 368), Etkin replies to the Bedouin elder "in broken Arabic, the residue of what he had managed to learn during the time of the [1936] riots and the [1948] siege [of Jerusalem]" (Oz 1965, 28). In both stories, the Oedipal rebellion merges with a rejection of anachro-nistic political patterns that blur the sharp political opposition be-tween dominant majority and dominated minority. But Oz, empha-sizing the ambivalence inherent in this reality, sets the minority posi-tion in a tension-fraught context, both criticizing and identifying with Etkin, the representative of the founding generation of the kibbutz.

An especially telling manifestation of the deterritorialization car-ried out by the Other in escaping the definitional strictures dictated by the majority culture is found in the play of ethnic and sexual iden-tities. Like Yehoshua's fire watcher, for whom "it is not himself but some stranger who wanders . . . between the two stories of the house" (Yehoshua 1975, 366), the nomad is portrayed as a person of hetero-geneous identity: "His garb is a mixture [*sha`atnez*]: a short, patched European jacket over a white desert robe" (Oz 1965, 26), and his voice "has a silken quality, like a woman's."

The pivotal figure in Oz's plot is Geula, a female member of the kibbutz. Her half-fantasy of an erotic encounter with the nomad and her addiction to the fiction that a rape has actually taken place are presented as a way to attain a release that has eluded her until now. Her conduct in the relationship is permeated with ambivalence and double messages: attraction, temptation, rejection, blatant flirting, along with authoritarian rebuke—"What are you doing here? Stealing?" (Oz 1965, 34)—and commands, which the Bedouin obeys in utter submission. When Geula touches his arm and the nomad realizes the degree of confusion pervading her motives, he cuts off the communication; backing off from the stereotype of the minority speaking the language of the majority, he reverts to his native Arabic (35–36). Like the Oedipal resolution that the forest watcher's pseudo-moral struggle represents in Yehoshua's story, here the libidinal compensation provided by the fabricated rape leads to its own pseudo-moral conclusion: violence against the nomads. It makes no difference whether the narrative voice here is that of an eyewitness privy to special information or of a different, omniscient narrator; in either event, the very presentation of this dynamic of majority and minority, and in particular of the majority as minority and of the erotic and linguistic power relations entangling them, amounts to denaturalizing this relationship and placing it in a critical perspective.

When the nomad has gone, Geula looks up at the military planes flying overhead, representatives of the dominant majority culture— but her gaze, the story says explicitly, is "unwilling" (Oz 1965, 36). The blinking lights of the planes and the thumping of the drums are juxtaposed and interwoven in a single leitmotiv that blurs the boundary between minority and majority. Geula, rapt in ecstatic release after her meeting with the nomad, is unaware that her body is blocking a viper's hole. And her fatal encounter with the viper, ending in her death by snakebite, occurs in part because the snake is not deterred by the airplane's flashing lights. Even the mightiest symbols of sovereignty do not prevent him from killing the girl who arouses his anger, an anger that, the story tells us, is "not arbitrary" (40). This fundamental disruption of the majority's relationship to itself and to the minority is further hinted at in the title "Nomads and Viper" and in other analogies between man and animal that are woven into the text.

The allegorical drama wherein Geula finds not only death but also, possibly, redemption (her name means "redemption") should accordingly be taken as a warning: the majority runs a grave risk in behaving as minority. The viper, the embodiment of the real minority in the story, stares unblinking; Geula, representative of the pseudo-minority, has her eyes closed. The phallic symbol of the viper brings to its climax a story of political blindness fraught with dangerous and far-reaching implications.

In portraying the narrator as a writer and the heroine, Geula, as a poet, the story makes a critical comment on the relationship between our perception of reality and its representation in literature. The metaliterary examination of the erotic and literary relationship between Geula and the narrator (30–31) in fact lays bare the very devices that make the story a work of minority literature. Geula's aesthetic reservations about the narrator's oeuvre in no way contradict the quite different value, at once collective and individual, that she ascribes to them. The narrator's practice of buying recent books of poetry for her as a birthday present and of leaving them in her room surreptitiously and with no written dedication points to a balance between an anonymous, public sensibility and a personal, intimate gesture. But this confusion between the private world of literature and the public, political domain ultimately leads to disaster. It is through her poetry that Geula expresses her feeling of reconciliation and release at the story's conclusion, reciting aloud to the imagined presence of the now-departed nomad; and it is this "poetic agitation" (40) that blinds her to the viper that ends her life.

The basic elements underlying a nation-state's inner legitimacy and sense of identity are a common ethnicity, a common history, and a common language. The process of building the Israeli nation-state, however, has also involved a struggle conducted in terms of national minority and majority. The presence of a national minority in a nation-state is not just a quantitative matter but has qualitative implications in the economic and social sphere as well. Oz's story, with its sensitivity to the dialectical role of the minority in the founding of the nation-state, illuminates in this way the struggle between the kibbutz and the Bedouins, who were "brought by famine" (25) in their quest for sustenance. Going beyond notions of ethnic or sexual distinctiveness, which may only blur the issue, such a portrayal depicts the minority's Otherness in terms of concrete interests that can clash with those of the majority.

The rule of sovereign power can afford a considerable measure of ignorance, and even deliberate "know-nothingism," with respect to the way of life and motives of the minority. A majority may, in principle, renounce its role as the axis on which everything else turns, a reductive center that sets all wheels in motion, explains everything, describes everything, imparts significance to everything. This sort of renunciation, however, is impossible if the majority persists in acting and thinking in terms of the collectivist, political, quasi-libidinal categories of a minority. Its centripetal orientation is, in fact, one of the main qualities characterizing a Jewish state as opposed to a state having a Jewish majority. The former, totally Jewish in character, will deny any constraint stemming from the presence of some other nation perceived as contradictory to its own interests; the latter, by contrast, will actively exploit the possibilities accruing to it in virtue of its majority status. Between Yehoshua's "Facing the Forests," which presents the majority as national minority, and Oz's "Nomads and Viper," which lays bare its own devices and warns against the dangers inherent in the discourse of a majority as national minority, the novella "Lev HaKaitz, Lev HaOr" (Heart of Summer, Heart of Light) (1966), by Amalia Kahana-Carmon, stands as a third option. This story, too, is a leading exemplar of Israeli fiction prior to the 1967 war; my brief portrayal of the particular discourse option embodied in it does not do full justice to the richness and complexity of the novella.

Two major elements of the story—the mystical vision of the boy Ronen Sokolov and his mother Hulda's falling in love with Dr. Baruchin—are repeatedly tied to national contexts having to do with the creation of a new kind of "Israeliness." Ronen's vision of "heart of summer, heart of light," an expression of his longing for personal and family happiness, has an atemporal status in the story.

The vision is conveyed in language that is both utopian and at the same time an echo of the traditional idiom of the revelation at Mount Sinai (Kahana-Carmon 1966, 237). It is, in fact, a moment constitutive of an intersubjective connection grounded in a common past ("mountains from ancient days") and interpretable here as an act of national integration. Like Yehoshua's student, the narrator in this story, the boy Ronen, also has the role of watcher and prophet. His self-appraisal—"Mine is only the utterance of Ronen [*neum Ronen*], the old child" (299)—is an echo of the biblical *neum Adonai* ("the utterance of the Lord"). Ronen is at once an expression of the national energy of the younger generation and a son entangled in his mother's love life. This Oedipal plot has both a political and a psychological dimension. Ronen's observation combines his mother's libidinal turmoil with the history of the photograph hanging in his school, that of Dr. Baruchin's father, the famous writer from the period of the National Revival (*HaTekhiya*). Dr. Baruchin's voice, full of life and "very Israeli," seems to Ronen to tear the Zionist writer's portrait (300) when the long-awaited telephone call from him finally comes at the end of the story. And when the phone call is over, the tear is mended and the picture is whole again. As the doctor's voice falls silent, it is rather the inanimate objects that have the power of speech—a thematic echo harking back to the first sentence of the story. The novella thus sketches the end of the Israeli Oedipal rebellion against its Zionist past. The utopian, visionary dimension that the story puts forward includes not only the deterritorialization of language through minority discourse but something more—a new voice, the oxymoronic speechless speech of inanimate objects.

As the story progresses, Ronen comes to see that the image of a majority Israeli culture, his ideal and that of those around him, is actually a crux, indeed, a kind of Archimedean fulcrum, which must be reexamined, as in the vision, to see what might lie beyond it. For Ronen, the starting point is the difference between his own family's way of life, which he sees as anomalous, and the Israeli norm (242). "I think," he says, "that to my mother, a native of a moshav [an agricultural cooperative settlement] in Emek Hefer, my father will remain a new immigrant till the day he dies, someone with no roots in the life of the country" (238). Slowly, the familial plot develops into a national allegory of Zionism versus Israeliness, of immigrant versus Sabra, and even of Jewish versus Arab existence. Kahana-Carmon lays out a broad panorama of oppositional minority stances, which are ultimately generalized into something transcending them, and even transcending Israeliness itself: "Were Father to change his name to a modern Hebrew name. Would things really be any different, I ask myself. Of course not" (238). Ronen's grandmother illustrates the struggle for dominance. She makes feeble attempts to learn Hebrew (241) and uses her pidgin Hebrew to attack the routine functioning of her son's household and to chide her daughter-in-law, Hulda, for the disrespectful way in which she received her as a new immigrant (245–46). She uses her own language politically within the Sokolov family, for it is a foreign language that only she and her son can understand (244). These elements and her invasion and occupation of Sokolov family territory during Hulda's illness illustrate the deterritorialization of Israeliness and Israeli Hebrew that the story carries out. When the vision of "heart of summer, heart of light" appears in all its splendor for the final time, at the end (299), it is set in explicit juxtaposition to the modest reality of an ordinary Israeli winter's day. In "Facing the Forests," the climax of revelation comes in empty silence; in "Heart of Summer, Heart of Light," the vision unfolds both in the silence of the revelation at Sinai and in a territory already in existence "somewhere else, off in the lands of the living" (298).

Myth assumes a central function in the story in consequence of a thematic pattern introduced in three stages: the option of minority discourse; the negation of that option; and, finally, an indication of the utopian solution that transcends it. The genealogical pattern, a principle that dominates the story and its various subplots, serves to formulate the story's central questions and even to lay out the framework for their solution. The myth provides the conflict and its solution within the framework of a pattern to be completed. Hulda's falling in love with the doctor explodes the by-now-degenerate family unit. An analogous function is assumed by the doctor's young Israeli voice, which comes in startling contrast to his aged appearance (255). And Ronen comments on the end of the relationship between his mother and the doctor in a similar vein: "The king is dead; long live the king" (289).

Through a variation on the legend of "Hulda and the Pit," which Micha Yosef Berdichevsky used in his story "BaEmek" (In the Valley) (Berdichevsky 1965, 127–30), this pattern is elevated to the status of a national myth. The legend exists in several versions. The following is given by Rashi:

> Once there was a young man who gave his pledge to a certain maid that he would marry her. She said: Who shall act as witness? And there happened to be there a well and a weasel [Hulda in Hebrew]. The young man said: The well and the weasel shall be witness to the matter. After some time he went back on his word and married another, and they had two sons. One of these fell into a well and died, and the other was bitten by a weasel and died. His wife asked him: What manner of thing is this that our sons have both died an unnatural death? Then he told her the whole story. (*b. Taanit* 8a; on the literary metamorphoses of the legend, see Sadan 1957, 367–81; Kagan 1983, 95–114)

Both the myth and its national implications are hinted at in the mother's name, Hulda, an uncommon name that evokes the heroine of the old legend; and in Sokolov's name, which alludes to the Zionist leader Nahum Sokolov (Kahana-Carmon 1966, 257). In Kahana-Carmon's story, as in the legend, a woman has two male children. The cyclic pattern of the myth converts the relationship between the mother and Dr. Baruchin into a kind of rectification of the breaking of the wedding engagement in the myth. The myth of "Hulda and the Pit" can explicate the story of Hulda and Dr. Baruchin as a breaking of faith with Zionism and the idea of the ingathering of the exiles. Thus, the connection between them takes place in a medium of Israeliness, combining elements of both betrayal and rectification. Hulda's neglect of Ronen's nonnative father, Pesach, coincides with her growing attachment to Dr. Baruchin, son of the writer of the national revival. The myth raises the concrete plot to a universal plane, thus limiting the significance of specific historical occurrences in the national allegory. The mystical, supratemporal vision of "heart of summer, heart of light" works to the same end. The story's utopian dimension recasts the specific historical situation as the point of departure for a dynamic of change: the descendant of the writer of a past national revival now heralds the new Israeliness; the vision of "heart of summer" begins to take form in the midst of an Israeli winter; and (to continue the series of oxymorons moving toward reconciliation) the boy-narrator describes himself as "Ronen the old child," while characterizing Dr. Baruchin as a young old man (255).

The tale of Leon, the uncle of Pesach's would-be business partner Alkalay, epitomizes the overall dynamic involved in the novella's tale of national minority. As a teenager, Leon was kidnapped and ultimately mustered into the "Club of the Lost," a unit in the Foreign Legion that, as Alkalay tells it, followed "fixed, secret, tried and true formulas for mixing and assembling a military unit like a drink, according to types and nationalities" (249). Leon's stormy life serves as a model for the boy's yearnings and triggers the fantasy in which Ronen explicitly says, "My father, they say, was an Arab; my mother, they say, a European lady" (249). One could almost take this as another version of the image of the Arab as Oedipal substitute. But the overall context of the novella also gives Ronen a more disillusioned perspective: it is he who both points out Leon's downfall and downgrades the possibility represented by Leon's enchanted life to the status of a mere childhood fantasy.

With Kahana-Carmon, as with Oz, the metaliterary dimension serves to undermine the natural relation between a given literary text and the reality to which it refers. In a conversation that takes place during a party at the Sokolovs' about the recent course of modern Hebrew literature, the speakers deal in categories that reveal "Israeliness" as a collective notion realized in fixed patterns of psychological plot types. But the main point of this passage is to criticize the anachronism to be found in the national functions of Israeli literature. This criticism comes across clearly in the attempt made by Lifshitz the furrier "to explain to them, too" (278)—that is, to the writers—his dissatisfaction with modern Israeli literature. It is a literature, he suggests, still immersed in its own closed, introverted world and cut off from the bustling Israeli reality of Dizengoff Street, the herd mentality of a collective moving without center or destination, whose old aspirations have become obsolete. This new Israeli reality, he says, has no need of books. Lifshitz proposes, in effect, to replace the current function of Israeli literature with a new relationship between literature and national life. Amalia Kahana-Carmon's story points to the national limitations of the fiction being written by her contemporaries, making explicit reference to *Mot Lisanda* (The Death of Lysanda), by Yitzhak Orpaz, and to "Sheloshah Yamim Veyeled" (Three Days and a Child), by A. B. Yehoshua.

In a critique of contemporary Hebrew fiction, Baruchin's wife's main thrust concerns the degree of nonaffinity and unrepresentativeness of its typical plot patterns in relation to actual Israeli reality:

> Why, this week my daughter gave me a book. Called *The Death of Lysanda*. If you please, it is the story of an uncouth fellow named Naphtali Noi who lives in a rooftop apartment in a Tel-Aviv *that I do not know and do not wish to know,* he creates a fantasy girl and together they commit a murder. . . . The stories I come across these days—all of them have heroes who half-heartedly make love to a woman who, in the final analysis, they have no interest in, and the same for whatever else they do. Who are these people anyway? (Kahana-Carmon 1966, 276–77; my emphasis)

In dispute here is the degree to which the libidinal motivations of such plots truly represent the national reality of Israel. The novella uses this skepticism to point a way for Israeli literature to escape from the patterns of a minority discourse that confuses the libidinal with the political. Kahana-Carmon's story amounts to a denunciation of the kind of Israeli fiction that, like "Facing the Forests," embodies the oppositional stance of an absolute minority that realizes itself through perpetual destruction and shirking of responsibility.

The relationship to the Arabs is also examined in categories similar to Yehoshua's. Jaffa, built on the ruins of its Arab past, is characterized as "a city which no one voluntarily considers home any more" (Kahana-Carmon 1966, 247)—a description analogous to the world of Ronen's family and, more generally, to the Israeli existence that the story seeks to portray. Even Ronen's pleasure in the swivel chair in his father's store is just a pretense; like Yehoshua's fire watcher contemplating the ruined Arab village, Ronen wonders whether this "used to be an Arab banker's chair" (252). In contrast to Yehoshua, however, Kahana-Carmon suggests a path toward a solution. Her story, with its sensitivity to a situation in which the majority culture is under attack from a minority position and consciousness, shows where the way out lies: in a future solidarity of minorities. The story is not, of course, a prescription for acculturation, for assimilation of minority consciousness into a dominant majority culture. Rather, Ronen's recurring mystical vision can be seen as sketching a utopian framework that may someday integrate the various strands of the divided field of power. His utopia allows us to take the dichotomy "majority/minority" not as something eternal and essential but as a stage in a historical process leading to the elimination of this opposition. Taking a diachronic perspective in this way makes it possible to envision an attenuation of the dichotomy and, ultimately, its complete dissolution in a longed-for moment of mystical revelation.

It may well be that the title of the story, "Heart of Summer, Heart of Light," was formulated as an explicit semantic and ideological counter to Joseph Conrad's *Heart of Darkness* and its bleak vision. Unlike Marlow's journey to Kurtz, which leads toward a universal "heart of darkness," Ronen's story moves toward a "heart of light." This inverse parallelism may explain the grandmother's self-image as a white missionary sacrificing herself for the good of Hulda and the children—whom she sees as "the darkest of darkest Africa" (Kahana-Carmon 1966, 244–45). Just as Kurtz's goal of bringing the gospel of progress to the Africans proves a lie, so, too, are Ronen's grandmother's intentions perverted.

With its emphasis on the discrepancy between sign and reference, achieved through acts of linguistic deterritorialization, Kahana-Carmon's novella creates the effect of a defamiliarization of signs that opens up new possibilities for the creative imagination. Moreover, the defamiliarization fosters the development of a new kind of consciousness and sensibility (Kaplan 1990, 357–68; Deleuze and Guattari 1986, 17) that, in turn, points out the utopian potential of a new kind of national community. And indeed, the novella's systematically created tension between the muteness and inhibitions of spoken language and the new path opened up through the written medium of literary language unfolds in a utopian and mystical light. The vision of "heart of summer, heart of light" points out the possibility of a reterritorialization of language, of the emergence of a new and different relationship between national existence and territory.

This exploration of three works of fiction from the sixties is also an attempt to look back at a critical juncture in the development of Israeli culture. From a vantage point more than forty years later, these stories represent a moment of insight into the dialectic of building a nation-state on the foundation of an oppressed minority tradition. The search for a new Israeli identity, conceived in these stories as the rebellion of a minority against a majority, is presented together with a critical delimitation of the bounds of this quest. These stories signal different stages in the shaping of a majority consciousness through a critical examination of minority stances. They also point to the possibility of majority consciousness taking shape without resorting to the kind of a priori superiority that denies the majority any autonomous space. The Israeliness that emerges from these stories is not something static or rigid that sanctions and defines the national identity of the marginal Other. Indeed, almost the reverse is true: the kind of Israeli identity suggested in these stories becomes possible precisely by virtue of the marginal Other. These stories from the early sixties contributed toward subverting the commonly held illusion of the ahistorical, metaphysical validity of the concept of national identity.

A number of positive developments in Israeli society, harbingers of a liberation from the consciousness of majority as minority, occurred shortly before the 1967 war. A striking illustration is the successful struggle to abolish the military administration that still governed the Arab population of Israel. The arguments made at the time in favor of maintaining the status quo reflected the fundamental tension between the Jewish majority's attempt to grapple with the existence of a numerical minority and the actual magnitude of the physical threat attributed to that minority. The continuing occupation of the West Bank and the Gaza Strip in the aftermath of the 1967 war, however, completely derailed this development. During this period, the ideological significance of terms such as *minority* and *majority* took a crucial turn. The majority's political and military power was now palpable as never before. But faced with the stark demographic threat that accompanied control over a larger territory and a much larger population, the majority's consciousness of itself as majority became even more uncertain. The gap between the power field of sovereignty and the imagined field of national self-consciousness only grew wider. Geula's misfortune in "Nomads and Viper," like the outbreak of retaliatory violence on the part of the younger kibbutzniks, results from "forgetting" membership in the majority culture. Indulging this weakness, they are no longer capable of distinguishing their own libidinal aims from the social exercise of power. It is a mechanism that begins by engineering authority out of addiction to weakness and ends by abdicating the responsibility devolving upon the rulers as members of the majority.

Picture, Photograph, and Map: Shimon Ballas's Controversial Constitution of National Identity

Shimon Ballas immigrated to Israel from Iraq in 1951 and published his first novel, *HaMaabara* (The Transit Camp), in 1964: a work that described the *maabara*, or temporary settlement camp for new immigrants, in bitingly critical detail. Upon its appearance, Aliza Levenberg, a commentator who wrote on issues concerning the absorption of immigrants of Eastern and North African origin into Israeli society, chose to begin her article on the novel with a discussion of its dust jacket:

> Is it mere coincidence that the publishers chose to use a photograph on the cover of Shimon Ballas's *HaMaabara?* It would seem to be the case that not a single child pictured in the photograph—neither those sitting or standing at the entrance to the tent, nor the children reflected in the water of the large puddle outside it—actually lives in the *maabara* which is the setting for Ballas's novel. The novel does not describe every character that its author encountered during the year he spent in the *maabara* as a twenty-year-old, newly arrived from his native city of Baghdad. Despite this, the book has something of the sharpness of a photograph about it. . . . One senses that Ballas is drawn to the *maabara* which he abandoned . . . in order to be a witness. . . . The book is therefore, to a certain degree, a documentary work, even though no single character or single fact precisely matches the official register. There is probably no single person who conforms exactly to the descriptions given in the book. (Levenberg 1964, 22)

Levenberg's criticism reflects her Ashkenazi, female response to the novel, reporting her strong sense of its failure to achieve representational consistency and reacting strongly to the heterogeneous representation of reality that she finds inscribed here. On the one hand, Levenberg argues that Ballas's novel is a literary text that describes reality with the precision of a photograph. On the other hand, she complains, it does not, in fact, describe actual individuals living in the *maabara*. While the novel refuses to beautify reality, the far-from-sublime reality it does portray deviates, says Levenberg, from the actual state of affairs. It is documentary, but its facts do not conform to the official record.

The discrepancy that Levenberg identifies in the novel's means of representation reflects its violation of the basic code of the Israeli literary canon during the sixties. This discrepancy is already apparent at a thematic level: the other place described by Ballas is not the kibbutz, as is the case with Amos Oz's 1965 work *Makom Akher* (Another Place), for example; nor is it London or Tel Aviv. Rather, it is the *maabara* in Israel that stands at the forefront, as *maabarot* in Israel and communities in Baghdad continue to do in Ballas's second book, *Mul*

HaKhoma (In Front of the Wall) (1969). But there is little doubt that the most significant discrepancy that Levenberg's response signals relates to the blurring of the clearly defined boundary between documentary representation on the one hand and fictional literary representation on the other: a separation that was basic to the perceived consciousness of Israeli literature of the sixties as universalist fiction. Ballas tells the story of the Oriya *maabara* through the deliberate mixing of fiction with real facts, a mixture that includes, for instance, references to the role of the Communist Party in supporting the struggle of the *maabara* inhabitants. He also refers in the novel to the role played by a newspaper, here titled *Niv HeHamon* (The Idiom of the Masses), which is a transparent representation of the Communist Party organ *Kol Haam* (The Voice of the People).

These deviations from the canon are particularly noticeable in view of the similarities that Ballas's work of the sixties shares with canonical fiction. After writing in Arabic for a period of time, for *El Ityahad* (The Unity) and *El Jadid* (The New) (the newspaper and literary periodical published by the Israeli Communist Party), Ballas was first published in Hebrew during the early sixties in a collection of stories that also featured such authors as Amos Oz, A. B. Yehoshua, Amalia Kahana-Carmon, Yitzhak Orpaz, Yeshayahu Koren, and others whose work confirmed the status accorded to them as leading canonical representatives of writing associated with the "generation of the state" (*Dor HaMedina*). Ballas emulated such writers in many respects. He, too, published in journals such as *Keshet* (Bow) or *Amot* (Criteria), and his writing upheld the basic code that characterized Israeli literature during the late fifties and early sixties: a predominantly allegorical code where the story of the collective is represented by means of a personal or an individual story, which generally also bears features of a sexual or libidinal growth to consciousness, or *Bildungsroman*. Amos Oz's 1965 work *Arzot HaTan* (Where the Jackals Howl) and A. B. Yehoshua's stories "Masa HaErev Shel Yatir" (Yatir's Night Journey) and "Mul HaYearot" (Facing the Forests) are typical examples of collective narratives consistently articulated through individual, usually sexual, plots. The relations between the private and the collective plots admittedly vary: they may run parallel, interfuse, or even stand in contrast to one another, as in Amos Oz's work, for example. But Israeli canonical writers of the sixties consistently manipulate these two trajectories—the private and the collective—one alongside the other, throughout the duration of the text.

It is the Oedipal pattern that organizes the life of the collective (be the latter understood as the younger generation of the newly established state, its kibbutzim, or its society in general) as a narrative of quest and desire. This narrative is clearly structured, with a definite beginning, middle, and ending, which forms both an individual and a collective retrospective and a conclusion. The institutionalized authority of the collective (the regime, the kibbutz leadership, the police, the Jewish National Fund official responsible for the forests) is the focus of the private and Oedipal rebellion of the young generation challenging its fathers. Thus, like the Amos Oz story "Nomads and Viper" (1965, 25–41), where the moral confrontation surrounding the question of how to respond to acts of theft by Bedouins is revealed to be an Oedipal confrontation in which the younger members of the kibbutz challenge its older secretary, in Ballas's story "Rukhot Shevat" (January's Ghosts) (Ballas 1969, 41–54), the hero's participation in the Iraqi workers' struggle against exploitation is revealed to be an Oedipal struggle against the adults surrounding him, stemming from his desire to prove his manhood in the eyes of his beloved. In the story "Doda Aony" (Aunt Aony), the young protagonist discovers the adult world, the world of sex, at the same time that he discovers the national forgiveness of the Armenians in Baghdad (Ballas 1969, 55–59).

But even if Ballas's oeuvre over the course of the sixties appears to conform to the basic rules of the Israeli canon, with the Oedipal model enshrined first and foremost as a comprehensive code for narrative organization, this impression is merely a matter of surface appearance. For Ballas's most prominent use of the Oedipal story, a constitutive and almost permanent feature of the canon of the sixties, consists precisely in deforming the Oedipal structure, chiefly though interrupting or fragmenting it.

These gestures of fragmentation and deformation are already apparent in the fact that the Oedipal code does not succeed in achieving domination over the heterogeneity of plot structures that the stories create. The universalism that the story of desire lends to the concrete elements of plot relating to Baghdad and Israel cannot contain and constrain that mixture of fiction and documentary to which Levenberg refers and therefore cannot fulfill its role as a metaframe that unites story fragments or fractions. Something goes awry as Ballas proceeds to generalize and expand the individual story beyond the boundaries of the personal: the process of its being rendered universal does not proceed smoothly. Instead of writing a causally governed and sequential Oedipal story involving the rebellion against authority—one whose conclusion has the hero identifying with authority and accepting its decrees in order to constitute his own identity—Ballas writes something else altogether. His stories refuse the causal sequence of identity formation and choose instead to fragment the universalist aesthetic assumptions underlying the Israeli national narrative of the time. Even when a story is structured as an Oedipal story unfolding in time, the connection to the national space or territory of the land of Israel is rendered irrelevant. In one case, "Rukhot Shevat," which describes the hero's love for Odette and his decision to join the revolutionary cause in order to rebel against his parents' generation, the story is set in Baghdad: this setting, which frames the process of the Oedipal coming-to-consciousness, expresses neither fusion with nor rejection of the Israeli national space—it simply exists at a remove from it.

In a similar fashion, the story "Derech Preda" (Parting Way) (Ballas 1969, 7–40) describes the migration to Israel as a set of parallel partings, encompassing both the departure from revolutionary activity in the Communist underground and the hero's farewell to his adolescent bond with a prostitute from a Kurdish village. Given this background, the protagonist's decision to leave Baghdad is not motivated in terms of his desire to become part of the Jewish homeland in Eretz Israel but is linked to an awareness of political persecution that has nothing whatsoever to do with Zionism.

A prominent aspect of the aesthetics of *HaMaabara* as a novel concerns its structure: instead of one Oedipal character, whose struggle either fails or succeeds in accordance with the overarching Oedipal pattern, we find an economy of characters that refuses to be restricted to one axis—so much so that it is difficult to identify the protagonists with any certainty. Various characters represent various political forces: some seek to become absorbed into the life of the state as autonomous leaders of the *maabara*'s inhabitants, while others belong to the Communist Party or act as agents of the Ashkenazi establishment. The novel fails to identify which of these options is the appropriate one. In addition to a clear collective struggle between the inside (the *maabara*) and the outside (the Ashkenazi regime, termed the "Yiddish" regime in the novel), together with a more private struggle between the generation of the sons and the generation of the fathers, Ballas depicts areas of struggle that do not run parallel: struggles where inner realities are as important as the engagement with the ruling powers. Additionally, the moral evaluations attaching to the characters in the inner ring of the *maabara* are not clear-cut, definite, or unambiguous (Levenberg 1964; Moreh 1997, 331). Thus, for example, the collapse of the generation of the fathers during the process of migration prevents it from serving as a focus for the Oedipal revolt, while the duplicity of Haim Vaad, who seeks to become the leader of the *maabara,* is depicted in the novel as part of an inner conflict among the inhabitants that weakens their capacity to resist the authorities. This separation between the Oedipal struggle and concrete political polarization is partly conveyed through a parable that realizes Oedipal authority in the public/political arena: Moshe, one of the *maabara*'s idle loafers, tells the story of a mass brawl in Baghdad during which a castration occurred before the watching eyes of the policeman (a representative of the ruling power), but this castration crucially failed to constitute an act of political agitation (Ballas 1964, 142).

One of the clearest examples of the disruption of the Oedipal pattern in *HaMaabara* occurs in the seeming fusion, or at least the parallel, of Yosef Shabi's erotic desires and his collectivist quest to be an architect in Israel, the new national homeland. But these two seemingly analogical quests develop very differently: his attempt to write a letter to his beloved, Esther, is interrupted, while he comes to define his dream for integration into the collective as "a dream that sank into the filth of the *maabara*"—indeed, a parody of a dream: "When he built a storeroom next to his shack, he said to his mother: 'Here, I have built my first palace'" (Ballas 1964, 166). These two insights—one concerning his personal dead end, the other relating to collective hopelessness—do not appear in the novel as the product of an Oedipal conflict with a loving-but-stifling source of authority but surface precisely as Shabi meditates on the figure of his mother before dozing off (163).

Nor does the novel's conclusion resolve its conflicts; rather, it preserves them. The circular plot structure means that there can be no process of working through conflict, as the reader is returned full circle to the text's problematic point of origin: life in the *maabara*. Similarly, the struggles that develop over the course of the novel fail to bring about the constitution of a clear new identity. The struggle of the *maabara*'s inhabitants is unsuccessful, and the text of the novel's concluding section is replete with the smell of hashish, which "floated above the heads of those who were seated, spilled sideways, and eventually disappeared in a dense layer, just as reality disappears into the embrace of the illusion" (203).

Ballas's narrative strategy at this point is very close to what Homi Bhabha terms "mimicry" (Bhabha 1994, 85–92). Mimicry may be understood as a form of imitation that uses ruling or hegemonic modes of representation in a manner that always produces difference in addition to similarity; closeness, but from a vantage point of distance; and imperfect imitation. It is for this reason that mimicry constantly challenges the coherence of hegemonic identity. Instead of an organized Oedipal narrative, Ballas produces the likeness or imitation of such a narrative; thus he deploys strategies characteristic of the dominated classes who challenge the identity dictated by the ruling culture by partly assimilating its models, in an act of identification that produces only the semblance of likeness. Ballas writes like Amos Oz but not really like Amos Oz—he is a successor to Oz but at the same time subverts his predecessor. In contrast to Israeli identity, which appears as natural, homogeneous, local, and, above all, universal, Ballas raises a possibility that is explicitly heterogeneous: the option of being a local yet simultaneously an immigrant from the East—a "doubly realized" reality, as Ballas put it in a manifesto he composed together with Yaakov Besser, Itamar Yaoz-Kest, and Reuven Ben-Yosef (1977). In this conceptualization, one is simultaneously local and an immigrant, in complete contrast to the option dictated by hegemonic Zionist discourse, where one is thought to have been an immigrant in the past but ceases to be one in the present, in order to fashion a new and exclusively local identity—at the very least, one submits oneself to the provisions of such an identity. But against these norms of homogeneity and of universality (which are usually merely a camouflage for Western Zionist norms), which characterized the hegemony of Israeli culture in the past as they continue to do in the present, Ballas continuously emphasizes the heterogeneity of the notion of the "Jewish people," which, he insists, must include both North African and Eastern immigrants and Jews of Western and Eastern European descent.

In public statements he issued throughout the course of the sixties, Ballas strongly opposed the dichotomy between those who "absorb" the new immigrants, and who are constructed as a homogeneous and well-integrated entity, and the immigrants to be absorbed, who are always constructed as inferior. As an alternative, Ballas formulated a program for the cultural integration of the entire population of Israel. In contrast to the melting-pot description of the Eastern immigration to Israel, an ideology whose local Israeli variant is known as "merging exiled Diasporas" (*mizug galuyot*), Ballas pointed to the more universal constituents of what is actually an anachronistic and colonial intervention:

> Whereas the leaders of the West sought to "civilize" entire peoples through the force of their colonial domination, the equivalent process in Israel is sevenfold more frightening, not only because of the negative coercion itself, but because Jews are seeking to "civilize" Jews—despite the fact that both sides share a common Jewish culture. We face yet again that blurring of the notions of culture and civilization in a grave and potentially disastrous version. (1965, 67)

In the continuation of this statement, Ballas criticizes Professor Natan Rotenstreich, exposing the latter's academic authority as an agent of the hegemonic establishment:

> There is, in my opinion, certain one-sidedness in presenting the problem of merging the Diasporas as seen through the prism of the statements issued by the veteran community. For some reason, it seems to envisage itself as an integrated and reality-based community, which has taken upon itself the task of absorbing immigrants who are inferior to it in their spiritual and economic capacities. For some reason, these people (the representatives of established Jewish settlement in Israel) are unable to rid themselves of the sense that they are destined, supposedly, to be the "absorbing establishment," and that the community of immigrants must conform to their dictates. . . . This, as I have stated, is a one-sided vision.

In actual fact, one necessary conclusion that should be drawn concerns the fact that the entire population of Israel, at all levels, is in a process of general spiritual fashioning and crystallization. In my opinion, there should be no talk of merging without a simultaneous willingness for the process to be bilateral: both the established and the new publics must be called upon to merge. All rapprochement must take place between two points, two agents. All acts of love are based on the premise of two partners, at least. This is also the case for an act of merging: the responsibility for "rapprochement-love" cannot be demanded of one side alone. (67)

Ballas's comments emphasize how liquid his sense of identity is: he feels local identity in the Iraq he was forced to leave, but Israel is not wholly Other, different, or foreign to him. For this reason, he continues to define himself as an Arab Jewish writer, whose sense of belonging to Arab culture is not erased the moment he is absorbed into Israeli literature; he lays claim to both identities. In his articles as in his stories, Ballas refuses to construct narratives or identities that are stable and unified: instead of a clear, permanent Eastern identity of one kind or another, Ballas's texts fashion sets of unstable identities.

This type of "mimicry" presented, and continues to present, a massive challenge to the hegemonic apparatus of Israeli identity formation. Evidence of this may be found in the anxiety-laden responses of hegemonic criticism to Ballas, in its need, for instance, to label his writing "ethnic-social realism," having "socially didactic orientations" that are justified solely in light of the fact that "social oppression calls for a kind of social realism in its engagements with the social arena" (Shaked 1993, 167–68). But as Ballas himself points out, these kinds of reactions reduce his oeuvre to the status of a record of the suffering he underwent as an Eastern (Mizrahi) immigrant (Ballas 1992). The literary-critical establishment that reduces Ballas's poetics to a handful of hostile metastories regarding ethnicity or to a kind of left-wing anti-Zionism, and that deploys ready-made labels of identity in order to do so, has marginalized Ballas's work in the literary canon. It has facilitated attempts to police the subversiveness of Ballas's discourse by labeling it, unequivocally, as second-rate. Thus, for example, the heterogeneous economy of characters in Ballas's writing is seen by the criticism as a flaw: Ballas fails to provide a single, unifying point of reference (Arad 1964). This type of reservation also shows the difficulty faced by the literary-critical establishment in light of Ballas's refusal to encode clear identities through the provision of a central and sequential narrative, in which private time and collective time flow parallel.

Ballas does not merely reject the parallel between the two temporal axes (private and collective); he replaces these coordinates with spatial patterns. Instead of being committed to a shared temporal framework, within whose boundaries a conflict develops and is resolved, Ballas resolutely foregrounds the spatial patterning of the novel. Unlike Zionist hegemonic discourse, which continuously parades its rootedness in space—that is, in Zionist territory—as a function of temporal progression (where the ability to rule territory is a function of national renaissance over time), Ballas relinquishes the centrality of the temporal axis, thus disrupting the claim to power over national territory.

Spatiality in Ballas's writing is expressed, first and foremost, in his emphasis on the *maabara* as a place, rather than on its inhabitants, as the representational focus of the novel. The foregrounding of the *maabara* as central in itself, not as the by-product of a more elevated and more central encompassing Israeli reality, is already an act of subversion to the extent that it confers a permanent status on that which Zionist discourse holds precisely to be a paradigm of transience—the *maabara* as temporary way station. In contrast to the official definition of the *maabara* as a "passageway" (*maavar*, from the same etymological root as the word *maabara*) to full absorption in the life of the country, Eliyahu Eyni presents an alternative meaning in the novel, one taken from the book of Samuel, where Jonathan seeks to "go over unto" the Philistines' garrison: "And between the passes by which Jonathan sought to go over unto the Philistines' garrison, there was a rocky crag on the one side and a rocky crag on the other side" (1 Samuel 14:4). "This is the *maabara* for you! A rocky crag on one side and a rocky crag on the other! Go break rocks! Is that not exile?" (1964, 51) asks Eyni, thus substituting for the Zionist passageway, as proceeding from exile to redemption in the homeland, a form of spatial deviation—from a Zionist perspective—since the immigrants have simply substituted one type of exile for another. Haim Vaad, for his part, presents a Zionist interpretation of the *maabara* as an alternative and says to Salim: "Here you are talking about fate as if it is our fate to be forever in *maabarot.* I say to you that a glorious fate awaits us [Jews of Iraqi descent] in Israel" (101). Later, he expands on the role of Iraqi Jews as a bridge between Israel and the Arab nations of the region. But neither Eliyahu Eyni nor Haim Vaad has an unambiguously positive status in the novel: each of their positions, like so many other positions in the novel, appears as one option among many. The status of the *maabara* as a bridge between the immigrant and the homeland disappears completely, to be replaced with a number of options, even contradictory ones, and certainly also options that stand in opposition to the institutional policies of the absorbing culture.

The emphasis on spatial representation leads to a synchronic organization of the historical strata of the *maabara,* one atop the other. For this reason, the remains of the Arab village, the original site on top of which the *maabara* was built, are not displaced to make way for this new phase in the Zionist narrative. Instead of a narrative logic that layers new on old through the erasure of the old, Ballas constructs a space that fuses all the different layers together: the remains of the Arab village, ruined during the 1948 war; the *maabara*; the poverty-stricken suburb, housing veteran Israelis, that lies next to it; and the courtyard of an old house "exposed to the four winds" (168), where the unemployed of the *maabara* come to meet the unemployed of the suburb.

The spatial organization peculiar to Ballas reveals his employment of accepted means of spatial representation—the picture, the photograph, and the map—to fashion identity in his stories. In contrast to the Oedipal strategy, which fashions private and collective identity into one sequence—say, the childhood or adolescence of the protagonist in Baghdad presented in plot sequence until its completion—the means that Ballas chooses to employ, the photograph and the picture, signify splitting, separation, and mediation between an original and its narrative representation. Thus, Ballas emphasizes the absence of a stable core that might anchor identity, as well as its lack of coherence and unity. The story "Mul HaKhoma" (In Front of the Wall) (1969, 70–89) develops in relation to a photograph of Latif, a former political comrade in the Communist struggle in Iraq, that the hero finds on the floor of a ship. The story blends an account of the protagonist's relationship with Latif and their common political activities with the description of a visit to political prisoners in a Baghdad jail. Scrutiny of the photograph returns the protagonist to different layers of his biographical and political self and triggers a process of self-evaluation that ends in a second interrogation of the picture, which reminds the protagonist of the demonstration during which Latif was killed. The fashioning of the hero's identity does not play itself out against the backdrop of collective judgments but with respect to a photograph; thus the importance for the story of continuous temporal development is minimized. The story's temporal conceptualization mixes early and late and renders the spatial organization of the photograph into an alternative that replaces a plot that develops over time. Looking at the photograph interrupts the causality of the temporal sequence and splits the identity of the observer off from any type of causal sequence, displaying a discrete beginning and a uniform trajectory of development. The latter type of causal sequencing is replaced in Ballas with a kind of multilayered and simultaneous presencing of discrete biographical moments.

A more fully developed example of Ballas's use of spatial patterning is the story "Nof Yerushalmi" (Jerusalem Landscape), also included in the collection *Mul HaKhoma* (1969, 94–103). At first glance, this story appears to conform to the canonical mold, because it is constructed around the parallel between the hero's artistic quandary as he seeks to draw a "Jerusalem landscape" in post-1967 Israel and his problematic relationship with his girlfriend, Tamar. The struggle to find the correct aesthetic code parallels the struggle for Tamar's heart. But, by the conclusion of the story, it becomes clear that the problem of the artistic representation of Jerusalem is, in fact, the problem of the artistic representation of Jerusalem after the war, and the quest for the appropriate visual mode of representation of the city is a pretext for allowing the artist to mourn his friend who died in the battle for Jerusalem. As far as the sequential patterning of the story goes, coming to terms with the private and collective price of the national war of 1967 involves a stepping back from contemporary national reality in order to achieve artistic distance. The protagonist Gad's greatest artistic achievement consists in doing that which is artistically appropriate, even if it is not destined to win him public approval: he produces an abstract representation of Jerusalem, which relieves him of the constraints of concrete reality and which, in his words, "frees his imagination from its chains" (131).

This story presents an intractable challenge to the demand for continuity between the private and collective narratives, which is one of the dictates of the hegemonic code. Ballas focuses his story on a type of distancing visual representation; in the words of the protagonist: "I am a landscape artist, Clara, a landscape that is perceived through the senses rather than the eyes, a landscape that does not exist in reality" (123). The picture, like the photograph, serves to mediate between the two stories—the private and the national—in a manner that prevents one from being read through the other. Using this strategy, Ballas fashions a type of identity based on the heterogeneous, the contradictory, the discontinuous, the irredeemable. Again and again in his writings, the photograph and the picture catalyze the development of a given story. Again and again, they disrupt, in a fundamental and principled manner, identity formation based on the merging of the individual, erotic, personal, or artistic story with the collective or national story. Instead, they construct a form of identity that is problematic, distanced, and nonuniform, through positing artistic representation as a kind of splitting off or a distanced and alienated mapping.

The picture and discussion of it also serve as the basis for a process of personal clarification in the novel *Hitbaharut* (Clarification), which Ballas wrote about the 1967 war and published in 1972. Its hero, Yaakov Drori, of Jewish Iraqi descent, was not himself drafted into the army, but the war nevertheless brought about significant changes in his personal life. (The husband of his ex-wife, the man who broke up their marriage, was killed in the war, leading to a rapprochement between Yaakov and his ex-wife, the mother of his child.) At a certain point in the development of the novel, forms of spatial representation—namely, the pictures in Yaakov's house and maps of the Sinai newly opened to Israeli construction (Yaakov is a civil engineer who designs roads)—help differentiate between his personal story and its national counterpart, so that his process of "clarification" occurs independently of the story of the national war; it neither is supported by nor conflicts with the latter.

The picture, like the map, is always split between its appearance as a coherent and uniform representation of the reality depicted, on the one hand, and its status as an articulation, on the other hand, a mediated visual representation of reality that proceeds on the basis of a series of parallels and differences that bridge the external reality and its representation. It is for this reason that the map foregrounds the lack or gap between the representation and that which is represented: it is, in Graham Huggan's words, "a manifestation of the desire for control rather than an authenticating seal of coherence" (1990, 127). That is, the map is not a reflection of reality; rather, it is a form of the desire to represent reality. It is not the thing itself but rather the attempt, the striving, to touch the thing itself. The picture and the photograph foreground the *process* of constituting reality over the end product of that process. They emphasize the heterogeneity of identity against the portrayal of identity as original and seamless, and they encode an awareness of the gaps, mediations, and lack of continuity that are integral to the process of identity formation.

In his autobiographical text, "Yaldut Shebadimyon" (Imaginary Childhood), first published in 1977, Ballas distances himself from an acceptance of the originary story, the story of childhood, as the basis for identity formation in the present, as this process is held to occur in the accepted communicative models of hegemonic culture:

> Are the two houses I grew up in [in Baghdad] still standing? A young Iraqi friend I met in Paris was unable to answer my question, but he showed me a map of the city—the kind of map distributed to tourists. I found there streets and gardens, bridges, squares and residential blocs, undifferentiated. "Do you have another map," I asked him, "a map of twisted and intertwining alleys like a dense spiderweb? I could draw such a map for you on paper, because I remember every twist, every niche, every arch, every window and the angled contours of every building where men used to stand and piss."
>
> "Many suburbs have been destroyed," said my friend laconically. "Perhaps your suburb was also destroyed."
>
> Is it important whether it was destroyed or not? For me, it will exist to all eternity. The world of childhood is an a-temporal world which exists in the imagination more than in reality. It is an experiential whole that you cannot divide or exhaust by verbal means.
>
> We are used to telling logical stories. Our language is subservient to set rules and to temporal concepts. Everything has a reason, and the ties of causality run like scarlet threads through the sentences which drop from our lips, otherwise no one would understand us. How shall we recount a dream? How shall we recount an a-temporal experience?

You cannot retell the experiences of childhood except at the price of entrapping them in time, at the price of binding them tightly within the bonds of cause and effect. Such are the childhood stories that we read. They are stories. A fading shadow, or a polished bubble, of imaginary experience. We do not invest the stories of childhood with much credibility, just as we do not invest much credibility in dreams. People whose power lies in inventing fictions are even less credible when its comes to recounting things as they happened—how much more so, things that happened in their childhood. ([1977] 1979, 144)

Instead of acquiescing to the ideal of an authentic Israeli origin, Ballas's stories gesture toward points of origin that are problematic, mediated, and noncontinuous, and they do so using pictures, photographs, and maps. By means of a self-consciousness rooted in the "dual reality" of an Israeli author whose very point of departure lies in the awareness of his double origins, Ballas challenges the hegemonic perceptions of the literature of the "era of statehood" as it was expressed in the sixties. He refuses to partake of the illusion of a "native" Israeli literature, secure in its self-representation as a new, progressive, but also local and authentic offshoot of universal literature.

Chapter 7

Hebrew in an Israeli Arab Hand: Anton Shammas's Arabesques

The Majority as Minority

Anton Shammas's *Arabesques* is undoubtedly one of the most radical and amazing examples of the dynamics of the relationship between majority and minority to grow out of Hebrew literature. Even the fact that Shammas is an Arab writer writing in Hebrew can be read as a protest, aimed principally at the ambiguous multiplicity that is perhaps the paramount characteristic of Israeli public discourse today. A wealth of examples could be mustered to prove that Israel, though behaving like a nation of rulers and conquerors, still relies heavily on the argumentation and rhetoric of a minority struggling for its very existence. Undoubtedly contributing to this phenomenon is the speed with which Israeli Jews made the transition, immediately after the Holocaust, from a persecuted minority to a ruling majority in their own state. But other considerations exist as well: for example, the way in which Jewish history, steeped in suffering, figures so intensely in the worldview of present-day Israel or in the Israeli "fortress mentality" vis-à-vis a largely hostile Arab world. What has developed, as a result, is a surprisingly flexible mode of public discourse, able to adapt itself to almost any dialogical situation. Depending on the requirement of the particular confrontation, it can speak in the voice of an impotent minority in need of reassurance or in the voice of a majority confident of itself and its power. In one way or another, then, almost any text found in present-day Israel is liable to fall into the same mode: a blindness to the fundamentally asymmetrical power relationships it enunciates. This holds even, and perhaps chiefly, for texts expressing sympathy for or solidarity with the Palestinian cause.

Anton Shammas, an Israeli Christian Arab, has published a Hebrew novel, a text written in the language of the conquerors. The reaction of the Israeli Jewish writer Amos Oz, cited in the introduction to this book, is based in large measure on the historical fact that Hebrew is the language of Zionism, the national liberation movement of a Jewish minority in the Diaspora that founded the State of Israel. Shammas was born after Israeli independence, an Arab and an Israeli citizen, in the village of Fasuta in the Galilee, and he linked his destiny and his literary career to Hebrew literature and culture. *Arabesques* is his first novel, though he has also published two books of poetry and a children's book, as well as translations from Arabic. He also contributes to Israeli newspapers and periodicals.

The identity of an Israeli Christian Arab does not line up in any simple way with the main political forces at work in Israel and the Middle East and, in fact, stands somewhat apart from them. From this special viewpoint, Shammas has constructed a novel that presents a challenge to his Hebrew-speaking readers. As an "Israeli Arab," Shammas is a member of a minority group, but as a Christian, he falls outside the Islamic mainstream of the minority that, at least according to the prevalent Israeli conception, tends more "naturally" to be identified with the Palestinians. On top of this, he writes in Hebrew, the language of the dominant Jewish culture, which is itself a minority within the predominantly Arab Middle East. This peculiar position, which Shammas likens to the image of a Russian babushka doll (Shammas 1986a), gives him a unique perspective on Israeli public discourse, simultaneously from within and from without. With this cultural and political flexibility, Shammas can develop an authorial voice that forces his readers to take a fresh look at their cultural assumptions and expectations. The principal critical and popular responses to Shammas, for example, tend to represent him as either an Arab author writing in Hebrew or a Hebrew author of Arab extraction. Shammas, however, sees himself as neither: he defines himself as someone unable to decide whether Israel represents homeland or exile. For an Arab author to be writing in Hebrew is highly unusual in the Israeli cultural landscape and is undoubtedly connected with a blurring of the traditional boundaries of Israeli national culture. Yet, as a writer, Shammas rejects these polarized images. He responds on another plane entirely and puts forth his own Israeli identity as his personal utopian resolution to the dilemma.

As has frequently been remarked, Shammas may well have created the most truly Israeli novel yet written. But that Israeli essence is imagined through an intricate web of negations. From an Israeli viewpoint, at once Jewish and Arab, great significance attaches to this analytical and demystifying negationist stance. The member of a minority within a minority within a minority, Shammas has used the figure of the arabesque as a richly articulated vehicle for minority discourse; such richness is indispensable considering the complexity of the Israeli reality with which Shammas is grappling. As we shall see, this figure has two principal aspects: the one negative, a striving for demystification, and the other positive, an attempt to develop a language adequate to the problems of a minority. This duality reveals how Shammas's decision to write in the Other's language provides a glimmer of hope, a possible way out of the political and cultural dead end in which Israeli society now finds itself.

The analysis here of *Arabesques* attempts to respond to the challenge presented by the novel's negationist stance. The comparison between the textual flow of the novel itself and paraphrases of it illustrate the opposition between Shammas's *Arabesques* and any attempt to restate it synoptically. The extent to which this opposition is politically charged is quite apparent: we need only note the asymmetry of a Jewish Israeli text passing judgment on a Hebrew text by an Israeli Arab. And, in fact, a dual consciousness underlies this chapter. On the one hand, there is an awareness of the power implications of the hermeneutic acts we perform in imposing hierarchies of meanings on the text. On the other hand, paraphrase is inevitable, even if one takes for granted the irreducible heterogeneity and uniqueness of the text (Jay 1986). The division into sections that may seem abrupt, the discontinuous shifts of topic, the fragmentary nature of the exposition, and the avoidance of any sort of harmonious, well-rounded interpretation all constitute a partial response to the unique challenge of the arabesque as a vehicle for minority discourse.

Who Are You, Anton Shammas?

The status of the narrator—his identity, his values, his potentialities, and, especially, his relation to the narration—is one of the focal points of this semiautobiographical novel. As part of the "communicative contract" that he offers his readers, Shammas deliberately undermines the authority and unity of the narrative voice in his novel. A sharp, formal split differentiates those chapters whose titles mark them as belonging to the "narrative" portion of the book from those chapters that comprise the "narrator's" portion. The narrative sections unfold the history of the multibranched Shammas family, starting from the early nineteenth century (when the patriarch of the family moved to the Galilee from Syria), on through the period prior to the founding of the State of Israel in 1948, and up to the present-day Israeli occupation of the West Bank and the Gaza Strip. The "narrator" portions relate the journey of the author, Anton Shammas, from Israel to America, to take part in the International Writing Program held annually in Iowa City. This formal thematic split signals the possible absence of conventional, causal links between the narrator and his narrative.

In no small measure, Shammas's novel is organized like a detective story. The Israeli Christian Arab Anton Shammas and his Palestinian doppelgänger Michel Abayyad, from the Center for Palestinian Studies in Beirut, are in effect trying to track each other down. Shammas the narrator is named after his cousin Michel Abayyad, who himself had been named Anton Shammas but, soon after birth, was kidnapped from his natural mother, Almaza, to be raised by a childless couple of "the old Arab nobility" in Beirut (Shammas 1986, 232; quotations follow the Hebrew original where they differ from the English translation [Shammas 1988]). From a newspaper article, Shammas the narrator learns of a certain Surayya Sa'id, a blond-haired Christian woman who converted to Islam and married the son of Abdallah Al-Asbah, one of the heroes of the Great Arab Revolt of 1936. Shammas surmises that she is none other than Layla Khouri, the same woman his father brought, in 1936, from the village of Fasuta in the Galilee, to Beirut to live with the Baytar family, and who had later been a servant in one of the wealthy neighborhoods of that city. In

1948, Layla Khouri had paid a very brief visit to Fasuta, only to be expelled to the West Bank by the Israeli army. Surayya Sa`id—that is, Layla Khouri—had been a servant in Michel Abayyad's house when the adopted boy was growing up and was secretly in love with him. On the very night in 1948 when Layla returned to Fasuta from Beirut, Michel Abayyad's parents were blackmailed into revealing the terrible secret of their adopted son and were forced to send the young Michel to America.

Shammas himself labels this an "Arab soap opera" (52). But in the "narrator's" portion of the book, the story reappears. During Shammas's emotional meeting with Michel Abayyad in Iowa City, Abayyad tells his own life story—a story very similar to the one Shammas had extracted from Layla Khouri. But Abayyad's version is not precisely the same as the "narrative" version. It is set a year later (in 1949 instead of 1948), and the servant in the Beirut house of his childhood is identified not as Layla Khouri but as Shammas the narrator's own aunt Almaza.

Abbayad's narrative casts the entire book in a new light. Michel Abayyad returned from America to Beirut in 1978 to join the staff of the Center for Palestinian Studies in Beirut. There he made the acquaintance of Nur, Anton Shammas's cousin, who suggested to Abayyad that he try to locate his natural mother, the same woman who had suddenly appeared at his adoptive parents' house in 1949 to claim her missing child. But the Beirut of 1978, caught up in civil war, was not the ideal place for such a search. And the fact of having grown up with Almaza, the bereaved mother, influenced Abayyad so strongly that he came to identify completely with her lost son, Anton. Based on Nur's stories, Abayyad decides to write the fictitious autobiography of Anton Shammas and to inject himself into the story in the role of Anton, Almaza's dead child. And now the reader is given a hint that the "narrative" portion of the novel referred to above, including the whole Abayyad–Shammas affair as told by Layla Khouri, is the invention of Michel Abayyad the writer. Here, at least, we seem to have reached secure epistemological ground: the "narrative" portions of the novel are to be taken as a fabrication. But Shammas the author has not yet exhausted his Chinese puzzle of boxes within boxes. The chapter summarizing the "narrator's" section of the novel not only reveals that the "narrative" portion is a fiction; it also includes a statement by Shammas the author that the "narrator's" portion is itself a fiction. Shammas strips Abayyad of the authority of reliable narration and reveals his own authorial presence even in passages spoken directly by Abayyad. Thus, any identity between the "narrative" parts of the novel and the fictitious autobiography written by Abayyad is represented as, at best, an uncertain possibility. And so the novel acquires yet another layer of reliability, undermining in turn the reliability of all preceding layers.

By this point, the notion of a causal link between the two portions of the novel has been so seriously undercut that it is impossible to tell which is the "authentic" Shammas: the Shammas of the "narrative" part or the Shammas of the "narrator's" part. There is a temporal discrepancy between the two versions regarding the moment at which Shammas becomes acquainted with Abayyad's story, which comes relatively early in the "narrative" version, quite late in the "narrator's" version. And yet the two are presented as separate events. In fact, any differences between the two versions can be taken equally as a contradiction or as a simple matter of mutual indifference. Each story line has its own claim to reality, and the reader has no way of determining which "reality" is "genuine."

There are, in fact, two Anton Shammases in the novel. Both appear in the book as protagonist-narrators; both are writers by profession; each calls the other's authority into question. It would be hard to overestimate the importance of this literary gesture. Here, the very composition of the novel mirrors Shammas's ambivalent position vis-à-vis the question of his own personal and national identity. And here, too, he takes an important step in encountering the fundamental tensions of Israeli public discourse: the dual representation of the Jews as majority and minority calls for the creation in the novel of a new type of literary Subject, a Subject who, confronting this duality, is capable of taking steps toward determining its real nature. Indeed, given the absence of such a determination, he can turn even this weakness to his advantage, using it as an analytical tool to crack the duality and attempt to change it.

The Israeli Arab as Palestinian and the Palestinian as the Israeli Jew's Jew

The self-identity of the Israeli was formed by Jews who were trying to build a state with a Jewish majority that would, in the framework of a liberal democracy, respect the identity and rights of all Israelis, Jews and Arabs alike. This formula included both the ideal of a democratic state and the ideal of a Jewish state with a Jewish majority and a Jewish character, a place of refuge for the Jewish people. The seeds of a contradiction are all too evident here, and they sprouted and grew over the years. The Arab inhabitants of Israel, in fact, were never citizens with truly equal rights. Confiscation of lands, constant pressure from the security forces, neglect of education in the Arab sector— these are only a few examples from a long history of discrimination. The temporary and partial compromises that attempted to reconcile the contradictions became more and more unworkable over the years. The problem was exacerbated by reduced Jewish immigration, with demographic projections indicating that the Jews were likely to lose their majority status in the not-too-distant future. The dramatic climax came in 1967, when Israel conquered Gaza and the West Bank. The desire to strengthen the ideal of a Jewish state was now reinforced by the desire to hold onto the occupied territories (though inhabited by over a million Arabs), and the inevitable result was to undermine Israeli democracy while suppressing the Palestinians and their national aspirations.

With the Israeli sense of identity caught in this dynamic and contradictory situation, the act of writing an Israeli novel becomes a highly complex cultural process. And given the bewildering array of sides and opinions in the current Israeli scene, all emotionally charged and almost totally politicized, any attempt at literary criticism becomes extremely difficult. It is not easy to carry on an incisive political dialogue in a charged situation where all the interlocutors are interested parties, automatically slotted into this or that political pigeonhole. Nor is it any easier to carry on a struggle against an occupying power whose past history and present consciousness preclude any neatly categorical analysis in terms such as strong/weak or ruler/ruled. Indeed, as has been pointed out repeatedly in the two previous chapters, Israeli public discourse disguises the power of the dominant majority precisely by adopting the linguistic and behavioral style of a minority as a way to circumvent temporarily the contradiction alluded to above, where the image of a small, democratic Israel fighting for a homeland for the oppressed Jewish people conflicts with the image of a great Israel engaged in deliberate suppression of the Palestinians. An outrageous expression of this ambivalent imagery can be seen in the protests of the Jewish settlers in the occupied territories at their "abandonment" by the Israeli government, as well as in the rhetoric of self-styled persecuted victims that accompanies their anti-Palestinian activities.

The occupation has created a cultural matrix in which these contradictions have become blurred. One measure of how deeply rooted this culture is at present can be seen in the overwhelming use in Israel of Arab workers for manual labor, which has in turn led to a large measure of rhetorical overlap in Israeli discourse between the categories of class and nationality. Later, mainly in the 1990s, Arabs were joined by migrant workers from Eastern Europe, Africa, and East Asia, and the cultural matrix became even more complicated. The ideological and cultural aspects of these phenomena, especially their literary manifestations, evince an opposition between minority and majority that does not always coincide with the opposition between weakness and strength (Biale 1986, 146). The dynamic flexibility of the opposition minority/majority—the mutual dependence between minority and majority, their relative degrees of power, as well as a special sensitivity to the link between cultural and linguistic identity on the one hand and sovereignty and political legitimacy on the other— finds expression through the discourse of the arabesque. The importance of this dynamic opposition can be seen most of all in the great strength it imparts to a minority confronted with the defense mechanisms of a majority that, however powerful, feels itself perfectly entitled to minority status and consciousness.

A special way of seeing and reacting must be developed in order to crack open this smooth and flexible battery of defense mechanisms, to criticize the presuppositions of the dominant discourse from the outside without losing the vantage point of a participant involved personally in events from the inside. To do this in a novel, it is crucial to determine first what identity and authority are available to its narrator. Shammas makes these issues the central focus of his novel and tries to delineate the true Israeli image through a dialectical juxtaposition of an Arab image and a Jewish image.

The mutual undermining of the "narrative" and "narrator's" segments of the novel is largely responsible for the uncommon dual effect Shammas has created: on the one hand, powerful emotional involvement in both segments; on the other, the abstract viewpoint from which both parts are formulated. It is from this viewpoint that Shammas formulates his own identity, through a systematic dialectical negation, almost to the point of absurdity, of the national significance of his own ancestral roots. In one of the most entertaining parts of the novel (Shammas 1986, 15–16), Shammas presents his family's ancestry as a hodgepodge of periods, religions, and nationalities. The founder of the family, who emigrated from southwestern Syria to the Galilee only at the beginning of the nineteenth century, did so chiefly because the rival family in his old village was trying to kill him. The Christian inhabitants of Fasuta in the Galilee had been persecuted and oppressed by the Muslim inhabitants of nearby Dir El-Qasi, which was renamed Moshav Elqosh after the Israeli War of Independence. The village of Fasuta itself was built not only on the ruins of the Crusader fortress Pasova but also on the still earlier ruins of the ancient Jewish village Mifshata, where a number of priests had settled after the destruction of the Second Temple. Thus, any attempt at a positive statement, based on a present-day political interpretation of the past, contains the seeds of its own negation. Shammas parodies the genre of dynastic political genealogy. And so the text, in purporting to do justice to the political interests of all the parties involved, actually satisfies none of them. In this way, Shammas sidesteps the traditional terms of the debate, which has conventionally focused on stating the comparative merits of the historical claims made by each of the parties.

Shammas thus exposes the distorted conception of time underlying Israeli public discourse, and he criticizes this conception from a perspective for which he must pay a certain political price. Shammas parodies and thus rejects the whole framework of historical privileges and justifications and structures the debate instead in futuristic and utopian terms. In this he assumes a risk, evincing a certain weakness, given a volatile political situation articulated precisely in terms of historical questions such as "Who was here first?" This is not a lack of sensitivity to the concrete political realities of the conflict; rather, it is an exercise in political tactics, in which Shammas relinquishes one position of strength to gain a better one.

In his political essays, Shammas returns repeatedly to the demand that the Jewish state finally adopt the political agenda of an Israeli state, a democratic homeland for Jews and Arabs alike (Shammas 1986b). Yet, at the same time, he demonstrates sensitivity to the legitimate fears and aspirations of Israeli Jews. His call for an Israeli state as opposed to a Jewish one is actually more a call for a reversal of priorities, an inversion of the hierarchy whereby Jewish considerations automatically take precedence over democratic ones. But the challenge announced in Shammas's novel, a challenge aimed in part at the Israeli Left, involves something more: a special sensitivity to the dialogue he is conducting with the presuppositions underlying even the leftist point of view. Shammas develops his Israeli identity as an Arab by confronting his own identity with the Israeliness of the Jews. In fact, his primary demand of Israeli Jews is that they change the rules of the game; that, as Jews, they reexamine the function that keeping old scores and accounts has in confusing the issues of their political and moral situation today. This is, however, no more than he demands of himself as he develops his own Israeli identity by rejecting much of the contemporary significance of his own historical and genealogical roots.

In the novel, the essence of Shammas's confrontation with the Israeliness of the Jews is embodied in the confrontation between Shammas, the protagonist-narrator, and Yosh (Yehoshua) Bar-On, the Jewish Israeli author who travels with Shammas to Iowa City. Shammas has hardly bothered to hide the fact that the prototype for Bar-On is the Israeli author A. B. Yehoshua. The latter is presented satirically in the novel and, indeed, is seen in much the same light as Shammas saw Yehoshua during the stormy debate between the two that was carried on in the Israeli press about a year before the publication of *Arabesques* (although the actual writing of the novel may have been completed before the debate itself). The Israeli author Bar-On appears in the novel as a somewhat ridiculous figure, with racist beliefs and impulses, engaging in inner monologues that are strung together from colloquial or literary clichés. One of the high points of the real-world debate between Shammas and Yehoshua came in a newspaper interview, when Yehoshua, who is identified with the moderate-liberal wing of Israeli political opinion, made the following suggestion: after the creation of a Palestinian homeland in the occupied territories, of which he approves, Yehoshua proposed that Shammas find full expression for his nationalism by packing up and moving to the newly formed Palestinian state (Yehoshua 1985). In a series of replies that drew many others into this debate, Shammas tried to show Yehoshua that his suggestion was akin to Meir Kahane's proposal to ensure the Jewishness of Israel through an organized expulsion of the Arab population. The unwillingness of Yehoshua and of many other Israeli liberals to acknowledge the Arab Shammas as a full-fledged Israeli, whose native land is Israel, just as theirs is, was proof for Shammas that the majority is not inclined to relinquish the Jewish primacy of the State of Israel, even at the risk of sacrificing its democratic character. In the novel, Shammas focuses on how liberals fall into the trap of racist discourse patterns. It is precisely for this reason that he conducts the satire with considerable sophistication—the better to expose the two-faced nature of Israeli public discourse.

In Paris, en route to Iowa City, Bar-On wonders what Shammas's reaction would be "if he only knew that to myself I think of him, proud Palestinian-Israeli-Arab that he is, as 'my Jew'" (Shammas 1986, 72). In fact, both epithets, "Palestinian" and "Jew," belong here to the same discursive universe of stereotyping and discrimination. It is crucial that Shammas refuses to label himself a Palestinian. In the novel, he rebuts attempts to define him as a Palestinian by noting, among other things, that as far back as the 1948 war, his father did not consider himself a Palestinian refugee. Bar-On does define Shammas as a Palestinian, thus feeding the discriminatory stereotype of the Israeli Arab as having "alien" loyalties. To be sure, Bar-On is presented as wishing to show empathy for the plight of an Israeli Arab writer. As the satire brings out clearly, however, Bar-On's inner monologue derives from both his feeling of genuine empathy with a fellow minority, an empathy based on the similarity between Shammas's situation and that of the Jews as a national minority, and the racist stance of a superior majority, revealed in the unconsciously derogatory use of the phrase "my Jew."

Arabesques in Time, Arabesques in Space

Does the novel open with Shammas speaking of the death of his grandmother Alya on April 1, 1954, in the village of Fasuta? Or is he instead speaking of the death of his father in Haifa, in April 1978? In fact, Shammas is doing both at once, a fact that has profound implications for his treatment of time in the novel. The interweaving of earlier and later events is a structural principle of the novel; Shammas exploits it chiefly as a means of realizing his cyclical conception of time. The numerous digressions, the twists and turns, the sudden predestined meetings all conform, in one way or another, to the Arabian iconography of the arabesque. This phenomenon stands out particularly in the "narrative" parts, which revolve mostly around the village of Fasuta. But a careful reading of the "narrator's" portion, which describes the trip to Iowa City, also reveals the figure of the arabesque. Even in such a straightforward matter as Shammas's travel journal, things are not as they seem: for one thing, the entries are not always in chronological order. The connections among events within each part are highly complex, as is the relationship between the two parts. The static arabesque frees the chronological flow of time in the plot from any necessary involvement with such notions as redemption or progress. As mentioned above, Shammas questions the validity of relying on his own family genealogy as a basis for present-day political judgments; at the same time, he stands opposed to present-day manifestations of Zionism. Instead, he offers his own Israeliness as an alternative, embodying a more modest and far less apocalyptic conception of time.

The traditional figure of the arabesque, pervading the structure of the novel at every level, brings Shammas's representational mode close to a pure statement of formal relations. In the arabesque, Shammas has found a way to relate to the past without falling victim to its nondialectical universalism. Thus, when he describes the hardships of the Arab refugees of 1948, he attempts to shift the moral debate from considerations of precedence, of who or what came first, to confrontations with undeniably concrete instances of human suffering. The two-dimensional nature of the arabesque motivates the description of the oppression of Palestinian women without minimizing its urgency or gravity within the overall web of political oppression depicted in the novel. Thus, for example, in describing the hardships endured by Layla Khouri, Shammas has interwoven her mistreatment by Israeli soldiers in 1948 and 1981 with her misfortunes at the hands of Arab society (for example, her betrayal by a member of Shammas's family and her sexual and apparently financial exploitation by the woman Sa`ada). Layla the Palestinian is portrayed in the novel as a commodity passed from hand to hand, from government to government. In this respect, her existence parallels another arabesque, the cyclical course taken by Abayyad, the boy who was kidnapped into adoption and was himself treated as a commodity, whose loss first brought misery to his poverty-stricken natural parents just as it would later to his wealthy adoptive parents. Thus, the arabesque takes the fetishization of the individual and the dominance of exchange value and weaves them into a fabric of human relationships existing in a context of social and political repression (JanMohamed 1986, 79). This unfolds against the background of the Zionist revolution, with the political realignments and the social and economic modernization that accompanied it, all culminating in the abandonment of the village and its uncommercialized way of life based on use value.

But the arabesque does not serve only a negative, critical function; it also bears a positive, utopian message. It acts as an analogue, in the area of the visual arts, to the position of Islamic "contractualism" in the social sphere. The distinction between Islamic contractualism and Western corporatism is a close parallel to the distinction between the collective *Gemeinschaft,* based on personal relationships, and the impersonal and achievement-oriented *Gesellschaft* usually associated with modern technological society. In contrast to Western corporatism, with its preference for hierarchical structures in which a limited number of conclusions are drawn from a limited number of premises (on the model of geometry), the cyclical rhythms of the arabesque could be said to characterize an "indefinitely expandable" structure. The arabesque provides a framework within which it becomes possible to reduce the apparently "chaotic variety of life's reality" to manageable proportions, yet without "arbitrarily setting bounds to it." Shammas's arabesque style displays the general features of Islam's traditional atomism, an atomism representing an "equal and coordinated responsibility of all possible individuals for the maintenance of moral standards" (Hodgson 1974, 344–47).

This moral atomism, and in particular the special kind of reduction that does not stifle the individuality of certain details, is the key to understanding Shammas's arabesque discourse. In a striking passage in the novel, Shammas writes:

> That was Uncle Yusef. On the one hand a believing Catholic, whose heart, like that of Saint Augustine, was firm and secure, as if the Virgin herself had promised him that his years were but links in a chain leading to salvation and redemption. And on the other hand he believed, as if to keep an escape hatch open, that if dust were to return unto dust, and the jaws of death were gaping, that the twisting, elusive, cyclical periodicity of things would have the power to withstand death. But he was unaware of these two opposing aspects coexisting within himself; he saw them only as a unitary whole. (Shammas 1986, 204)

Shammas's novel forces these two types of discourse, linear and cyclical, into a confrontation involving not synthesis but an attempt to extract the best from each. Shammas presents himself in the novel as someone in a position both to clarify this duality of the coexistence of Christian time and quasi-pagan time in Uncle Yusef and to enter into the Christian conception of time as a path leading to salvation (204). But this intermediate stance, in fact a continuation of Uncle Yusef's position, represents a source from which Shammas draws strength. From within this static arabesque of time, but with one foot already on the outside, Shammas is in a position to continue striving toward his goal of a utopia, without paying the price of a nondialectical universalization of the past. Undoubtedly, dehistoricization can be made to serve the purposes of those interested in perpetuating the status quo of oppression, through a deliberate confusion of the notions of development, contingency, and the potential for change (JanMohamed 1986, 77). But the arabesque, whose cyclical nature has the power "to withstand death," enables Shammas to keep a firm grasp on the absolute reality of suffering and of human existence, whose universal validity is not altered or obscured by its relative position in time. The arabesque creates the effect of static motion, motion without progress. This is its way of "withstanding death" and of undermining attempts to develop a rigidly teleological concept of "national time." It must be emphasized that the great flexibility of the arabesque does not disconnect it from the process of generalization and reduction involved in the creation of a "national Subject." But it is never committed to a rigid representation of a national Subject, fixed in space and time, and is therefore free to become an autonomous critical tool, endowed with its own absolute and self-sufficient validity. With its power thus not contingent on the exclusive authority of some national Subject, it becomes an effective weapon for the minority.

Standing both inside and outside the arabesque, Shammas freezes history; he does this to forge a critical dialogue in which both sides are precluded, in their argumentation, from appealing to selective generalizations based on decontextualized bits of history. Shammas denies Israeli Jews the right to justify present wrongdoing by past grievances, and he holds himself to the same standard. Others have not been so careful. Edward Said, for example, rightly criticizes the distortion of history implicit in Zionist claims about the Palestinians, but he falls into the same trap himself in his discussion of the enactment of the Law of Return (which imparts automatic Israeli citizenship to any Jewish immigrant) when the State of Israel was established. He views the law as racist, as a reflection of the inherently discriminatory character of the State of Israel, ignoring the fact that the Law of Return, like affirmative action in the United States, was enacted in an attempt to discriminate in favor of a disadvantaged minority, persecuted and uprooted Jews everywhere (Said 1986, 45; Shammas 1986a, 44–45). Shammas, too, is conscious of the law's racist implications. But he expresses this awareness in a completely different way from Said, and with sensitivity to its dialectical dimensions, by proposing that the law in its present form be repealed in the not-too-distant future and remain in force only for immigrants from distressed Jewish communities.

The nonmimetic geometrical abstractions of the arabesque are intimately linked to the function of spatial patterning in the novel. The entire journey to America, in fact, shows elements of a search for roots and spiritual identity. But here, too, the cyclical arabesque is brought into play, the same motion without progress, wherein every destination immediately becomes the point of departure for a new quest. The writers participating in the International Writing Program are housed in a dormitory suggestively called the Mayflower, a name that hints at a connection between Shammas's ideal conception of Israeli identity and the model of a society of immigrants embodied in America and its young history. At the same time, Shammas has come full circle: he comments, while discussing a letter to his Jewish lover, Shlomit, in Israel, that only now, in Iowa City, "over twenty years after I left my childhood house, do I feel, for the first time in many years, that I can conjure up my childhood house in the village, its smells and sights and sensations, for I am able for the first time to describe it to Shlomit, who never set foot there" (Shammas 1986, 133).

Shammas invests his layover in Paris en route to Iowa City with a special function. First of all, during this intermezzo the novel introduces the figure of Amira, the Jewish writer from Egypt. In fact, the images of women in the novel, including Shammas's Lebanese cousin; his Jewish Israeli lover, Shlomit; and Layla Khouri, the Christian woman converted to Islam, make up a representative sample of Middle East geography. There is a large degree of overlap here with the range of male figures. All these serve to lay out, in effect, a map of the different local and national images constituting the cardinal terms in the system of oppositions that collectively define Shammas's Israeli identity. A planned reunion in Paris with Shammas's female cousin from Lebanon represents a new possibility for Shammas to express his identity as an Arab. But at first the meeting does not come off. This is another example of the dialectical process, where a possibility is presented only to be rejected, by which Shammas develops his own identity. Indeed, as a "replacement" for his cousin, Shammas immediately makes contact with her opposite: the Jew Bar-On, who is also staying over in Paris.

The Gospel according to Uncle Yusef, or Hebrew as the Language of Redemption

Uncle Yusef's arabesque tales are described by Shammas in these words: "They flowed about him in a stream of illusion which linked interior and exterior, beginning and ending, reality and fiction" (Shammas 1986, 203). The arabesque, which makes no claim to represent any reality outside itself, is by that very token a fine vehicle for conveying a variety of heterogeneous materials. This constant confusion of domains and categories characterizes the lesson Shammas learns from his uncle's legacy. As he puts it, his uncle has given him all the keys to extricate himself from the arabesque and enter another existence—all the keys but the final one. The key to salvation lies in bringing together the two halves of a single whole, a juncture that comes only once in a lifetime. But the incompleteness in Shammas prevents him, as he puts it, from relying with confidence on any possibility of salvation whatsoever. Like the almost inextricable confusion of fiction and reality, epitomized in the contradiction between the two halves of the story, the novel presents a series of illusory solutions in the form of sets of twins, or near twins, who are intended to complement and complete each other. All this illustrates the novel's clear-sighted appreciation of the political potential of the arabesque. The bond between Shammas the Christian Arab and Bar-On the Jew should be sought not in some sort of messianic eschatology but rather in a close analysis of the Israeli experience and the utopian elements already present in it.

The stories told by Shammas's Christian Arab family from Fasuta depict a static existence, a dimension highlighted even more by the orality of these stories, telling of family life in the village in the years before (and even after) the founding of the State of Israel. Oral literature acquires its cultural significance in relation to the time frame in which it is told. Here the time frame of the storyteller is also the political and moral time frame, in which Shammas the author wrote and published his book. In this way, Shammas simultaneously emphasizes the oral sources of his stories and the radical change that he himself introduces in moving from a traditional oral tale to a written story. Only rarely in the novel does he deny his identity as an Israeli writer and pretend to be a naive folk narrator. Over and over again, Shammas stresses the tension between his connection to oral tradition and his commitment to writing. Indeed, sometimes the very act of storytelling, as in Layla Khouri's case, can undermine the stability of reality. Shammas needs both oral and written narrative to come to terms with his own national literary tradition and to open a gateway to the utopian conception of modern Israeli nationhood outlined in his novel.

What he does is to rework in writing those stories he heard orally from Uncle Yusef, in order to formulate through them a present reality. As remarked earlier, the atemporal, arabesque rhythms of the oral tradition serve as a touchstone for evaluating the nondialectical attitude toward time found in Israeli public discourse. With this in mind, it is noteworthy that Israeli critics reacting to *Arabesques* have largely ignored the revolutionary function that Shammas gives to the blending of oral and written modes. They delight in the folklore and reject those parts that have contemporary political relevance (for example, Laor 1986). But this pattern of disregarding a part of the novel provides interesting testimony precisely to the novel's effectiveness. To maintain the regular structure of their response, the novel's readers have had to cut the work into its two parts and blur the connections between them.

The duality with which Shammas displays his oral sources, a blend of estrangement and closeness, parallels the duality of his relationship to Hebrew literature and, indeed, complements it. In distancing himself from his oral sources, Shammas is forcing his way into written Hebrew literature as an outsider demanding equal rights with the insiders. The conceptual framework that best illuminates the relationship between Bar-On and Shammas is the world of literature and books, a world epitomized by the gathering of writers participating in the International Writing Program. Bar-On, at work on a book about an Israeli Arab, asks to make use of the figure of Anton Shammas. He wants to portray the Arab in his story with real empathy and not reduce him to a stereotype. But the motives underlying this—for example, his desire that his Arab character should play a leading role in a study of the image of the Arab in modern Hebrew literature— only accentuate Bar-On's stereotypical attitudes toward his Arab characters. The stereotype, of course, is in general an extreme expression of domination. And so, as Shammas shows us, Bar-On's desire to change the surface formulation of the stereotype without addressing the presuppositions of his own discourse leads him, at best, into a new variation on the same stereotype. At one point, Bar-On announces his intention to write "about the isolation of the Palestinian Israeli Arab, an isolation greater than any other" (Shammas 1986, 84). This would appear to reveal a special sensitivity to the fate of his protagonist, but the larger context of Shammas's novel makes it clear that it is just another indication of Bar-On's unwillingness to give up control over the representational molds available for the depiction of this fate.

Bar-On's highly practical, utilitarian attitude toward the Other is illustrated by his reaction to Shammas's attempts to preserve his own independence in the face of Bar-On's domination. Bar-On proposes to treat Shammas's private life as an object to be exploited in the creation of his novel. Even when Bar-On gives up on Shammas, he still clings to the same Palestinian stereotype. And so, at one point, he seeks a functional replacement for Shammas, finding it in a Palestinian writer also taking part in the writing program; and when things fail to work out with this Palestinian substitute, he leaves America and returns to Israel. But just as the fictional autobiography of Shammas written by Abayyad the Palestinian does not count in the novel as the definitive text determining Shammas's identity, so, too, Shammas provides Bar-On the Jew with misleading information about his life. Shammas develops his own Israeli identity by liberating it from the various political interpretations threatening to swallow it up. And thus he keeps both Abayyad the Palestinian and Bar-On the Jew at a distance, allowing neither to gain control over the representation of his life story.

A number of Bar-On's comments on his own forthcoming novel are strikingly applicable to the novel *Arabesques* as well; and the deliberate obscurity that shrouds the whole matter of textual interrelationships, in comparing Shammas's own text with other texts developed within it (that of the Palestinian and that of the Jew), emphasizes their predominant status as mere collections of images rather than as representations of some external reality. In this way, through the world of literature and books, the ideological dilemma of Shammas's identity is translated into a struggle between texts. The arabesque novel, in its rejection of the authority of all representation, focuses our attention on the internal dynamics of the political, national, and cultural images involved.

Shammas is contrasted with Bar-On in the context of the writing program, at a time when both authors are at work on their own new books. At the writing of *Arabesques,* however, Shammas was also engaged in a confrontation with Bar-On's real-life counterpart, the Israeli writer A. B. Yehoshua, whose story "Facing the Forests" was discussed in the previous chapter. Interestingly, the central episode of

Yehoshua's story concerns the burning of a forest, the forest being one of the paramount symbols of Zionist reconstruction. This particular forest was planted on the ruins of an Arab village that had been destroyed in 1948, and it is set on fire by an old Arab villager with the silent cooperation of an eccentric Jewish fire warden.

The arabesque binds literature and metaliterature, the literary text itself and the critical discourse responding to it. And so Yehoshua's story enters Shammas's novel, along with the important article, discussed in the previous chapter, that was written in response to "Facing the Forests" by the critic Mordechai Shalev (1970). Shalev criticized the fact that the figure of the Arab in Yehoshua's story, with its political and moral overtones, fulfills a much more general Oedipal function: the Arab serves as a means for the young man to carry out an Oedipal revolt against the generation of his fathers. In essence, Shalev claims that the moral issue, the eviction of the Arabs from their land, is only a pretext for raising the real question: Whose life has the greater vitality, the Jew's or the Arab's? Shammas portrays Bar-On (Yehoshua) as trying, in his new novel, to accommodate the critic Shalev. But Bar-On is unable to see that the attack against him was directed largely against the imposition of individual psychology on what is properly a political and collective matter. Yehoshua's story is thus seen as exploiting the figure of an oppressed Arab in order to fulfill the spiritual needs of an Israeli Jew. The same point is further emphasized by the fact that Yehoshua's Jewish protagonist is an anti-hero, an eccentric existing on the fringes of society. Even in the protests of the younger generation of Israelis against the injustices accompanying the realization of the Zionist dream, Shammas tells us, the image of the Arab is exploited when a dominant majority ignores its responsibility to examine its own past with maturity and integrity.

Which One Is the Other's Ventriloquist?

In principle, what we are dealing with here is a variation on the Hegelian paradigm of the master-slave relationship, whereby the master's consciousness of himself as master is conditioned by the slave's acknowledgment of the master's superior status. Yehoshua's "Facing the Forests" and Bar-On's clinging to the stereotype of the Palestinian both emphasize the role played by the figure of the Arab as the key to the identity of the Israeli Jew. But a situation whereby the Israeli "master" draws on a dual consciousness as minority and majority complicates considerably any attempt at interpretation, and it renders equally problematic the strategies open to those assigned to the role of "slave" in this dialectic; for the Israeli "master," the Jewish majority, in conformity with the Hegelian paradigm, has attained this status only after winning a life-and-death struggle for independence and continues to derive its self-consciousness and legitimacy from its still-recent past as an oppressed minority.

But the Hegelian "slave" in the novel—that is, the Israeli Arab—is just as dependent on the Israeli "master" for his own consciousness. The narrator's confrontation with Bar-On is especially relevant here. After Bar-On's hurried departure from Iowa City and return to Israel, Shammas is beset by guilt and the sense of having missed an opportunity. Despite the struggle he wages against Bar-On, with Bar-On ultimately recast as his satirical victim, Shammas's life is fundamentally dependent on Bar-On. Shammas is afraid that his meeting with Abayyad could be taken by Bar-On as an attempt to enlist Shammas in the Palestian Liberation Organization; he interprets this as an important clue to his own identity, which cannot exist without the presence, at once threatening and soothing, of Bar-On the Jew. Just as he feels betrayed when Bar-On prefers the Palestinian to himself (Shammas 1986, 152), so he reflects: "How could I react without Bar-On breathing down my neck? How could there even be a situation, good or bad, where Bar-On was not breathing down my neck?" (232). The fact that Shammas is set in opposition to a master who is himself a slave, namely, the Israeli Jew, limits the spiritual and revolutionary power that normally accrue automatically to the slave.

It is hardly an accident that the blatantly material dimension of Arab life in Israel and the occupied territories, with the Arabs visible and prominent as manual laborers, finds as little genuine political expression in the novel as it does in real life. As an Israeli Arab, Shammas, too, must confront the dual consciousness of the Israeli Jewish master-slave, and in consequence, he has difficulty crystallizing any sort of revolutionary consciousness. As Fredric Jameson has said, there is a certain advantage to having an overall map of a given situation, a map drawn from the realistic materialist viewpoint of someone who fulfills it in his own work. Shammas has such a map but cannot take advantage of it. Neither Yehoshua nor Shammas can allow himself to take advantage of the national allegory that characterizes the materialism of Third World literature, "where the telling of the individual story and the individual experience cannot but ultimately involve the whole laborious telling of the experience of the collectivity itself" (Jameson 1986). As mentioned above, Shalev has criticized the story "Facing the Forests" for substituting an external political dimension for its Oedipal concerns. Shalev's attack can now be reinterpreted as an attack on Yehoshua's deviation from the national allegory that is permitted him as an Israeli author belonging to the majority culture.

For Shammas, the arabesque, with its flexibility and "freedom from any myth-based symbolism," is the appropriate vehicle for coping with the problematic status of allegory in this literary and political situation. He is suspicious of the validity of the Israeli national allegory, both for the Israeli Jew, with his uncertain identity as master, and for himself as a half-slave whose role and identity are no less uncertain; and his suspicion finds expression in the novel in a heterogeneous and discontinuous arabesque of allegorical patterns, many of them Christian, interwoven with passages of local documentary narrative. For Shammas, the allegorical image of the New Testament cock before it crowed at dawn to signal that Peter had denied his Lord Jesus (Matthew 26:75) introduces into the novel a fascinating blend of mutually incompatible interpretations, reflecting both Eastern and Western traditions. The reality depicted in the novel repeatedly rejects the promise of redemption implicit in this mythic image. The arabesque blends fact and fiction, realism and romance, tragedy and soap opera, with bits of the real-life biography of the author Anton Shammas thrown in. All this keeps the reader continually alert not to expect the ideological satisfaction that a traditional, fixed literary genre is able to supply.

In several senses, Anton Shammas's *Arabesques* both conforms to and deviates from the patterns of a minor literature, as defined by Gilles Deleuze and Félix Guattari (1986). In accordance with this pattern, *Arabesques* is not subject to the authority or the conventions of standard literary genres. First, this Hebrew novel written by an Arab "doesn't come from a minor language; it is rather that which a minority constructs within a major language" (Deleuze and Guattari 1986, 16). In the hands of the Israeli Arab Shammas, Hebrew, the mythic language of Zionism, undergoes a process of deterritorialization—the first definitional component, according to Deleuze and Guattari, of a minor literature.

Deleuze and Guattari's discussion of the release of the fluid material of desire (of the libido) from its imposed representation focuses mainly on the dominating representation of the "Oedipus complex." The Freudian unconscious, they claim, is a capitalistic construction that supports the internalization of a given set of power relations. Psychoanalysis granted the Oedipus complex a kind of a final territory and the status of law, and as a result, the capitalistic world granted the analyst the power of a tyrant, who also charges fees. But the "flow" of desire, whose existence proceeds beyond its psychoanalytical representations, enables Deleuze and Guattari to observe the unconscious even when it lacks definition or any social identity. Therefore, they argue, these libidinal energies, which have been transformed through a process of territorialization into frames of nation, family, party, and so forth, can also be deterritorialized, which will undermine and fragment identities. The prelingual and presocial status of the material of the unconscious endows it with the political potential to dismantle social identities (Deleuze and Guattari 1985). This "politics of desire" endows minor literature with a prominent revolutionary role (which Deleuze and Guattari call schizophrenic), whose ultimate representative they find in Franz Kafka, and which can create, with the participation of an appropriate reader, a kind of "revolutionary machine" that breaks down identities and the authority of laws and institutions. Minor literature such as Kafka's gains most of its power from its capability to deterritorialize the major language through the destruction of lingual codes, achieved by breaking down and displacing accepted meanings while trespassing over accepted and acknowledged borderlines. Such deterritorialization, which activates territory in its primary, literal sense, is visible in minor literature's undermining of the supposedly natural triadic connection of ethnic identity, national language, and national territory.

Yet this characterization, which at first glance appears to fit the case of Shammas rather well, is somewhat deceptive. Although Shammas does carry out a process of deterritorialization of Hebrew, at the same time he reterritorializes it as the language of the Israel.

The second component of a minor literature, whereby everything (including the individual) is viewed in political terms, also marks a divergence between Deleuze and Guattari's definition and Shammas's novel, with the special situation from which it springs. For Deleuze and Guattari, the "political" means a liberation from the unified authority of an autonomous subject, a notion that they apply to Kafka. Politicization plays a significant role in Shammas's novel, too; it is a major effect of the mutual undercutting performed by the narrators of the two halves of the novel. Shammas, however, does not politicize everything. His intermediate stance here can be seen both in the novel's critical response to Yehoshua's politicization of the Oedipal pattern in "Facing the Forests" and in its refusal to see itself as a national allegory.

Nor does Deleuze and Guattari's third definitional component, whereby "everything takes on a collective value" (1986, 17), make the case of Shammas any easier to characterize. This notion of collectivity is to be understood in terms of the opposition between a nonreductionist, "collective assemblage of enunciation" and the reductionist concept of a (national) subject (18). In fact, "collectivity" in Deleuze and Guattari's sense is at variance with the dual effect of the arabesque, which simultaneously preserves the independence and particularity of atomic bits of experience while carrying out a reduction, albeit open-ended, that organizes and unites them. Deleuze and Guattari's antireductionist stance carries a price: a disconnection from the inherently reductionist, utopian project of nation making. Indeed, in their discussion of the collective component of a minor literature, they suggest that an author on the margins of the community is more able "to express another possible community and to forge the means for another consciousness and another sensibility" (17). By contrast, Shammas does not construct his Israeli utopia from some totally Other consciousness or sensibility but from the existing, contradiction-ridden inventory of present-day Israeli reality.

But all these differences shrink into insignificance as Deleuze and Guattari proceed to expand the scope of their definition enormously, claiming that the term *minor* "no longer designates specific literatures but the revolutionary conditions for every literature within the heart of what is called great (or established) literature" (18). From here it is only a step to their conception of minor literature as a "machine of expression," a tool for producing mere effects, with no center of gravity (18), thus divorcing it from any possible utopian dimension. Like minor literature, the arabesque is characterized by a lack of obligation to any sort of representation or mythic symbolism. Yet the arabesque does not discard the dream of a national utopian act; indeed, it requires it, for the utopian dream creates by contrast a context and a target against which the arabesque can level its attack on uncritical, restrictive reductions. In fact, the arabesque undermines the dichotomy that, according to Deleuze and Guattari, any minor literature must address, between an extreme reterritorialization of language through symbols and archetypes (their example for the political results of this process is the Zionist aspiration) and the process they ascribe to Kafka, a radical deterritorialization of language "to the point of sobriety," culminating in "a perfect and unformed expression, a materially intense expression" (19). Shammas's Hebrew arabesque takes up, at the sociopolitical level, the question Deleuze and Guattari had formulated at the linguistic level, that of evaluating "the degrees of territoriality, deterritorialization, and reterritorialization" (25) practiced in Hebrew (the mythic language informing the genesis of Zionism) and in other languages in a similar position. Faced with these conflicting demands—an extreme deterritorialization "to the point of sobriety" versus a concern for relative degrees of re- and deterritorialization—the arabesque can suggest a dynamic middle way. Shammas's paradigm concedes the importance of the concept of a nation-state, but only as articulated through the arabesque: not as an absolute and rigid notion, defined once and for all, but in a much more critical and flexible sense, as something evolving and responsive to the dialectical process.

The differences between Shammas's model and that of Deleuze and Guattari could serve to outline a theoretical discussion of the principles implicit in the arabesque as a vehicle for minority discourse. A good example of the especially pertinent benefits afforded by the arabesque is the way in which Shammas turns to real advantage his own weakness as "slave" vis-à-vis an ambiguous "master." Hebrew culture's battery of defense mechanisms, which thwarts the development of a revolutionary consciousness, is appropriated by Shammas and used for a different purpose: to illuminate the quandary of the slave forced to choose between assignment to a niche in the master culture, thereby condemning himself to imitation, assimilation, and loss of identity, and adherence to his traditional culture, which would force him into the position of a rejected "savage." Indeed, it is precisely within this unique sort of majority culture, which pretends to be a minority culture and thereby absolves itself of its real responsibilities and commitments as the master culture, that Shammas can realize Jacques Derrida's ideal "to speak the other's language without renouncing [his] own" (1986, 333). We should not forget that Hebrew Israeli culture, by virtue of being the dominant majority's culture, attracts the minorities who must function within it. But when it represents itself as a minority culture, it undermines its own authority to reject whatever is defined as the Other culture. Bar-On, who, in his search for a literary subject, shifts his attention from Shammas to the Palestinian from Nablus, compares the two. He himself admits to being troubled by Shammas's complex, multiple identity, whose existence transcends the stereotype and violates the binary opposition between Bar-On and the Other:

> But my previous hero [Shammas] does not define himself as my enemy, at least not in the accepted sense of the word. And this constitutes a difficulty for me. By contrast, I feel closer to the problems of this Palestinian, and I hope I will not be proved wrong, but my heart tells me that he is the one I will succeed in setting down in writing. (Shammas 1986, 152)

Arabesques places Israeli Jews in an uneasy position. On the one hand, they cannot merely dismiss Shammas or ignore him as someone totally Other, especially in light of his virtuoso command of Hebrew as a literary medium and his vigorous participation in the Israeli mass media as journalist, polemicist, and author. On the other hand, Shammas's violation of the accepted boundaries of Hebrew culture makes it difficult for Israeli Jews to identify easily with him or to adopt him as one of their own. This background shows how the novel forces a fundamental revision in some of the political assumptions underlying Israeli public discourse. The fact that a novel like *Arabesques* exists at all undermines the traditional view of Hebrew literature as a Jewish national literature. Through the interweaving of oral and folk elements into the narrative, the novel contributes to a process of deterritorialization, challenging the long-standing total coincidence of the Hebrew language with its Jewish subject matter. The Hebrew reader, unable to reject Shammas's challenge out of hand, must either undergo a kind of internal split or develop temporary defense mechanisms (for example, putting folklore and politics in clearly separate boxes or making the absurd demand that Shammas become a traditional Zionist). The phenomenon of Arab authors writing in Hebrew is still in its infancy, but the trend has already been joined by other writers, such as Salman Massalha, Na`im Araydi, and Muhammad Ana`im. And on the Jewish side, it is noteworthy that parallel attempts to overcome canonical linguistic boundaries have been made by writers such as Yoram Kanyuk and Yisrael Eliraz, who have actually published Hebrew works under Arab pseudonyms. Shammas secures this subversive move, undermining the basis of Hebrew canon through the novel's specific poetic strategies as well. The special effect the novel creates by including oral and folkloric elements exposes—and also participates in—the deterritorialization process, which undermines the constant congruence of Hebrew language and Jewish topics.

Shammas's novel methodically ruins the possibility of perceiving it as coherent and stable. The strong effect of deterritorialization it creates, which breaches the boundaries of the Hebrew canon, is anchored finally in the undermining of the identity of the Subject constructed in the novel. The Subject often typical of major national literature—due to, among other things, its moral autonomy, which enables its acceptance as a representative of authentic national identity (Lloyd 1987, 19–26)—here undergoes penetrating critical trial. The inability to detect the stable, autonomous identity of the character Anton Shammas in the novel prevents its readers from perceiving it as a representative expression of crystallized national identity and foregrounds it as a minor literature that subverts the canon of the major literature.

It is important now to turn our attention to the other side of the coin, shifting from the deterritorialization to the reterritorialization of Hebrew. "It is essential this time to have an Arab, as an answer to silence," Bar-On muses,

an Arab who speaks in the language of grace, as the exiled Floren-
tine once termed Hebrew. Hebrew, as the language of grace, in contrast to the language of confusion which raged around the world
with the fall of the Tower of Babel. My Arab will build his tower of
confusion on my own lot. In the language of grace. In my opinion
this is his one chance for salvation. Within the accepted limits, of
course. (Shammas 1986, 83)

We have here a paradox, a simultaneous striving to speak in the
Other's language without giving up one's own. Thus Hebrew, the old-
new language, which Shammas, following Dante, calls the "language
of grace," turns out to offer a political salvation for the Israeli Arab.
But it can also suggest a political and existential solution to the confusion of "Jew" and "Israeli." The kind of synthetic Hebrew wielded so
ably by Shammas, a popular and modern vernacular, is in fact also a
new language, created by the Other. The very artificiality of Shammas's language, sometimes even verging on parody, undermines the
"self-evident" presuppositions of the entire discourse and encourages
the cultural and political reconceptualization so essential to the life
and discourse of Israeli Jews.

Curiously, this process reenacts, in a sense, the creation during
the early days of Zionism of a national Jewish consciousness within
the Hebrew literature of the late nineteenth and early twentieth cen-
turies, as writers strove to re-create Hebrew as a new synthetic language and a source of modern national identity. At the beginning of
Zionism, this synthetic language fulfilled a prominent role in the ideological practice of the Jewish national minority that wished to use it
in the constitution of a normative conscience of a national majority
aspiring to reach a normal existence in its own land. Therefore, the
written language, the artificial "language of the book," was perceived
as the natural language of Hebrew literature at this historical stage in
the development of national consciousness and action (Berdichevsky
1960, 108–9; Miron 1987, 112–13).

Now, generations later, when this phase of the process of territorialization of Hebrew as the national renaissance language has been
completed, Shammas points to the next stage. This work of linguistic
invention serves Shammas in his attempt to build a new-old language
as a bridge toward the re-creation of an old-new nation. As an Israeli

Arab writer breaking into the linguistic and literary citadel of the Israeli Jews, Shammas calls into question their claim to exclusive possession of the traditional language of Zionism. He accepts Hebrew as
the language of present-day Israelis. Acknowledging this revision in
the canonical definition of Hebrew literature amounts to acknowledging the radical changes that the Zionist national Subject must undergo to cope with the sharp contradictions besetting the Subject in
its new historical situation. The immediate (though not exclusive) expression of these changes is an admission of the need to force the values of the Jewish state to approximate better the concrete norms of a
truly democratic society.

   In *Arabesques,* Shammas's affair with Amira, the Jewish woman
writer from Egypt, arouses Bar-On's anger. Bar-On sees in this love an
intolerable threat to the established boundaries delimiting his national culture. But Amira has no material connection to the reality of
Israel; therefore for her, existing as a member of the Jewish minority
in Alexandria, living in an Arabic and French milieu, Hebrew is indeed the language of the dead past. But for Shammas and Bar-On,
Hebrew, as the language of Israel and the Israelis, is the "language of
grace," a language capable of reconciling and uniting them. A Dutch
author visiting the writing program wants to speak with Shammas
about "this schizophrenia wherein Bar-On and [Shammas] are but a
single individual" (Shammas 1986, 130); and a Norwegian writer
acutely observes "that they have not yet made up their minds which
one is the other's ventriloquist."

   The language of grace, which is supposed to effect a fusion of
Shammas and Bar-On, also reminds us of how the arabesque maps
out the future of this special confrontation between master and slave.
As previously remarked, the possibility of this fusion is latent in the
very ambivalence of the confrontation. Shammas's arabesque does
not aim to liberate the slave through a mere reversal of master–slave
roles; for, let us recall, a truly Hegelian freedom would involve an
Aufhebung of the entire opposition. The promise held out by the
arabesque's composition "figure[s] forth eternity, presenting the in-
finite complexity and movement of existence and at the same time resolving it in total harmony of detail with detail and of part with whole
so that all that movement is seen in overall response. . . . The innu-
merable details are each felt as precious, yet no one item stands out

to dominate the whole" (Hodgson 1974, 510). But the dangers involved in a shift from Hebrew as the language of the past to Hebrew as "the language of grace" are not negligible. To be sure, the Israeli dream presented here is no Canaanite movement, no apocalyptic vision of liberation from the fetters of Judaism through an aggressive severing of historical roots. To the contrary: Shammas's Hebrew arabesque represents a utopia, emerging from a detailed, critical confrontation between the cultural demands of past and present. But the confrontation is fraught with danger. Indeed, when the husband of Shlomit, Shammas's Israeli Jewish lover, discovers Shammas's Hebrew love letters to his wife, their affair explodes, shattering a delicate and dangerous balance across both familial and national boundaries (Shammas 1986, 85). From a language of grace and redemption, Hebrew thus risks once again becoming a language of censure, sanctioning racist fears of the Other, whose sexual prowess overcomes the "master's" wife.

The arabesque is a remarkable blend of two conceptions of temporality: a critical approach to time, having no necessary commitment to history or to any promise of progress toward redemption, with an adherence to a static and cyclical temporal continuum. Shammas's Israeli identity is constructed from multiple negations and a critical relationship to prevailing interpretations of the past and future. His arabesque appropriates Hebrew as the language of Israelis. This is an approximation of a relatively autonomous entity present and capable of bringing about a better future. In the current Israeli situation, the arabesque serves as a model for minority discourse, one whose flexibility stands it in good stead even in a contradiction-ridden labyrinth that sometimes appears to have no exit. Shammas's book points the way to a utopian unification of the language of Arabs and Jews, a unification that is only a contingent possibility, subject to human and political constraints. And yet, coming as it does in the dark days of the occupation of the West Bank and Gaza, the deep sensitivity of Shammas's challenge may open a door to hope.

Chapter 8

Of Refugee Gals and Refugee Guys:
Emil Habibi and the Hebrew Literary Canon

National Minority Literature

The discourse on the relationship between national majority and minority groups often takes place through a language of deception and
repression. The use of these political and cultural categories, "majority" and "minority," generally tends to exploit a semantics of numbers
that blurs the actual power relations between a majority and a minority within a single political system. The numerical distinction between a minority and a majority is, in the final analysis, a kind of euphemism, a "cleansed language" that permits us to avoid the fact that
we are dealing with a power relationship rather than a numerical one.
This is a relationship between the strong and the weak, between those
who are in power and control the political mechanisms and those
whose basic national identity places them in a position of inferiority.
Even the most liberal democracy, which places the rights of the minority above all other considerations, cannot cancel out the essential
inferiority in the status of the minority group member.

The strategic outline of the forces in a minority-versus-majority
situation allows us—as has been argued before—to see the relations
within the culture as political power relationships, developed at various levels and in different spheres, one of which is the institution of
a literary canon. The reservoirs of authority that adhere to the canon,
that is, to those literary texts that, in a given culture and period, have
been deemed worthy of preferential status, are a concretization of
this kind of cultural politics. These texts are dispersed by means of
the institutionalized mechanisms of society (schools, universities,
media) and often gain the approval, or at least a priori legitimation,
of its "cultural agents" (publishers, editors, literary critics).

The decision of which texts to incorporate in a literary canon by its very nature involves the rejection of texts that are not considered worthy of inclusion. Both original and translated texts undergo a selection process under the auspices of the literary canon. A work that is translated is, in effect, a work that has been deemed worthy of translation into the language of the canon and thus achieves canonical status. Modern Hebrew literature has adopted, in various forms and on different levels of orthodoxy, the majority of the canonical decisions of Western literary culture. The Western classics are, on the whole, considered worthy of translation into Hebrew. The questions that may arise during this process usually pertain to arguments over the internal hierarchy among different national literatures, among different literary periods, or among various trends and styles. The case of Eastern or Third World literature is different. There, the basic question of setting aesthetic value resurfaces. Western critics often assume that their aesthetic values are universal dictates, beyond any specific aesthetic norms. In so doing, they give these values an apparently apolitical, disinterested authority. In this way, Eastern texts are subjected to a Western value system, which demands for itself an universalist authority covering both Western and Eastern literary production.

This is still the status of many Palestinian literary works written in Israel, which, even after being translated into Hebrew, are still stigmatized and marginalized. These texts are positioned within a canon that basically continues to comply with the universalist norms that have guided the central current of Hebrew literature since Brenner and Berdichevsky. The lukewarm response of readers and critics to these works, many of which deal with questions of Palestinian nationalism and relations between Jews and Arabs, is made all too often in a language of generalizations, evoking multiple political motivations (even if these are not always consciously political) that underlie these kinds of aesthetic judgments.

The Infiltration of Palestinian Literature into the Hebrew Canon

Notwithstanding the trend to downgrade Palestinian literature, the last decades of the twentieth century have seen a movement in the opposite direction. Numerically, more Palestinian works are being published in translation. Culturally, the presence of Arabic works in the Hebrew literary field is a *fait accompli*. It may be said that, in translation, many Arab/Palestinian works have become a part of the Israeli literary canon written in Hebrew. From the perspective of the power struggle underlying this cultural clash between a majority and a minority, it appears that as the Arab minority in Israel emphasizes and expands its Palestinian identity, its significance grows within the dominant Hebrew culture, which is controlled by Jews. The *intifada* has especially heightened this phenomenon, since, as the Palestinian identity of the Arab minority in Israel is strengthened, the sense of outrage against Arab/Palestinian marginalization by the majority Jewish culture is reinforced. As the border between majority and minority in Israel grows increasingly indistinct through the growing and deepening attachment of the Israeli Palestinians to the Palestinian environment of the West Bank and Gaza, their influence as creators of a minority culture in Israel is further emphasized.

The lengthy occupation has contributed significantly to this ongoing process. Before 1967, for example, the existence of the military administration expressed the confused and embarrassed stance of a Jewish majority that continued to relate to itself (through its historical self-perception) as a suffering national minority, as demonstrated in the previous three chapters. Safeguarding the Subject's integrity was achieved, in majority rhetoric and iconography, by effectively demonizing the minority in its midst, by seeing "them" as specifically Eastern, Oriental Others. *They* posed a threat to the majority, and this necessitated the imposition of an antidemocratic military administration. On this level of collective identity and communal symbols, a gradual moderation before 1967 eventually brought about the cancellation of the military administration. Then, after the 1967 war, the continued occupation of the East Bank and Gaza Strip contributed to the relative strengthening of the position of the Arab minority within Israel, when a Jewish majority of no more than 5 million was in control of 2 two million Palestinians. Thus there opened up, on both sides of the divide, further opportunities for the development of cultural confrontations between a minority and a majority.

From an Israeli Jewish perspective, the occupation changed the cultural orientation of the Palestinians who were Israeli citizens, those who had remained in Israel after the 1948 war. The political changes and the growing awareness of Palestinian identity in the territories gave the Palestinians a broader space in which to maneuver politically and strengthened their sense of cultural power. The growth of the image of Palestinian power during the long years of the occupation served a function in foregrounding the Palestinians (including the Israeli Palestinians) in the consciousness of majority Jewish culture and in polarizing attitudes toward them in Israeli society. Nevertheless, progress has been and hopefully will be made in changing a previously almost universally negative attitude. One marker of this process, and a significant one, is the speed with which Israeli culture accepted the signing of the Oslo Accords, in effect legitimating the Palestinian entity.

The encounter through which the literature-in-translation of the minority group infiltrates the majority's literary canon takes place mainly inside Israel and inside Hebrew culture. Works that were created, however, in the context of a specific majority/minority relationship can participate in other cultural fields as well. Thus, Israeli/Hebrew works in English translation have taken on a significant role in the relationship between Israel and the Jewish Diaspora and in the presentation of a Jewish Other to a Christian world. Similarly, Palestinian works that have been written in Israel conduct a relationship both with Arabic literature and culture and, in translation, with Hebrew literature and culture.

Lillian Robinson has been quoted to the effect that the literary and cultural canon is a kind of gentlemen's agreement, behind whose pleasant, aesthetic facade hide political, hierarchic, national, and other interests (Robinson 1989, 572). Therefore, in trying to change the canon, it is sufficient to employ those kinds of strategies to which a gentlemen's agreement may be vulnerable.

Emil Habibi, an Israeli Palestinian author, recipient of the 1992 Israel Prize, provides one example of an author of a minority group who is present, through translation, in the language of the majority. He examines official, public Israeli naming practices as a way of controlling geopolitical reality, but the means he uses are entirely personal and ungovernable—they are his own memories.

One of the highly visible processes of molding a nation, used by the young State of Israel, is the creation of a new imaginary geography. With this purpose in mind, just after the establishment of the state, new names were given to new Jewish settlements set upon the ruins or in the vicinity of Arab towns and villages that had been destroyed or deserted during the War of Independence or in its wake. Yet the transition from the Arab name to the Jewish name was in many cases only partially successful. Sometimes places were renamed by changing the Arab name only slightly, an implied restitution of the lost Jewish presence in the land of Israel. Instead of completely wiping out the original Arabic name, in many cases the Hebrew name that was given (while attempting to re-create the biblical or Mishnaic name) also preserved in its sound or in its meaning the Arabic name. This incomplete transition from Arabic into Hebrew stemmed from a desire, similar to that of the colonist, to give the conquered sites a taste of exotic Otherness and to make the domination of the conqueror into a spectacle of control. Thus, Kibbutz Baram, established on the site of an Arab village, took not only its location but also its former name: Bir'am. Yet alongside this colonial entrapment in the charms of the Orient was a desire to show that, through the giving of a new name, the old biblical or Mishnaic names were being returned to these sites. Thus, cities such as Ashkelon, Eilat, and Beer Sheva were named to echo biblical glory, to territorialize Israeli/Israelite presence, and to replace decades- and perhaps centuries-old "Eastern-sounding" names such as Majdal and Um Rashrash, which, paradoxically, were often closer geographically and etymologically to the biblical sites and names than their Hebrew replacements. The Arabic name thus continues to exist, as it were, under erasure. Despite the apparent suppression of one territorial history in favor of another, more doubtful one—visible testimony of Israeli power and control—the repressed (name) was bound to return.

The palimpsest of discrete layers of names and their associated histories thus created is one of the interstices by which Habibi and other Palestinian writers infiltrate and overturn the consensual gentlemen's agreement of the majority. For example, Habibi points to and insists on the remembrance, and thus the continued existence, of the Arabic name, repeatedly pointing to incommensurable histories, one in Hebrew and one in Arabic:

The street was called HeHalutz (The Pioneer) Street, "Tali'" in Arabic. That is why we are not allowed, for historic reasons, to translate the name into Arabic. Unlike our Jewish brethren who took a lot of the old Arab street names in the city and translated or even changed them. Thus El-Natzra (Nazareth) Street became Israel Bar Yehuda Street; and King Faisal Square, in front of the Hijazi Train Station became Golani Brigade Street. But when they wrote the name in Arabic on the sign, like most signs in the country, they wrote it in bad Arabic spelling, so it came out H'atibat Julani, which means Julani's fiancees. And I, before I had acquired the necessary military information, was of the impression that Julani was some Israeli Don Juan who had many mistresses and so as not to seem rude they were called "fiancees." (Habibi 1988, 38)

The process of infiltration into Hebrew culture of Israeli Palestinian works developed partly because the Arabic literature in Israel, as a literature of a weak minority, finds ways (some of them quite elusive) through which it can enter into the culture of the powerful majority as a "minor literature" written in the language of a "major literature." To maximize the potential for breaking through from the rejected margins to the canonical center, a minority will act, whether consciously or unconsciously, in cultural patterns that bring it ever closer to the position of the majority. Yet, to infiltrate the majority culture from a position of weakness and rejection, which questions the restrictive authority of the canon, a minority may not be satisfied with a simple strategy, based on a linear, slow, and gradual accumulation of power. To maximize the power potential granted to it as the weaker partner, the minority may identify weak links in the majority's cultural environment. As the minority repeatedly strikes at these sensitive points, the majority culture's apparatus is forced to give them legitimization, consideration, and importance. A successful strike at an Achilles' heel signifies, in effect, the contraction of the available space for the majority culture to play with in its struggle to confront and reject the minority culture (Hever 1989, 30–33).

As in Anton Shammas's case, the infiltration of Palestinian writers into the Hebrew cultural context is often achieved through the strategy of writing their works in Hebrew. Although such writers as yet are numerically not very significant, this phenomenon has already brought about an extension of the collective consciousness of Hebrew literature, slowly transforming it from a literature that defined its parameters according to the ethnic Jewish identity of its writers to a literature that bases its concept of itself on the Hebrew language of its authors or their presence within the cultural dialogue of Israeli reality and the presence of their works, in translation, in Hebrew.

Emil Habibi's Universalism

Emil Habibi's work is a decisive example of a Palestinian literary oeuvre that has attained an important status within Hebrew culture. Translations of several of his works, among them stories from his *Sextuplets of the Six Day War* (1988; 1986), his famous novel *The Pessoptimist* (Opsimist in Hebrew) (1984), his book *Ahtaye* (Pity) (1988), and his tale *Saraia, Daughter of the Evil Demon* (1993), all in Anton Shammas's translation, have earned Habibi a central place in the minds of Hebrew readers. The epitome of this process of acceptance was the awarding of the Israel Prize for Arabic Literature to Habibi on Israeli Independence Day 1992. From the perspective of the Hebrew reader of contemporary Israeli literature, his place in the canon of Israeli/Hebrew literature has been confirmed both through his public prestige as an Israeli intellectual and by the presence of his works in translation in the present-day Hebrew literature.

In the story "Rubabeka," which appeared in *Sextuplets of the Six Day War*, written after the 1967 war, Emil Habibi describes a character, a secondhand-goods saleswoman, who insisted on remaining in the homeland in 1948, in Haifa's Wadi Nisnas district, and never left there. Now, after 1967, she yearns to reunite with her people who are living as refugees. The narrator praises Rubabeka as someone who, in her own special way, has carried on the struggle of Palestinian nationalism. She is described as one who was ready to sacrifice the most important things in her life just to be part of the national struggle and to remain close to the homeland. Through the description of the impressive character of Rubabeka, the writer criticizes his fellow Palestinians who were not able to appreciate her and who accused her falsely of living off her countrypeople's suffering by selling the goods that the refugees had left behind when they fled: "When you were involved in political issues, she would get excited and was ready

212 Refugee Gals and Refugee Guys

to fulfill any role given to her. And when one of you was arrested, she was at the jail to visit him even before his mother. She would bring you food and do your laundry" (Habibi 1988a, 57–63).

On the allegorical level, the story is extremely critical of those who attacked the Palestinians who remained in the State of Israel after 1948 and saw them as traitors and collaborators (Massalha 1992). You Palestinians, the author claims, were so involved in high politics, while she took upon herself the really important action, the act of survival. Rubabeka's story is told from a universalist perspective: her contribution to the Palestinian struggle is presented on the same level as the author's critique of the weakness exhibited by his fellow Palestinians. The whole array of phenomena is judged not only from a narrow, particularist angle of national interests but also from a universal value system of morality and justice. These values are presented in the story as being valid beyond any specific historical or national context, even if by remaining loyal to them the author is forced to criticize his own people. On the one hand, the Palestinians slander Rubabeka, their own countrywoman; on the other hand, they themselves do not behave very well. Through this device, Habibi produces narrative patterns that are excellently adapted for positive consumption by the majority Hebrew-speaking culture. Habibi's text, with its self-critical approach and its sympathetic presentation of women's issues—a theme that is given at least as much, if not more, weight than the theme of the national struggle in the story—is very suitable for the universalist expectations of a majority culture that wields the power and demands that all those under its control adhere to these universal, Western values.

In his other books, such as *The Pessoptimist* and *Ahtaye*, Habibi develops similar thematic structures, placing at their heart a position of self-criticism of the Palestinian nation while presenting strong female characters who carry out a central role in the struggle to achieve national aspirations (Elad 1993). In *Ahtaye*, Habibi also aims his comic barbs at the Arab League. Just as he criticizes the brutal translation of Arabic place names into Hebrew, in keeping with his universalist criterion of self-criticism, he also criticizes the extreme Arabization of Hebrew/Israeli names. On the one hand, he questions the process by which the State of Israel confiscates land from the Palestinian memory by renaming places with Hebrew names (Hever 1989); on the other hand, in the eyes of the Hebrew reader, he applies a similar principle of criticism and questioning to the Arab side:

> In passing I am reminded of that Libyan student, who asked me after a lecture at the University of Milan: "What is your position on the question of the Tel El-Rabiah action?" and all the Palestinian students burst out laughing, and explained to me, that the man had translated Tel Aviv to Arabic, "Tel El-Rabiah," and that what he was the referring to was the coastal road attack, near the Country Club on the outskirts of Tel Aviv, which ended in great confusion. As far as acquired knowledge is concerned, there is no difference between our brothers the Jewish historians of Haifa, and this Libyan student, aside from the fact that this one only translates in words whereas they translate both in words and in deeds. (Habibi 1988, 38)

In the story of Rubabeka, the individual, particular woman is no less important than her status as an allegorical representation of the symbol of the struggle. This positioning of the woman as a central character, along with the self-critical approach that Habibi uses, has made his writing appeal more strongly to the majority Jewish culture. *The Pessoptimist* and *Ahtaye* were well received by the Jewish critics when they appeared as novels, as well as when *The Pessoptimist* was put on as a one-man show by the actor Muhammad Bakri. The reaction of the majority culture emphasized the universal element common to Jews and Arabs in these works. Many critics pointed out repeatedly that the character of the "pessoptimist," the Palestinian who survives under Israeli rule, is similar to the character of the evasive Jew surviving through his wits in the Gentile world—a character immortalized in the works of Mendele Mocher Sfarim and in the stories of Shalom Aleichem. Thus, the majority culture's spokespeople have created a universal base, common to Jew and Arab alike (Bar-Kadma 1950; Zach 1988). The emphasis on the artistic achievement as universal has obliterated and repressed the fact that what is being shown is a power relationship between an oppressive majority and an oppressed minority, which was being vehemently attacked by the Palestinian author. The universalist rhetoric was just a way of hiding this attack. The majority culture reactions became especially blunt, however, in response to the adaptation of the novel into a play. H. Novak (1986), for example, juxtaposes her resentment of the play's political stance with her admiration of the artistic achievement. This critical tendency is testified to in Aharon Megged's 1987 article, which takes a different stand and criticizes the general tendency to applaud Habibi's achievement. Megged resents the Israeli audience's enthusiasm, which ignores—or accepts—the harsh political criticism the play addresses to the State of Israel and the events accompanying its founding.

In another example, when the Hebrew translation of Sahar Khalifa's Palestinian novel *The Sunflower* (1987) appeared, critical essays in Hebrew showed similar patterns. They lauded the universalist connection that the novel presents between the struggle of the women for liberation from the oppression of Palestinian men, in the context of a self-critique of Palestinian society, and the Palestinian struggle for freedom from the oppression of the Jewish occupation. In this context Sahar Khalifa was presented as obeying a respectable tradition of self-criticism of one's own people, similar to the tradition that developed in early Hebrew literature, for instance, in the works of Yosef Haim Brenner (Ben-Ezer 1988). A similar thematic structure may be found in the novella "All That Remains for Them," by Rhasan Kanafani (1988), where a Palestinian brother and sister both end up killing. She kills her oppressive husband, in an act of liberation as a woman and in revenge for his having betrayed the national struggle, and he kills an Israeli soldier, as an act of national liberation.

The apparent universalist rhetoric of Habibi's work contributed to his acceptance into the Hebrew canon of the majority culture. The reactions of the literary and theatrical critics are both an indication of the reactive pattern he arouses among the majority culture and part of the process of consolidation of this pattern. For someone whose base position vis-à-vis the majority culture is that of a rejected outcast, this strategy appears to be highly effective—he overcomes the rejection by finding a universal common denominator that includes him, as a member of the Palestinian national minority, *and* the majority Jewish culture. There are powerful similarities between the mode of representation of women in the majority culture and that in Habibi's work. A majority-culture example is Amos Oz's *Ladaat Isha* (To Know a Woman) (1989), which deals with a secret agent, a retired member of the Israeli secret services, who in the second stage of his life is confronted with the need to mature emotionally as a man in order to find an emotional link with a woman. The private career of the hero as a lover and his national career as a secret agent are examined in close conjunction, from the general, universalist perspective of the question of love and its application to both the professional and national existence. Oz raises these issues within the framework of a universal concept of adult existence, indicating wholeness and emotional maturity.

In most cases, a national majority literature will present characters who enjoy ethical autonomy. These characters are based on an array of universal values and offer the reader of the majority culture the option of identification or rejection on the basis of a common interhuman value system that is not specifically relevant to the particular national circumstances surrounding the writing and the reading of this literature. The minority literature that co-opts itself into this particular approach is usually forced to pay a heavy political price, since this movement toward universalization blurs its position of political inferiority, oppression, and antagonism, as well as the power-related opposition between it and the dominant majority culture. The minority creation of the universalist common denominator represses the lack of common ground, that is, the inequality between the minority and the majority culture.

Undermining the Majority Culture

Habibi's path, however, is far more subtle and complex. On the one hand, he writes a minority national literature that co-opts itself into the majority literature, gaining its acceptance while paying the political price for doing so. However, he also uses the universal representation to subvert the pillars of faith of the majority culture. He places the universalism on the surface of his story and uses it to gain acceptance by the majority culture, but in the background, behind the scenes, is often a completely separate drama, one that aims its subversive action in a totally different direction. Thus, the technique of foregrounding the tale of the woman, while making the narrative universalist, also produces the subversion of that universalist code, questioning, dismantling, and violating it, through the device of an alternative story that refuses to accept the narrative framework suited to the universalist demand of the majority culture.

The story of Rubabeka is, as already mentioned, the story of a woman who participates in the national struggle, but at the same time it is the story of someone who carries on the struggle in her own way and, as such, is scorned by Palestinian society. Rubabeka is a representation of the national mother figure, who is exalted as an accepted national symbol that represents motherhood as a kind of national service. But in the final analysis, we discover, through Habibi's narrator, that she achieves her role as national mother symbol at the price of her family role as real mother: "When her husband emigrated and took the children she insisted on staying with her paralyzed mother. That was the first tale of leaving" (Habibi 1988a, 59). To achieve her national role, Rubabeka is ready to pay the price of disconnection from the family framework. Furthermore,

> after five years, when her mother had died, we heard that her husband refused to acknowledge her and wasn't interested in having her back. You never believed her when she said she had no interest in leaving her house. You just winked at one another and made faces. The rumor got around that she was having an affair that's what you were saying. You claimed that it was impossible for her to remain in the Wadi for no apparent reason. (59)

Palestinian society is presented in the story as unable to accept the possibility of a woman's story having a purely national motive, one not connected to some private tale of love. The real story of Rubabeka is neither a national story nor a private love story. It remains a riddle, a secret. This feminine secret presents the option of a private tale that refuses to fit in simply with either the national narrative option or the private one—or with a combination of the two. Through this device, the feminine story contributes to undermining the unity of the universalist tendency. The feminine story of Rubabeka refuses to fit in with the demands made of it and, in so doing, undermines and dislocates the stability of the universalist generalization that sees a common ground between men and women and between Palestinian and Jew.

The story that builds this generalization is itself fragmented, disturbed, dislocated, incomplete, and lacking in closure. Rubabeka wrote the secret reason for her remaining in the Wadi after the war of 1948 in those "letters that I used to write—as she admitted herself—

without ever sending them anywhere" (62). Now, after the 1967 war, when the possibility of reuniting with the 1948 refugees has arrived, she hands over the collected letters to the narrator. Yet for all that, the story systematically avoids supplying a full explanation for her steadfast endurance in remaining in the Wadi. The incompleteness of her story is explained by the narrator through the story of his grandmother, who always began her stories to her grandchildren from the middle and "we never managed to remain awake until the end. She would also fall asleep before the end, and so we never knew the beginning or the end of the story about 'Hassan the Mischievous.' And when we grew up we started remembering Grandma and the story we called 'The Unfinished Tale' and we would laugh loudly, as if it were a totally obvious thing that a story had a beginning and an end" (62). The narrator, who is also a writer, insists on keeping the secret enclosed in Rubabeka's letters under lock and key and emphasizes that he has a right to keep the secret from us—"so that this story will remain 'unfinished' until we write its ending, together" (63). In so doing, he emphasizes his position that the final authority to tell the story belongs to Rubabeka. He received direct permission from her to tell the current tale, which uncovers only a part of her feminine secrets. And the future fulfillment of the possibility that her full story will be written by the two of them is dependent entirely on Rubabeka's will to do so.

In this way, the female character created by Habibi avoids being implicated in the Oedipal narrative (in which there is a clear hierarchy of power relations and authority among the characters of the "family," as well as a clear structure of beginning, middle, and end) both on the national and on the general level, a narrative that tries to create a linkage between the liberation of women and national liberation. The woman as defined by Habibi holds onto her independent status, which cannot be integrated into universalist generalizations. The purposely unfinished story of the woman allows Habibi to set pitfalls or disturbances within his universal narrative that make it difficult for the majority-culture reader to interpret and digest his stories as ordinary universalist texts, as such a reader would read texts of a minority literature, which are easily accepted and integrated by the majority culture without threatening it or questioning its authority. On this universalist front, the Palestinian woman fills the role that has been apportioned her, as a member of a minority, by the Jewish hegemony. In this role, she takes part in the Oedipal narrative, with its built-in family power structure, and incorporates the libidinal and the national in a single allegorical drama.

Just the fact that the narrative places a woman at its heart, assigning her the role of undermining and subverting the Oedipal narrative, creates in the final analysis a state of feminine subversion of the masculine character of Jewish hegemony. Therefore, the nationalist subversion that Habibi creates is double-pronged, directed against the oppression of the Palestinian woman both by the Israelis and by Palestinian men. Rubabeka's feminine secret, that constant which usually constitutes femininity in masculine hegemonic systems, here sets up the separation between her private world and the public/national world and places her in opposition to both the masculine hegemony and the Jewish hegemony. At the same time that this is a story that can be accepted by the majority culture as minority literature, Habibi styles his tale in such a way that it also becomes a subversive story, one that undermines its simple acceptance by the reader of the majority culture.

The subversive approach of Habibi's stories is clearly apparent in another story from the collection *Sextuplets of the Six Day War*, "At Last . . . the Almond Blossom" (Habibi 1988a, 45–55). This is a story based on dualities. It tells of two friends, Mr. M. and the author, whose close friendship was terminated after the founding of the State of Israel. This rupture came about when M. became a high school teacher, "and how could one keep one's position in the State of Israel, but that one must cut off any connection with a friend or a relative that was not acceptable to the establishment—even though he might be thy brother, son to the same mother and father" (46–47). The story develops as a classic national allegory: the founding of the State of Israel is described as a turning point that renders the teacher a split subject who must disconnect from his boyhood friends and repress his memories. After 1967, Mr. M. tries to repair the broken connection. During all the years that he lived in Israel, cut off from his past, he used to drive to work past Maale El-Abhariye on the way from Nazareth to Haifa. Now, after 1967, while driving along the winding route of Maale El-Laban on the way from Nablus to Ramallah, he remembers an old incident from his youth about a youthful friend who loved a girl from Jerusalem or Bethlehem. "The friend's sweetheart split the branch in two, gave him half and kept the other half herself. They made an oath to keep the two parts of the branch, and to meet the next spring, when the almond trees were in blossom. At that point he was meant to bring his parents so as to ask for her hand in marriage" (52).

Mr. M.'s aim now is to complete the story and find the friend of his youth who was in love with the girl. But what he doesn't recall is that he was the lovesick youth, and that he received the half of the almond branch himself. Thus his efforts are actually a search for himself, for a way to reconnect to his earlier identity, which existed before the war of 1948. But in contrast to the ex-sweetheart, who remembers it all, Mr. M. is presented as lacking any historical awareness. When he comes to visit her, she tries unsuccessfully to awaken his memory and to bring him to a recognition of the past and of her. But he, who is so set on recovering the connection to his past, cannot remember anything. She hints at the truth but does not expose it, continuing to keep it hidden as a feminine secret. Once more, the woman carries the burden of the national struggle on her back. Up to this point in the plot, the story appears to develop as a national allegory that subsumes man, woman, and their private erotic memory to the national narrative. But from this point, the woman refuses to function as a complementary agent for the man. The woman—and the author follows her example—aborts the completion of the allegorical narrative as a tale of a couple. The woman holds onto the national memory without the erotic coupling becoming subsumed in a simple way into the national narrative.

In "Shaato HaTova Shel Masood" (Masood's Happy Hour with His Cousin) (1986), also from the collection *Sextuplets of the Six Day War*, Habibi repeats a similar thematic model while he develops the clash between the political and the personal existence of the Palestinians who became citizens of the State of Israel. The child Masood, nicknamed "Radish," who lives in the State of Israel, undergoes a major change in his life. Masood is the son of a family with neither friends nor acquaintances. They do not belong to any of the local *hamulas* (extended family clans), and thus his position in the neighborhood is negligible. Then a visit by family from the West Bank suddenly makes him a person of great family standing, which raises his status among the neighborhood children. But this shift in his life has a dual effect, the two aspects of which cannot be integrated. On the one hand, Masood becomes very much connected to his West Bank family through links that were established by means of the occupation of the territories in the 1967 war; in this light, it may be said that the occupation raised his status among his peers. On the other hand, along with all the other neighborhood children, he believes that Israel should withdraw from the territories, an action he now is afraid will cut him off from his West Bank family and return him to his earlier position of lacking roots and family ties. The source of authority for the political truth of the necessity of the withdrawal is his sister, "the philosopher":

> He would ask anything he liked and she would answer him. Like her he was much excited by the prospect of the withdrawal and like her he was certain that it would happen to him and that it was inevitable.
>
> Only one question he was afraid to ask his sister, "the philosopher," for fear she might slap him across the face and he would fight with her unnecessarily, or perhaps for some other reason altogether: Will I, when they withdraw, go back to being what I was, without a cousin? (Habibi 1986, 37–38)

In this story, too, the woman holds the secret of the ability to stick to the homeland even when the price is an existence in the shadow of an apparently irresolvable contradiction. The child prefers to live his life avoiding this contradiction. In contrast, the woman, his sister, is presented as one who knows how to choose between personal interests and the national interest, and who maybe even knows the hidden secret of how to resolve and clarify the relations between the personal/familial interest and the national/public interest.

The Family Story as National Subversion

The family carries an important role in the building of a national identity and the struggle to uphold it. In *The Pessoptimist*, however, by pointing out the origins of the family, Habibi once more undermines the standard allegorical meaning that one might expect for the family as part of the national narrative. He chooses to describe Said's family as "a well-established and distinguished family whose heritage can be traced back all the way to some Cypriot slavegirl from Aleppo" (Habibi 1984, 15). He also describes it as a family where it was customary for "our fathers to divorce our mothers all along the line" (16). The ambivalent meaning of family lies in its being a "pessoptimistic" family that integrates opposite perspectives of time. The family's "pessoptimism" is well presented by Said's mother's reaction to his brother's tragic death, which is that it was preferable this should have occurred than that her daughter-in-law should have run off with another man (21–22). Similarly, Said reacts with typical "pessoptimism" when the officer from the Lebanese guard slaps him across the face, and he, who had hurried back to the border with his friends, whispers, "Better it should have worked out like this than any other way!" (51). But it immediately transpires that the "pessoptimistic," ambivalent approach is connected to the character of the woman— Gazale, the gazelle—whom he met on the way, and to whom he promised that he would return with arms and ammunition necessary for the national struggle. Now that he's been slapped, he clarifies that his tears are for Gazale, who lost him, her lover, in Beirut. His "pessoptimistic" ambivalence sets aside a separate space for the love story, which does not necessarily join with the national narrative.

The personal, private distress of the refugees, the victims of the national misfortune, is exposed in a similar fashion:

> The Palestinians had turned into refugees whom the young local women were not attracted to spend their mercies upon. Therefore I turned to the young female refugees, since supposedly the refugee gals go for the refugee guys. But they were attracted, unlike us, to the mercies of other men. So they had no interest in us. Since this was the case, I returned to the State of Israel without quenching my thirst. (51)

In using the humorous "the refugee gals go for the refugee guys," Habibi incorporates a critique of the Jewish state alongside his self-critique of the Palestinians. At one and the same time, he presents a wicked parody of the Israeli militarist-chauvinist slogan "The best guys go to become pilots," which was then continued in parlance "and the best gals go for pilots!" and he criticizes the contempt exhibited by the Arabs toward the Palestinian refugees. Yet, also in this case, the universalist parallelism between self-criticism and criticism of the enemy does not conclude the discussion. Said's basic supposition is that nationalism is equal and parallel to private Eros—that the young Palestinian women are supposed to be attracted to the refugees, the symbolic bearers of Palestinian suffering. But in reality, this linkage between the private and the collective/national sphere is disrupted. The young women do not accept the refugee men, and the hero decides to return to Israel.

The character of Yoad, Said's sweetheart, stands out in *The Pessoptimist* for the complexity of its characterization. On the one hand, she serves as a fixed object of desire; on the other hand, she is a character who splits into three parts: "Yoad returned and lo and behold she was not Yoad" (217). Twenty years later she returns in the image of her daughter, who is described as one who "appears as a man among men" (195). In the tale of Said's marriage to the Tanturaean woman, Said continues serving Jacob, the Jew. In other words, he places himself in national bondage in order not to lose his private world and to be able to continue his life with his Tanturaean lover (116). The tale of the escape of the mother and her son, the fighter, who had tired of his parents' clandestine existence, is apparently a national incident that receives a suitable family-based treatment. In point of fact, however, the escape story is left underdetermined; it is not clearly resolved (155–56), and the symbolic significance of the woman and her family remains unclear.

By means of these techniques, Habibi manages to write texts that carry a double-edged political status: on the one hand, they are acceptable to the canon of the majority culture through their universalist appearance; on the other hand, they subvert that culture by allowing the Palestinian voice a special place, an independent existence that cannot easily be reduced to the universalist framework. This particularist voice is not created through allegory or symbolism, which is subjected to the universalist narrative and incorporated into it, but rather by dislocating and undermining the narrative through unfinished stories that refuse closure and do not play by the rules of the Oedipal game. A powerful example of this appears in the character of the woman who lived in a village and denied she was the daughter of her father, a "Present Absentee" who was in hiding in the village. The national Palestinian situation forced the daughter to live a feminine life without a father, since her father was a "Present Absentee," whereas the father did not live as a man with the woman who was the mother of his children—only after his death could she appear in public as his wife (205–6). Thus, the situation of the struggle and national oppression forced her to forgo, during her husband's life, her role as a woman. Yet, when he died and she could identify herself publicly as his wife, she could fulfill her role only as a widow.

Specifically because of the national struggle, Habibi avoids producing in his stories a simple and unsophisticated feminine portrait that will easily fit in with the Western majority culture's expectations of an oppressed minority culture. In the final analysis, there are no clear Oedipal conflict relationships in his works, as a struggle either between a son and his father or between generations. Instead, Habibi uses the female character to present a struggle that, when stripped of its external attributes, refuses to allow a parallelism between the libidinal narrative and the political narrative.

In a minority literature, as mentioned, there is a tendency to write texts that mobilize the libido in favor of politics. This is a tendency of positioning the collective Subject as a product of collective literature, written as a national allegory, which blurs the distinction between the personal/private and the public spheres. In many ways Habibi follows this path, and in his stories, the libido is mobilized in the service of the national narrative; for example, love for the homeland in *Ahtaye* is also erotic love. Ahtaye, the girl who was raped and abandoned, who walks the streets in rags with her illegitimate child in her arms, is "none other than the homeland, the miserable homeland" (Habibi 1988, 134). But, at the same time, Habibi presents the image of a woman who does not incorporate herself easily into the web of expectations of the integrating majority culture. This kind of problematic connecting link between the libidinal and the political appears in *Ahtaye*, for example, when the narrator mocks the Jews for suspecting political motivations behind the Arabs' natural reproduction rate— "and they believe that we don't sleep with our virtuous wives except through a directive straight from Abu-Ammar [Arafat] (if we are respectable) and one from Abu-Jihad, at least (if we are not that respectable)" (35). A similar function is fulfilled in the novel by the ironic description of the blonde woman in the Mercedes. When it transpires that a woman is the instigator of the act of defiance (as the narrator tells us, the rumor is that she organized the allegorical "traffic jam" in Haifa), it turns out that she is actually a Jewish woman who joined the Palestinian revolution abroad (74).

Saraia, Daughter of the Evil Demon: The Tale and Its Opposite

Saraia, Daughter of the Evil Demon, Habibi's last book to be translated into Hebrew, is in many ways a prime example of a minority literary work that infiltrates into the majority literature. Saraia is exposed in the story, but similar to other women in Habibi's oeuvre, she also remains always a secret that refuses to be fully unraveled. The central thematic device of apportioning the female character a double role of both expressing the universalist ethic and undermining it on the particular level is brought here to its fullest development. Saraia, the woman, the demon's daughter, is given the central role in the *khurafiya*, the traditional folktale, that Habibi relates. From the beginning, however, she performs a dual function. On the particular level, Saraia is an essential element of the biography of Habibi, the author and the narrator, and she is also a partial allegory for the Palestinian nation. She is also a universalist symbol of utopian longings and dreams. On the one hand, she cries out allegorically: "The homeland has missed its sons, O Abdallah. Have you forgotten us so quickly?" (Habibi 1993, 29). On the other hand, using the language of personal biography, the narrator tells us that "half a century ago, Saraia would take my hand and lead me up the Wadi of Lovers, and she warned me that it was time to return to the tents of her tribe" (37).

The narrator promises us, the readers, that if his friend should return from his impossible quest to start his life with Saraia again from the beginning, then he will relate the continuation of this *khurafiya* to us. In the second ending, however, which is placed right next to the first one, the narrator signs off the story with the blessing to his readers: "See you in the next *khurafiya*" (169). This dual structure of an unending end expresses a tendency throughout the book for one tale to include its opposite within itself. In this doubling, the narrator figure is telling us (and there are at least two narrator figures, who are not always easily distinguishable) that this is the breakdown of the clear distinction between the practice of storytelling and the discussion of its poetics; thus, this story is presented as a traditional folktale that has been adapted to a modern idiom.

The time is the summer of 1983. The days of the Lebanon war offer the narrator, the fisherman-author (Habibi's alter ego in the story), a chance to reassess his personal biography and local Palestinian history. Amid the hallucinatory images that appear to him as he sits and fishes on a reef off the coast of Akhziv, he attempts to bridge the gap of a generation and re-create the memory of his relationship on Mount Carmel with Saraia, the daughter of the demon. Between him and Abdallah, his own alter ego (both as a partner in the story and as a co-narrator), there develops a familial and national web of memories, forgetfulness, and repression in which the longings for Saraia and the feelings of guilt for not having been there for her fill a central role.

The story shifts between a desire to face historical and personal truths in a sane and balanced manner and a systematic attempt to evade them. The fate of the refugees of 1948 is represented, for example, by the story of Brother Jouad and the breakdown of his mother, who could not bear to see her family separated as a result of the war. The collapse of authority and of the spiritual and political tradition of Palestinian society and the longing for its reinstatement are raised through the nostalgic evocation of Uncle Ibrahim and his mysterious cane.

The love story of the hero with Saraia, the mysterious daughter of the demon, which apparently moves toward its linear end, ultimately disrupts the expectation that it generates in the reader for an ending to the *khurafiya*. But the real disruption that is generated here is the actual denial of the formal demand for (or convention of) an ending. The ending as the signifier of the formal boundaries of the plot is questioned, and in its stead the reader is offered two alternatives. As in the storytelling technique of Scheherezade, the narrative framework in this story is only a kernel for a broader framework, which in itself is part of a larger structure. Thus Habibi plays with a series of conventions that direct the expectations of a Western/Jewish reader: source versus translation, reality versus imagination, the story versus its process of creation, the folktale versus its modernist adaptation.

In contrast to his earlier books, Habibi has suggested that *Saraia, Daughter of the Evil Demon* was written with the Hebrew reader already in mind. With the assistance of Anton Shammas, the translator,

Habibi applies techniques that undermine and reexamine the hierarchic division of labor among writer, translator, and reader. Thus, for instance, the act of translation of the Arabic text into Hebrew is thematized when, in full view of the readers of the translation, Habibi discusses the abilities of the translator, Shammas. In so doing, Habibi extracts Shammas from his invisible status as translator, who normally remains behind the scenes, and reinstates him in the foreground of the text. Instead of the usual union between reader and translator as against the author, the author here creates a pact with the readers over the head of the translator.

As before, in this story Habibi utilizes the ambivalence of the Israeli/Hebrew discourse. Once again, he struggles with the use of double meaning in Israeli discourse when it describes the current Israeli landscape alongside the repressed Palestinian memory landscape. He shows sensitivity in his awareness that the evidence of memories of the repressed past in the Hebrew names upholds repression itself as an ambivalent act. The repeated use of the doubling semantics that present the Hebrew Akhziv in close proximity to the Arab El-Ziv, for example, or Tel Shikmona alongside Tel El-Samakh, bursts through this gap in the discourse, cancels the sense of normalcy and naturalness of the act of repression, and turns it into a temporary, artificial decision that could be reconsidered. Thus, Habibi expropriates the "natural" authority and primacy of the national majority group (who hold the power) to allot names to the sites of its own home landscape. This dual, subversive status of the language is strongly apparent in the book in the purposely artificial Hebrew devised by Shammas: the spiraling syntax, which at times gives a sense of being incorrect; the exaggerated and sly use of quotes from Hebrew literary works ("From one year to the next this," a quote from a poem by Natan Zach, is attributed, of all things, to a song about the refugees by the Lebanese singer Fairuz); and, in general, a language that repeatedly jars against the assumed tolerance of the Hebrew reader. As it questions the limits of tolerance, the language produces a double-pronged effect. On the one hand, it is a heightened and artificial language that calls attention to itself as a conscious imitation of Hebrew, the language of the dominating power (Bhabha 1994, 85–92); on the other hand, it tries to enter the linguistic network in order to undermine and subvert it and its political presuppositions. Once more, it creates for itself a special borderline existence that is subversive and provocative, managing to be at once a part of the canonical norm and outside that norm.

The National Allegory and Its Negation

The flexible position of the story and its unclear boundaries allow Habibi, through the translator Anton Shammas, to enter into a tense and provocative dialogue with the Hebrew reader. As in his earlier books that were translated from Arabic into Hebrew, and as in some of his short stories, in *Saraia, Daughter of the Evil Demon*, Habibi challenges the Hebrew reader in the format of a dialogue between two narrators who describe their personal story against Palestinian history but also as a part of it. On the one hand, this is a story written by an author from a national minority culture, whose clear political commitment and typical use of an aesthetic of national allegory do not appeal to the Western aesthetic norms that dominate the majority Israeli culture. On the other hand, this is also a story that is meant to arouse sympathy in the Hebrew readers, and perhaps even solidarity based on universal truths. Since Habibi is primarily telling an internal, autobiographical story, in which he once more defines the suffering of his people through a distancing irony mixed with deep pain, the critique of the Israeli actions during the War of Independence—the destruction of Arab villages, the horrors of the expulsions, and turning the Palestinians into refugees—does not distract him but at times even encourages him to develop in his story a wholesome dose of universalist self-criticism against his own people (e.g., the collaborators). Thus, once more from a universalist position of distance, he observes the Eastern folktale as a Western aesthetic, literary possibility.

This dualism exposes the Hebrew reader to a text that is very difficult to categorize. Habibi can be read by the Hebrew reader both internally and externally, both as part of the Israeli canon and as external to it. Whether conscious or not, his writing is designed to attack the shifting boundaries of the Israeli canon, which Habibi's writings in translation have been instrumental in opening up. The way Habibi infiltrates the majority culture and literature as a minority author is through his activity in the linguistic/cultural heart of majority culture.

Habibi's ambiguous position in relation to majority culture is most emphasized in his dual relationship to the national allegory, the expression of collective commitment, as the natural weapon of the national minority author. Only in old age, when he has awakened from the dream of the Soviet "new world," does he come back in repentance to search for Saraia, who represents, among other attributes, truth, the homeland, and the hope for national liberation. His forgetting Saraia is portrayed not as a willful act but as a result of weakness and passivity. The allegorical national expression completes the picture and points at national suffering as the reason for the author's disguising himself as one who has forgotten the truth. The accusations against him for having dealt with "bread and the philosophy of bread" (i.e., Marxist historical materialism) he dismisses with the claim that "we have no safe world of our own, not even the hint of one" (142). Here, as well, Habibi's text displays its dual approach. On the one hand, he tells the allegorical tale of Saraia, and on the other hand, he denies it. On one side the national allegory is upheld; on the other it is rejected: no occupation kept me away from Saraia, the narrator tells us, as much as what happened that night when Saraia didn't release herself from my arms and did not return to her tribe. He interprets this unusual act as an overly powerful devotion to Saraia, whom he dismisses as a decorative, dressed-up Eastern beauty who only sullies him.

But this statement is already involved in a process of questioning the uniformity and authority of the allegorical continuity. Now he already tries to speak his mind without breaking the tale, because "this tale is not a series of philosophical deliberations on the nature and quality of a past that has gone, but rather a sensual concretization like the slowly rising dough lying flattened out next to the oven that will be lit in the evening" (143). Habibi attempts to extricate his allegory from the collectivist steamroller and identify in it concrete moments of personal meaning. Therefore, the main quality he identifies in himself, his personal hesitation at the final moment, is both the basis for his demand to stop postponing the reunion with Saraia and to accept his responsibility and thus become a part of the collective story and the signifying acceptance of a personal, simple, and mundane reality. For this reason, in the final analysis, he describes his ultimate desire in the same dual language of private and public reality that he defines as "public tolerance" (146).

A clear expression of this dualism is apparent in the representation of time in the tale. On the one hand, the story of Saraia is described through a series of incidents that occurred in the biographical past of the narrator. For instance, when the graveyard attendant reports to him that the grave of Souad the Second, his deceased daughter, has been visited by a woman he has never seen before, "a withered woman in the fall of her life, wearing a black, transparent scarf around her head" (Habibi 1993, 55–56), this is an incident from the past. Habibi, however, uses the storytelling present of the writing to disguise the difference between what actually happened and what is to be expected or desired. The transfer from oral storytelling to the written text involves a transfer to a new set of rules. The written text, Habibi claims, has its own laws. Instead of the novel he had dreamed of, "I came up with these confessions that are now in your hands" (61). In defining the writing process, he points out "that he does not write, oh Mr. Angel-of-Death, but from the power of gravitation; like a stone that has been dislodged from its moorings high up on Mt. Carmel" (62). These confessions tell of the end of the writer in a language of biblical future tense (*waw* converse—the letter *waw* precedes the word in the form of the past, thus creating future tense), which presents the death and burial of the writer from a dual perspective: what has already taken place but is told as something that is going to happen. This continuity, which leads to the ongoing biblical present of "And Saraia comes down from the mountain" (62), gives the occasion of her appearance a dual status of longing and reportage. The concrete, personal, biographical event is presented as also obeying the general allegorical law of gravitation that controls it. This duality is most clearly present when Habibi turns to the refugees, the absentees:

> And behold his stone, as it roles down from the top of Mt. Carmel, it hits a snag and changes its track: Please, my dear absentees, you should not allow yourselves to be content with the homeland as a female djinn that you take with you to bed, believing you are free to do whatever you will with her shape and form. Because nymphs only

exist in paradise, but Saraia is made of flesh and blood, even if she
has been consigned to the dunghill of forgetfulness! (63)

Between Two Watermelons

Saraia's political existence in the hazy zone between the dominant
Jewish Israeli culture and Israeli Palestinian culture is often foregrounded in the text. The possibility of infiltrating the majority culture by means of this duality of particularism and universalism is
presented from the start of the book as a dilemma—one that Habibi
had dealt with several times in the past—of the minority author, who
is forced to carry two watermelons in his arms: the watermelon of
politics and the watermelon of literature. In this book, Habibi turns
this dilemma into the axis of his writing. This is a book about the
limitations and possibilities of political and cultural action among
the Palestinian national minority that survived in Israel after the War
of Independence as second-class citizens and as objects of official
persecution. The tension between the two watermelons is maintained, and Habibi's universalist self-critique does not lead him to
deny his responsibility as a writer committed to bettering the fate of
his people. His criticism of his own political path, especially in the Israeli Communist Party, does not lead him to deny the necessity for
political commitment in his writing but rather to a redefinition of
his political commitment as an author and of the political role of the
author.

Along with her other attributes, Saraia is an allegory of continual
searching and striving. But after the multiple hardships of his search
for Saraia, the main narrator of the story reaches the awareness that
Saraia was already his from the start. Once more, the allegorical authority is undermined. It now transpires that the allegory of the
search is not a given structure but an artificial construct. The search
for Saraia was fictitious, since the narrator who was searching for her
was responsible for her imprisonment by not attending to her needs.
As an alternative, he praises the intellectuals and creative artists who
did not neglect or imprison their utopian hope but knew how to treat
their Saraias in a dual manner of one who both "sets her free and refuses to replace her with another" (Habibi 1993, 169). The actual nar-

rative plotline, with its reversals and contradictions, gives rise to the possibility of taking a political stand and finding a path of action by walking a tightrope.

As already mentioned, the ending is also the basis for the ongoing story. The act of writing is often likened to digging a tunnel that constantly runs into dead ends; thus "I have no other choice if I want to save myself, but to go on digging" (27). This is a fluid position that attempts to hold onto a clear, unequivocal political and moral commitment and to create and maintain a space for individual liberty. Thus, for example, it may be asked: if once he had received a clear sign of life from Saraia, did her lover do all he could to find her? The answer is affirmative yet not unequivocal. In an attempt to overcome this ambiguity, the narrator suggests overturning the accepted wisdom that "catastrophes always come before the means for their avoidance can be found" (167), as well as not relating to the act of fiction as a cure for misfortunes and catastrophes, one that supplies renewed hope in the wake of specific concrete disasters. Instead, he suggests, in effect, seeing the act of storytelling as an act of utopian commitment, without any relationship to any specific catastrophe. But, as might be expected, the negation of the utilitarian utopia, the cure for specific catastrophes, brings with it an unwillingness to end the story. The story is thus an obstinate aspiration along the unpaved route to the dual solution. On the one hand, it is an expression of the effort to supply answers to the suffering of the wars. On the other hand, it is a suggested solution that once more breaks the direct and immediate commitment to suffering and wonders whether "we have already become so accustomed to the sounds of war, and we can differentiate between one war cry and another. Have we become addicted to the war cries, from one war to the next, . . . to such an extent that we cannot hear the other music? Can we not decipher the other wave length?" (167). Thus, Habibi directs his principle of storytelling in the light of the same duality that is faithful to the particularist suffering of his people even as he undermines it in the name of a commitment to a universalist value system.

This tense middle road characterizes Emil Habibi's place in Israeli culture: a strong opponent of the policies of the Israeli establishment, yet a recipient of the Israel Prize for literature. His acceptance of the award led to widespread condemnation from the Arab world, which nevertheless joins the Israeli establishment in recognizing the aesthetic qualities of his work. The duality that encompasses both the author and his oeuvre was also apparent in the manner in which Israeli culture accepted Habibi as a winner of the Israel Prize. As might be expected, there were right-wing protests—one expressed, for example, by the Israel Prize for Physics laureate, who is a right-wing ideologue, against awarding the prize to someone who, to his mind, questioned fundamental precepts of the state (Neeman 1992). This kind of political interpretation worked to reject Habibi from the legitimate circle of Israeli culture. But the attempts by critics from the other side of the political spectrum, the liberal Left, to legitimate Habibi were carried out by way of an attempt to disguise the political aspects of his texts (Hareven 1992). This was a continuation of the same act of misinterpretation, since the denial of the political dimension in Habibi's writing and the attempt to base it solely on universal aesthetic qualities is, in the final analysis, not that dissimilar to the right-wing critiques. In both cases there is an attempt to reject him and to redesign him so that he may be acceptable to the legitimate Israeli culture. In the final analysis, Habibi remains on the borderline of legitimacy; the sharp political aspects of his work undergo processes of adaptation and castration, while the main way in which he infiltrates the Israeli canon is through a linking-up with the hegemony of the dominant culture, even as he undermines it.

Thus closes an uncontinuous cycle of resistance to the national Hebrew canon from the minor margins. Reuven Fahan's and Yitzhak Fernhoff's acts against Brenner's and Berdichevsky's canonical Subject at the beginning of the century return now, eighty years later, in the form of the Palestinian stance vis-à-vis the Jewish Israeli canon. The role played in the Jewish Diaspora by the peripheral writers, who created a nonradical version of Zionism, is now played within the culture of the sovereign state of Israel by the Palestinian voice. This cycle embraces many more fragments: Hebrew literature written in Poland between the two world wars; the "Canaanite literature" that developed during the struggle for independence; and the Mizrahi voice, which developed alongside Hebrew fiction of "the generation of statehood," the classics—albeit containing inner tensions—of Amalia Kahana-Carmon, A. B. Yehoshua, and Amos Oz.

References

Adondon [S. Y. Agnon]. "Bibliographia" (Bibliography). *HaPoel HaTzair* (The young worker), Tammuz–Av, 1908.

Agnon, S. Y. "Bineareinu Ubizkeineinu" (With our young and our old). *HaTekufah* (The era) 6 (1920).

———. "A Letter to David Zakai." Erev Shavuot 1939. *Yediot Genazim* (Genazim bulletin) 70 (1970).

———. *MiAzmi el Azmi* (From me to myself). Tel Aviv: Schocken, 1976.

Ahad Haam [Asher Ginzberg]. *Kol Kitvei Ahad Haam* (The collected writings of Ahad Haam). Tel Aviv: Dvir, 1943.

Almog, Shmuel. *Zionut VeHistoria* (Zionism and history). Jerusalem: Magnes, 1982.

———. *Zionism and History: The Rise of a New Jewish Consciousness.* Translated by Ina Friedman. New York: St. Martin's, 1987; Jerusalem: Magnes, 1987.

Alterman, Natan. "Magash HaKesef" (The silver tray). In *HaTur HaShveee* (The seventh column). Tel Aviv: HaKibbutz HaMeuchad, 1962.

Amir, Aharon [Yariv Eitam]. "HaBoker HaHadash" (The new morning). *Aleph*, October 1949.

Anderson, Benedict. *Imagined Communities.* London and New York: Verso, 1991.

Arad, Miriam. "New Novels Disappointing." *Jerusalem Post*, May 15, 1964.

Baer, Yitzhak. *Galut* (Diaspora). Jerusalem: Mosad Bialik, 1980.

Bakun, Itzhak. "Introduction." In *Y. H. Brenner, Mivhar Mamarim Al Yezirato HaSipurit* (Selected essays on his fiction), edited by I. Bakun. Tel Aviv: Am Oved, 1972.

———. *Brenner HaTzair* (The young Brenner). Vols. 1 and 2. Tel Aviv: Ha Kibbutz HaMeuchad, 1975.

———. *HaTzair HaBoded BaSiporet HaIvrit 1899–1908* (The young solitary in Hebrew literature 1899–1908). Tel Aviv: Agudat HaStudentim, 1978.

———. *Mitoch HaHavura* (From within community). Tel Aviv: Papyrus, 1982.

Bakun, Itzhak. *Brenner BeLondon* (Brenner in London). Beer Sheva: Ben Gurion University, 1990.

Ballas, Shimon. *HaMaabara* (The camp transit). Tel Aviv: Am Oved, 1964.

———. "Hearot Levikuah" (Comments to a debate). *Amot* (Criteria), August 1965.

———. *Mul HaKhoma* (In front of the wall). Ramat-Gan: Massada, 1969.

———. *Hitbaharut* (Clarification). Tel Aviv and Merhavia: Sifriat Poalim, 1972.

———. "Yaldut Shebadimyon" (Imaginary childhood). In *Baer HaTahtit* (Downtown). Tel Aviv: Sifriat Tarmil, 1979.

———. "Siha bein Yaakov Besser Le Shimon Ballas" (A conversation between Yaakov Besser and Shimon Ballas). *Davar* (Word), October 23, 1992.

Ballas, Shimon, Reuven Ben-Yosef, Yaakov Besser, and Itamar Yaoz-Kest. *Mamashut Kfula* (Double substance). Tel Aviv: Eked, 1977.

Barash, Asher. "Sifrut Shel Shevet O Sifrut Shel Am?" (Literature of a tribe or literature of people?). *Moznayim* (Scales), January 22, 1931.

Bar-Kadma, Emanuel. "HaOpsimist" (The pessoptimist). *7 Yamim* (*Yediot Aharonot* weekly supplement), October 31, 1980.

Barthes, Roland. *S/Z.* Translated by R. Miller. Oxford and New York: Oxford University Press, 1970.

Ben-Ezer, Ehud. "HaMahatzit HaHashuha Shel HaAm HaFalasteenee" (The dark half of the Palestinians). *HaAretz* (The land), July 15, 1988.

Benjamin, Walter. "Theses on the Philosophy of History." In *Illuminations*, edited by Hannah Arendt, translated by Harry Zohn. New York: Schocken, 1969.

Bennett, Tony. *Formalism and Marxism.* London and New York: Methuen, 1979.

Benshalom, Benzion. *HaSifrut HaIvrit Bein Shtei Milhamot HaOlam* (Hebrew literature between the two world wars). Jerusalem: HaMahlaka Leynyaney HaNoar Shel HaHistadrut HaZionit, 1943.

Berdichevsky, Micha Yosef. *Kitvei Micha Yosef Ben Gurion (Berdichevsky), Maamarim* (The writings of Micha Yosef Berdichevsky: Articles). Tel Aviv: Dvir, 1960.

———. *Kitvei Micha Yosef Ben Gurion (Berdichevsky), Sipurim* (The writings of Micha Yosef Berdichevsky: Stories). Tel Aviv: Dvir, 1965.

———. *Sipurei 1900* (Stories of 1900). Tel Aviv: Iriat Holon and Reshafim, 1991.

Berdichevsky, Micha Yosef, and Yosef Haim Brenner. *HaLifat Igrot* (Correspondence). Tel Aviv: Beit Dvora VeImanuel, 1984.

Bhabha, Homi. *The Location of Culture.* London and New York: Routledge, 1994.

Biale, David. *Power and Powerlessness in Jewish History.* New York: Schocken, 1986.

Brawer, A. Y. "Bineareinu Ubizkeineinu, Bemisgeret Hayey Mehabro" ("With our young and our old" in the context of the life of its author). In *Yovel Shay* (Festschrift), edited by Baruch Kurzweill. Ramat-Gan: Bar-Ilan University Press, 1958.

————. "Bineareinu Ubizkeineinu Leshai Agnon" ("With Our Young and Our Old," by Shai Agnon). *HaUma* (The nation), December 1973.

Brenner, Yosef Haim. *Yosef Haim Brenner Ktavim* (The writings of Yosef Haim Brenner). 4 vols. Tel Aviv: HaKibbutz HaMeuchad and Sifriat Poalim, 1985.

————. *HaKtavim HaYideem Y. H. Brenner* (The Yiddish writings of Y. H. Brenner). Edited by Yitzhak Bakun. Beer Sheva: HaKatedra LeYidish, Ben Gurion University, 1985a.

Brinker, Menachem. *Ad Hasimta HaTeverianit* (Until the Tiberian's lane). Tel Aviv: Am Oved, 1990.

Cohen, Israel. "Buchach Shel Agnon" (Buchach by Agnon). *Moznayim* (Scales) 30 (1970).

Deleuze, Gilles, and Félix Guattari. *Anti-Oedipus: Capitalism and Schizophrenia.* London: Athlone Press, 1985.

————. *Kafka: Toward a Minor Literature.* Translated by Dona Polan. Minneapolis: University of Minnesota Press, 1986.

Derrida, Jacques. "Racism's Last Word." In *'Race,' Writing, and Difference*, edited by Henry Louis Gates, Jr. Chicago: University of Chicago Press, 1986.

Doron, Yehoyakim. *HaGuto HaZionit Shel Natan Birenbaum* (Natan Birnbaum's Zionist philosophy). Jerusalem: HaSifria HaZionit, 1988.

Dubnov, Shimon. *Miktavim Al HaYahadut HaYeshana VeHahadasha* (Letters about old and new Judaism). Tel Aviv: Dvir, 1937.

Eagleton, Terence. "Ideology, Fiction, Narrative." *Social Text* 2 (1979).

Elad, Ami. "Avanim Al Mitzha Shel HaMoledet: Al HaSifrut HaPalasteeneet Bitkufat HaIntifada" (Stones on the homeland's forehead: Palestinian literature in the days of the *intifada*). *Alpaim* (Two thousand) 7 (1993).

Eliav, L. "Sefarim HaDashim (Reshimot Bibliografiot): Kerekh Hadash Shel HaTekufah" (New books, bibliographic notes: A new volume of *The era*). *Hayom* (Today), November 27, 1925.

Elkes, G. "Iton VaSefer" (Journal and book). *Reshit* (Beginning) 1, September 1932.

Evron, Boaz. "Hamaase Ubavuato HaAkademit" (The act and its academic reflection). *Yediot Aharonot* (Latest news), March 2, 1984.

Fahan, Reuven. *Mehayei HaKaraim: Tziyurim Vetipusim* (From the lives of the Karaites: Types and illustrations). Halitch: Akselrod, 1908.

Fahan, Reuven. "BeHararei Karpat" (In the Carpathian mountains). In *Mivhar Ketavim* (Collection), edited by Nurit Govrin. Givatayim: Massada, 1969. [The story was first published in serialized form in *Hayom* (Today), February–March 1926.]

———. Reuven Fahan to H. N. Bialik, February 11, 1930. In *Mivhar Ketavim* (Collection), edited by Nurit Govrin. Givatayim: Massada, 1969a.

Feitelson, Menachem Mendel. "Mehayei HaKaraim" (From the lives of the Karaites). In *Behinot Vehaarachot* (Inspections and observations), edited by A. B. Yaffe. Ramat-Gan: Massada, 1970.

Fernhoff, Yitzhak. *MeAgadot HaHayim* (From the legends of the living). Podgorzje: Hamizpe, 1908.

———. *Sefer HaMitnagdim* (The book of the Mitnagdim). Edited by Israel Cohen. Tel Aviv: Dvir, 1952.

Fichman, Yaakov. "Mikhtavim Al HaSifrut HaIvrit: Mikhtav Shevee" (Letters on Hebrew literature: Seventh letter). *Moznayim* (Scales), April 7, 1938.

Forgacs, David. "National-Popular: Geneology of a Concept." In *The Cultural Studies Reader*, edited by Simon During. London and New York: Routledge, 1993.

Foyerstein, M. "Hem Yagyu Mahar BaCamery" (*They will arrive tomorrow* at the Camery). *HaZofe* (The observer), February 9, 1950.

Frishman, David. "HaMekoshesh" (The wood gatherer). *HaTekufah* (The era) 12 (1921).

Gafni, Shraga [Eitan Notev]. "HaKrav Al Mivtzar Williams" (The battle of Fort Williams). *Aleph*, April 1950. [For English translation by Moshe Ron, see *The Other in Jewish Thought and History*, edited by Laurence J. Silberstein and Robert L. Cohn, New York: New York University Press, 1994.]

———. "HaShevah LaEloim" (Praise the lord). *Aleph*, May 1950a.

Gelber, Michael Natan. *Toldot HaTnuah HaZionit BeGalizia 1875–1918* (The history of the Zionist movement in Galicia). Vol. 2. Jerusalem: HaSifria HaZionit and Reuven Mass, 1958.

Gertz, Nurit. *Amos Oz.* Tel Aviv: Sifriat Poalim, 1980.

———. "Navadim VaTzefa" (Nomads and viper), units 2–3, and "Mul HaYearot" (Facing the forests), unit 7. In *HaSiporet HaIsraelit BiShnot HaShishim* (Israeli fiction in the sixties). Tel Aviv: Open University, 1983.

———. *Hirbet Hizah Vehaboker Shelemaharat* ("Hirbet Hizah" and the morning after). Tel Aviv: Porter Institute Publications and HaKibbutz Ha Meuchad, 1983a.

———. "HaKevuza HaKnaaneet Bein Ideologia Lesifrut" (The Canaanite group between ideology and literature). In *HaKevuza HaKnaaneet Sifrut*

VeIdeologia (The Canaanite group: Literature and ideology), edited by N. Gertz and R. Weisbord. Tel Aviv: Open University, 1986.

Goldberg, G. "Orot Meofel: Rishmei Keriah" (*Lights from darkness:* Reading impressions). *HaTzefirah* (Dawn), July 24, 1931.

Goldberg, Y. "Orot Meofel: Y. Warshaviak" (*Lights from darkness:* Y. Warshaviak). *Reshit* (Beginning) 3–4, November–December 1933.

Gramsci, Antonio. *Selections from the Prison Notebooks.* Edited and translated by Quintin Hoare and Geoffrey Nowell-Smith. London: Lawrence and Wishart, 1971.

Gruenbaum, Yitzhak. "Veshuv Nisayon" (An experiment, yet again). *BaDerekh* (On the road), September 15, 1932.

Gur, Israel. "Pirkey HaMahaze HaMekory BeIsrael" (Chapters in original Israeli drama). *Bamah* (Stage) (1982).

Habibi, Emil. *Sudasiyat al-yyam al-sittah* (Sextuplets of the Six Day War). Haifa: al-Ittihad, 1970.

———. *Haopsimist* (The pessoptimist). Translated by Anton Shammas. Jerusalem: Mifras, 1984.

———. "Shaato HaTova Shel Masood im Ben Dodo" (Masood's happy hour with his cousin). Translated by Yona Shilo. In *Makom Al Pnei HaAdama, Sipurim Arveem Bnei-Zmaneinu* (A place on the face of the earth: Arabic stories of our times), edited by Yosef Givoni and Sarah Surani. Jerusalem: Van-Leer Institute, 1986.

———. *Ahtaye* (Pity). Translated by Anton Shammas. Tel Aviv: Am Oved, 1988.

———. "Levasof . . . Parah HaShaked" (At last . . . the almond blossom). In *HaYalim Shel Mayim* (Soldiers of water), translated by Naim Araide. Tel Aviv: Maariv, 1988a.

———. "Rubabeka." In *HaYalim Shel Mayim* (Soldiers of water), translated by Naim Araide. Tel Aviv: Maariv, 1988b.

———. *Saraia, Bat Hashed Hara, Khurafiya* (Saraia, daughter of the evil demon: A story). Translated by Anton Shammas. Tel Aviv: HaKibbutz HaMeuchad, Siman Kria, 1993.

Halevi-Zweik, Yeudit. "Tekufat Germania (1914–1918) Beyetzirato Shel Shai Agnon" (The German era [1914–1918] in the writings of Shai Agnon). Diss., Hebrew University, Jerusalem, 1968.

Halkin, Shimon. *Mavo Lesiporet Ivrit* (Introduction to Hebrew fiction). Jerusalem: Mifal HaShichpul, 1958.

Hall, Stuart. "Gramsci's Relevance for the Study of Race and Ethnicity." *Journal of Communication Inquiry* 10 (1986).

Hareven, Shulamit. "Al Sifrut VeSifrut Poleeteet, Absurd Hu Ir Prazot" (About literature and political literature: The absurd is an unfortified city). *Yediot Aharonot* (Latest news), Tarbut Sifrut Omanut (Literary and cultural supplement), June 19, 1992.

Hazan, Leib. "Min HaMaytzar" (Out of the distress). *HaTzefirah* (Dawn), October 28; November 4 and 11, 1927.

————. *Geulah* (Redemption). Kovel: Sirton, 1930.

————. "Yahadut Polin Heikhan?" (Whither Polish Jewry?), *BaDerekh* (On the road), January 18, 1935.

Herder, Johann Gottfried. "Ideen zur Philosophie der Geschichte der Menschheit." In *Herder's Werke. Nach den besten Quellen Revidirte Ausgabe*, edited by H. Düntzer and A. Wollheim da Fonseca. Berlin: Gustav Hempel Verlag, 1879.

Hertzig, Hanna. "Lev HaKaitz Lev HaOr" (Heart of summer, heart of light). Unit 9. In *HaSiporet HaIsraelit BiShnot HaShishim* (Israeli fiction in the sixties). Tel Aviv: Open University, 1983.

Hever, Hannan. "Hai HaHai VeMet HaMet" (The living is alive and the dead is dead). *Siman Kria* (Exclamation mark) 19 (1986).

————. "An Extra Pair of Eyes: Hebrew Poetry under Occupation." *Tikkun* 2, 2, May 1987.

————. "Israeli Literature's Achilles' Heel." *Tikkun* 4, 5, September–October 1989.

Hirshberg, Y. "Hem Yagyu Mahar BaTeatron HaCamery" (*They will arrive tomorrow* in the Camery Theater). *Kol Haam* (The voice of the people), February 21, 1950.

Hodgson, Marshall G. S. *The Venture of Islam: Conscience and History in a World Civilization.* Chicago: University of Chicago Press, 1974.

Huggan, Graham. "Decolonizing the Map: Post-Colonialism, Post-Structuralism, and the Cartographic Connection." In *Past the Last Post: Theorizing Post-Colonialism and Post-Modernism*, edited by Ian Adam and Helen Tiffin. Calgary: University of Calgary Press, 1990.

Hurvitz, Yaakov. "Zeror HeArot" (A few comments). *HaAretz* (The land). February 17, 1950.

Jameson, Fredric. "Third-World Literature in the Era of Multinational Capitalism." *Social Text* 15 (1986).

JanMohamed, Abdul R. "The Economy of Manichean Allegory: The Function of Racial Difference in Colonialist Literature." In *'Race,' Writing, and Difference*, edited by Henry Louis Gates, Jr. Chicago: University of Chicago Press, 1986.

Jay, Martin. "Two Cheers for Paraphrase: The Confessions of a Synoptic Intellectual Historian." *Stanford Literary Review* 3, 1 (Spring 1986).

Jehlen, Myra. "Archimedes and the Paradox of Feminist Criticism." *Signs* 6 (Summer 1981).

Kagan, Zipora. "'BaEmek' (Tarsat)—MeAgadat 'Hulda Uvor' LeNovella Hevratit" ("In the valley" [1909]—from the legend of "Hulda and the pit" to a social novella). In *Meagadah Lesiporet Modernit Beyetsirat Berdichevsky* (From legend to modern fiction in the work of Berdichevsky). Tel Aviv: HaKibbutz HaMeuchad, 1983.

Kahana-Carmon, Amalia. "Lev HaKaitz, Lev HaOr" (Heart of summer, heart of light). In *Bikhefifah Ahat* (Under one roof). Merhavia: Sifriat Poalim, 1966. [The story was first published in *Molad* (New Moon) 23, 208–10 (December 1965).]

Kahin, B. "Meolam Hasifrut" (Of the world of literature). *HaTzefirah* (Dawn), January 28, 1927.

Kanafani, Rhasan. "Ma Shenotar Lahem" (All that remains for them). In *Gvarim Bashemesh* (Men in the sun), translated by Daniella Brefman and Yani Damianus. Jerusalem: Mifras, 1988.

Kaplan, Caren. "Deterritorializations: The Rewriting of Home and Exile in Western Feminist Discourse." In *The Nature and Context of Minority Discourse*, edited by Abdul R. JanMohamed and David Lloyd. New York and Oxford: Oxford University Press, 1990.

Katz, Yaakov. *Leumiyut Yehudit: Masot Vemehkarim* (Jewish nationalism: Essays and studies). Jerusalem: HaSifria HaZionit, 1979.

Keisari, Uri. "Hem Yagyu Mahar BaTeatron HaCamery" (*They will arrive tomorrow* in the Camery Theater). *HaOlam Haze* (This world), February 16, 1950.

Keynan, Amos. "Ivrim Velo Tzabarim" (Hebrews and not Sabra). *Aleph* (October 1949).

Khalifa, Sahar. *HaHamanit* (The sunflower). Translated by Rachel Halaba. Haifa: Mifras, 1987.

Kisilev, Y. "Al Hem Yagyu Mahar" (On *They will arrive tomorrow*). *Al HaMishmar* (On guard), February 2, 1950.

Kleinman, Moshe. "Mezakei HaRabim" (Contributors to the community). *HaMitzpeh* (The watch-tower), 29 Tevet 1908.

Knaany, David. "HaNiglot VeHaNistarot BeYezirato Shel S. Y. Agnon" (The revealed and the concealed in the writings of S. Y. Agnon). *Luah HaAretz* (The calendar of *HaAretz*) (1949).

Kressel, Getzel. "Reshito Shel Agnon Be HaPoel-HaTzair" (Agnon's beginning in "The young worker"). *HaPoel HaTzair* (The young worker) (1968).

Kubayanda, Josaphat B. "Minority Discourse and the African Collective: Some Examples from Latin American and Caribbean Literature." In *The Nature and Context of Minority Discourse*, edited by Abdul R. JanMohamed and David Lloyd. New York and Oxford: Oxford University Press, 1990.

Kurzweil, Baruch. "Mahuta UMekorotea Shel Tnuat HaIvrim HaTzeirim (Knaanim)" (The essence and sources of the "Young Hebrews" movement). In *Sifrutanu HaHadasha Hemshech O Mahapecha?* (Our new literature: Continuity or revolution?). Jerusalem and Tel Aviv: Schocken, 1971.

Laor, Dan. "HaFasutaim: HaSipur Shelo Nigmar" (The people of Fassuta: The story that does not end). *HaAretz* (The land), May 30, 1986.

"Leyl HaBehora Shel Hem Yagyu Mahar" (The premiere of *They will arrive tomorrow*). *Al HaMishmar* (On guard), February 1, 1950.

Levenberg, Aliza. "Hayey HaMaabara Mibefnim" (The Maabara's life from within). *Min HaYesod* (Groundwork), June 25, 1964.

Livnat, Pnina. "Hishtakfut HaTekufa Mitoch 'Bineareinu Ubizkeineinu,' 'Vesipur Pashut' Leshai Agnon" (The reflection of the era in "With our young and our old" and "A simple story," by Shai Agnon). *Maalot* (Degrees) 2, October 1976.

Lloyd, David. *Nationalism and Minor Literature: James Clarence Mangen and the Emergence of Irish Cultural Nationalism*. Berkeley, Los Angeles, and London: University of California Press, 1987.

———. *Anomalous States*. Durham: Duke University Press, 1993.

Lusternik, Malkiel. "Veod . . ." (And more . . .). *Reshit* (Beginning) 2, October 1933.

———. "Misaviv Lanekudah" (Circling the heart of the matter). *Reshit* (Beginning), 4–6, January–March 1934.

Luz, Ehud. *Parallels Meet: Religion and Nationalism in the Early Zionist Movement (1882–1904)*. Translated by Lenn J. Schramn. Philadelphia, New York, and Jerusalem: Jewish Publication Society, 1988.

Malkin, Yaakov. "Hem Yagyu Mahar" (They will arrive tomorrow). *BaMahane* (In the camp), February 9, 1950.

Massalha, Salman. "HaShed Yatza Min HaBakbuk" (The devil fled out of the bottle). *HaAretz* (The land), Tarbut USifrut (Cultural and literary supplement), March 20, 1992.

Megged, Aharon. "Facing the 'Opsimist.'" *HaAretz* (The land), February 22, 1987.

Meizel, Y. L. "Gibor Polanyah" (Poland's hero). *BaDerekh* (On the road), May 17, 1935.

Melzer, Emanuel. *Maavak Medini Bemalkodet: Yehudei Polin, 1935–1939* (A political struggle trapped: The Jews of Poland, 1935–1939). Tel Aviv: HaMahon LeHeker HaTfutzot, 1982.

Mendelsohn, Ezra. "Polin" (Poland). In *HaTefuzah: Mizrah Eropah* (The diaspora: Eastern Europe), edited by Yaakov Tzur. Jerusalem: Keter, 1976.

Mifelev, Nachman. "Levado Nishar: Tsiyur" (Alone he remained: A sketch). *HaTzefirah* (Dawn), March 31, 1921.

———. "Sipur Ivri Mekori" (An original Hebrew story). *HaTzefirah* (Dawn), June 1, 1928.

———. "Hu Lo Yireh Et HaAretz" (He will not see the land). In *Sefer HaShanah LeYehudei Polanyah* (The Polish Jewish yearbook), edited by Benzion Benshalom, Zecharia Zilberpfennig, and Zvi Fefer. Vol. 1. Kraków: Miflat, 1938.

Miron, Dan. *Bodedim BeMoadam* (Singular in their time). Tel Aviv: Am Oved, 1987.

Moreh, Shmuel (with Lev Hakak). "Yetziratam HaSifrutit Vehamehkarit Shel Yotsey Irak BeYrak UBeIsrael Bedoreno" (The literary and scholarly work of Iraqi's Jews in Iraq and Israel in our generation). In *HaIlan Ve-HeAnaf* (The tree and the branch). Jerusalem: Magnes, 1997.

Naiman, Y. M. "Hem Yagyu Mahar BaTeatron HaCamery" *(They will arrive tomorrow* in the Camery Theater). *Dvar HaShavua* (Davar's weekly supplement), February 23, 1950.

Neeman, Yuval. *HaAretz* (The land), May 25, 1992.

Novak, Hava. "HaOpsemism Shel Habibi—Veulay Shel Shalom Aleyhem" (Habibi's pessoptimism—and perhaps Shalom Aleichem's?). *Davar* (Word), October 20, 1986.

Ofrat, Gideon. *HaDrama HaIsraelit* (Israeli drama). Herzelia: Cherikover Publishing House and the Hebrew University, 1975.

Oz, Amos. "Navadim VaTsefa" (Nomads and viper). In *Arzot HaTan,* (Where the jackals howl). Ramat-Gan: Massada, 1965. [The story was first published in *HaAretz* (The land), February 7, 1964.

———. *Where the Jackals Howl.* Translated by Nicholas de Lange and Philip Simpson. Toronto, New York, London, and Sydney: Bantam Books, 1980.

———. *Ladaat Isha* (To know a woman). Jerusalem: Keter, 1989.

Parush, Iris. *Kanon Sifruti Veideologia Leumit* (Literary canon and national ideology). Jerusalem: Mosad Bialik, 1992.

Paulson, Ronald. *The Fictions of Satire.* Baltimore: Johns Hopkins University Press, 1967.

Pomerantz, Ber. "Eyma, Masuot" (Awe, beacons). *Reshit* (Beginning) 4–6, January–March 1934.

Rabbi Benyamin. "Betokh HaEreg: Dor Shileshim—Dor Tzanua" (Woven into the fabric: The third generation, the humble generation). *HaPoel HaTzair* (The young worker), June 3, 1909.

Rabinovitch, Yaakov. "Al HaSipur HaIvri" (On the Hebrew story). In *Masloley*

Sifrut (Routes of literature). Vol. 1. Tel Aviv: Neuman, Agudat HaSofrim, [1930] 1971.

———. "Al Am VaShevet" (Nation and tribe). *Moznayim* (Scales), April 30, 1931.

Ratosh, Yonatan. *Sifrut Yeudit BaLashon HaIvrit* (Jewish literature in Hebrew language). Tel Aviv: Hadar, 1982.

Rattok, Lily. *Amalia Kahana-Carmon.* Tel Aviv: Sifriat Poalim, 1986.

Rawidowicz, Simon. "Leshem Hidush Sifrutenu" (For the sake of the renewal of our literature). *HaOlam* (The world), December 2, 9, and 16, 1930.

———. "Shtei Sheelot Shehen Ahat" (Two questions which are one). *Moznayim* (Scales), March 12 and 19, 1931.

———. *Im Lo Kan Heihan?* (If not here, where?). Lvov: Brit Ivrit Olamit, 1933.

Reuveny, Aaron. *HaOnyot HaAhronot* (The last ships). Warsaw: Stiebel, 1923.

———. *Shamot* (Devastation). Warsaw: Stiebel, 1925.

Riv, A. "Gahelet HaYezirah HaIvrit: Lehofaat Amudim" (Ember of Hebrew creation: At the publication of *Columns*). *BaDerekh* (On the road), June 12, 1936.

Robinson, Lillian. "Treason Our Text: Feminist Challenges to the Literary Canon." In *Critical Theory since 1965*, edited by H. Adams and L. Searle. Tallahassee: Florida State University Press, 1989.

Sadan, Dov. "Leagadat Hulda UVor" (On the legend of Hulda and the pit). *Molad* (New moon) 15, 109–10, 111 (1957).

———. *Avnei Gvul* (Border stones). Ramat-Gan: Massada, 1964.

———. "Rosh Verishon—Rosh Mum Hoo Rishon? HaDugma: Zmihat HaManheegut BaZionot BeGalitzia" (Above all—but is not the Leader defected? The example: The rise of the Galitzian Zionism's leadership). In *Kvuzot Ilit UShchavot Manhigut BeToldot Israel UBeToldot HeAmim* (Elite groups and leading classes in the history of Israel and its people). Jerusalem: Magnes, 1967.

Sadan-Lowenstein, Nili. *A. B. Yehoshua.* Tel Aviv: Sifriat Poalim, 1981.

Sadeh, Yitzhak. "Hem Yagyu Mahar" (They will arrive tomorrow). *Al HaMishmar* (On guard), March 10, 1950.

Said, Edward. *Orientalism.* London and Henley: Routledge and Kegan Paul, 1978.

———. "An Ideology of Difference." In *'Race,' Writing, and Difference*, edited by Henry Louis Gates, Jr. Chicago: University of Chicago Press, 1986.

Shaham, Natan. "Bator" (In the line). In *HaElim Azelim* (Lazy are the gods). Merhavia: Sifriat Poalim, 1949.

————. "Shivaa Mehem" (They were seven), *HaElim Azelim* (Lazy are the gods). Merhavia: Sifriat Poalim, 1949a.

————. *Hem Yagyu Mahar* (They will arrive tomorrow). Merhavia: Sifriat Poalim, 1949b.

————. *They'll Be Here Tomorrow.* Translated by Israel Schen. Jerusalem: World Zionist Organization, 1957.

Shaked, Gershon. *Gal Hadash BaSiporet HaIvrit* (A new wave in Hebrew fiction). Merhavia and Tel Aviv: Sifriat Poalim, 1970.

————. *Omanut HaSipur Shel Agnon* (Agnon's art of storytelling). Merhavia and Tel Aviv: Sifriat Poalim, 1973.

————. *HaSiporet HaIvrit, 1880–1970* (Hebrew narrative fiction, 1880–1970). Tel Aviv: Keter and HaKibbutz HaMeuchad, 1977.

————. *HaSiporet HaIvrit, 1880–1980.* Vol. 2: *BaAretz UBaTefuzah* (Hebrew narrative fiction, 1880-1980. Vol. 2: In the homeland and in the diaspora). Tel Aviv: Keter and HaKibbutz HaMeuchad, 1983.

————. "Rodfim? Nirdafim?" (Persecutors? Persecuted?) In *Ein Maqom Aher* (There is no other place). 2d ed. Tel Aviv: HaKibbutz HaMeuchad, 1988.

————. *HaSiporet HaIvrit, 1880–1980.* Vol. 4: *BeHevly HaZman, HaRealism HaIsraeli, 1938–1980* (Hebrew narrative fiction, 1880–1980. Vol. 4: Times of suffering, the Israeli realism, 1938–1980). Tel Aviv: Keter and HaKibbutz HaMeuchad, 1993.

Shalev, Mordechai. "HaAravi KePitaron Sifruti" (The Arabs as a literary solution). *HaAretz* (The land), September 30, 1970.

Shammas, Anton. *Arabeskot* (Arabesques). Tel Aviv: Am Oved, 1986.

————. "Ashmat HaBabushka" (The guilt of the babushka). *Politika* (Politics) 5–6, February–March 1986a.

————. "Milhamti Betahanot Anshei HaRuah" (My fight against the windmills of the intellectuals). *Moznayim* (Scales) 60, 3, September 1986b.

————. "Al Galut Vesifrut" (On exile and literature). *Igra* (Roof) 2 (1987).

————. *Arabesques.* Translated by Vivian Eden. New York and Cambridge: Harper and Row, 1988.

Shavit, Yaacov. *The New Hebrew Nation: A Study in Israeli Heresy and Fantasy.* London: Frank Cass, 1987.

Shmueli. "Bikoret Sefarim, Bayit URehov" (Literary review on *House and street*). *Moznayim* (Scales), July 2, 1931.

Shoam, Haim. *Etgar UMeziut BaDrama HaIsraelit* (Challenge and reality in Israeli drama). Ramat-Gan: Bar-Ilan University, 1975.

Spivak, Gayatri Chakravorty. "Imperialism and Sexual Difference." *Oxford Literary Review* 8, 1–2 (1986).

Steinman, Eliezer. "BaNekhar" (In foreign parts). *HaTekufah* (The era) 12 (1922).

Steinman, Eliezer. *Esther Hayot.* Warsaw: Stiebel, 1923.

————. "Hearot Ketanot, Merkaz" (Minor remarks, center). *Kolot* (Voices) 3 (1923a).

————. "Mahshavot BiZmanan: HaYahas El HaMerkaz" (Reflections of their time: The relation to the center). *Kolot* (Voices) 5–6 (1923b).

————. "Mahshavot BiZmanan: MiSaviv LaMedurah HaYetomah" (Reflections of their time: Around the orphaned bonfire). *Kolot* (Voices) 5–6 (1923c).

Sternberg, Michael [Z. Z. Weinberg]. "Adam BaOhel, Sifrut" (A man in the tent: Literature). *Kolot* (Voices) 7 (1923).

Stierle, Karl. *The Reader in the Text.* Princeton: Princeton University Press, 1980.

Talmon, Jacob. *Mitos HaUmma VeHazon HaMhapecha* (The myth of the nation and the vision of revolution). Vol. 1. Tel Aviv: Am Oved, 1982.

Tammuz, Binyamin. "Hem Yagyu Mahar" (They will arrive tomorrow). *HaAretz* (The land), February 17, 1950.

————. *Holot HaZahav* (Sands of gold). Tel Aviv: Mahbarot LeSifrut, 1950a.

Thon, Yehoshua (Osias). "Sifrut VeShaar HaKsafim . . ." (Literature and the rate of exchange . . .). *Luah Ahiasaf: Measef Sifruti* (Ahiadaf calender: A literary collection) 13 (1923).

Twersky, David. "An Interview with Amos Oz." *Tikkun* 1, 2 (1986).

Urinovsky, Aaron. "HaTenuah HaIvrit Bishnat 1932–33 BePolanyah" (The Hebrew movement in Poland in 1932–33). *BaDerekh* (On the road), October 13, 1932.

————. "Reshimot A: Miflagtiut O Daat HaZibur HaIvri" (Notes A: Partisan loyalty or Hebrew public opinion). *BaDerekh* (On the Road). September 15, 1932a.

Warshaviak, Yehuda. "Bli Emunah" (Without faith). In *Bli Emunah.* Warsaw: Makor, 1928.

————. *Orot Meofel* (Lights from the darkness). Warsaw: Makor, 1931.

————. "Roman Polanee Mehayei Eretz Israel BaHove" (A Polish novel on current life in Eretz Israel). *HaTzefirah* (Dawn). May 21, 1931a.

————. "Av Antishemi" (Antisemitic father). In *Afilot* (Late blossoms). Warsaw: Makor, 1935.

————. "Beshulei Hitnaplut Ahat: Meyain Teshuvah Kzarah" (At the margins of one attack: A kind of a short answer). *Amudim* (Columns), July 1936.

Warshavsky, Yakir. "Yaldey HaVisla" (The children of Vistula). In *Maalot Umordot: Sipurim VeTsiyurim* (Ups and downs: Stories and sketches). Warsaw and Tel Aviv, 1925.

————. "Itim Hadashot: Perek MiSipur" (New times: A chapter of a story). *Hayom* (Today), December 25, 1925; January 4, 1926.

Warshavsky, Yakir. "BeMerhavei Polin: Rishmei Over Orakh" (Around Poland: Impressions of a wayfarer). *HaTzefirah* (Dawn), October 4 and 13, 1926.

Weinberg, Z. Z. *Bayit URehov: Shnot 1918–1926* (House and street: The years 1918–1926). Warsaw: Stiebel, 1931.

Werses, Shmuel. "The Hebrew Press and Its Readership in Interwar Poland." In *The Jews of Poland between Two World Wars*, edited by Yisrael Gutman, Ezra Mendelsohn, Jehuda Reinharz, and Chone Shmeruk. Hanover, N.H., and London: University Press of New England, 1989.

Yakubovitz, A. L. [A.L.Y.]. "LeHofaat BaDerekh" (At the publication of *On the road*). *BaDerekh* (On the road), September 15, 1932.

Yehoshua, A. B. "Mul HaYearot" (Facing the forests). In *Ad Horef 1974* (Until winter 1974). Tel Aviv: HaKibbutz HaMeuchad, 1975. [The story was first published in *Keshet* (Bow) 5 (Spring 1963) and later was included in Yehoshua's collection *Mul HaYearot* (Facing the forests). (Tel Aviv: Ha-Kibbutz HaMeuchad, 1968). An English translation of the story, by Miriam Arad, appears in Robert Alter's anthology *Modern Hebrew Literature* (New York: Behrman House, 1975), from which page references and translations (with some emendation) have been taken.]

———. "HaKavim HaAdumin Shel HaSmol HaZioni" (The red lines of the Israeli left). *HaKir VeHahar* (The wall and the mountain). Tel Aviv: Zmora-Bitan, 1985.

Yizhar, S. "The Story of Hirbet Hizah." Translated by Harold Levi. In *Caravan: A Jewish Quarterly Omnibus*, edited by Jacob Sonntag. New York: Yoseloff, 1962.

———. "The Prisoner." In *The New Israeli Writers*, edited by Dalia Rabikovitz. New York: Funk and Wagnalls, 1969.

Zach, Natan. "HaSofer Kebadai Emet" (The author as inventor of truth). *Yediot Aharonot* (Latest news), Tarbut Sifrut Omanut (Culture and literature supplement), July 1, 1988.

Zeligman, R. "Al Lashon Vetarbut" (About language and culture). *HaTzefirah* (Dawn), June 12, 1931.

Zemer, Avraham. "LeTakanat Shuk HaSefarim HaIvri" (Organizing the market of Hebrew literature). *HaTzefirah* (Dawn), June 25, 1928.

Zilberpfennig, Zecharia. "Mai Miflat?" (What is the refuge?). In *Sefer HaShanah Leyehudei Polanyah* (The Polish Jewish yearbook), edited by Benzion Benshalom, Zecharia Zilberpfennig, and Zvi Fefer. Vol. 1. Kraków: Miflat, 1938.

Zilbertal, Moshe. "Hem Yagyu Mahar BaCamery" *(They will arrive tomorrow* in the Camery). *BaShaar* (At the gate), February 9, 1950.

Zohar, Zevi. "LeAliyat Z. Z. Weinberg Leeretz Israel" (On the immigration of Z. Z. Weinberg to Eretz Israel). *BaDerekh* (On the road), July 6, 1934.

Index

"Adama" (Berdichevsky), 35
Aestheticism, 14
Agnon, S. Y.: on Fahan's *From the Karaite Lives*, 44; in Galician cultural revival, 19; on Galician literature, 59; and national minority literature, 7. *See also* "With Our Young and Our Old"
Ahad Haam (Asher Ginzberg): debate with Berdichevsky, 12–18; "Teudat HaShiloah," 12, 13, 15
Ahtaye (Habibi), 211, 212, 213, 223–24
Aleph (Canaanite publication), 106
Al HaMishmar faction, 74
"Al HaSipur HaIvri" (Rabinovitch), 70
Allegory, national. *See* National allegory
"All That Remains for Them" ("Ma Shenotar Lahem") (Kanafani), 214
Almog, Shmuel, 11, 12, 31, 33, 34
Alon, Yigal, 120
Alterman, Natan, 123
Amir, Aharon, 105, 106–7, 110
Amot (journal), 162
Ana'im, Muhammad, 201
Anderson, Benedict, 2, 26, 105, 145
Antisemitism: Agnon's "With Our Young and Our Old" on, 63; in Galician educational system, 34; in Poland in the thirties, 95; Warshaviak's "Av Antishemi" on, 97; Warshavsky's "Itim Hadashot" on, 80; Weinberg's *Bayit URehov* on, 86
Arabesques (Shammas), 175–204; Michel Abayyad, 178, 179, 187, 193, 195; Amira, 190, 203; arabesque as representational device in, 186–90, 196, 198, 199, 203–4; Yosh Bar-On, 184–86, 190, 191, 192–95, 200, 203; contractualism and corpo-

ratism contrasted in, 187; ethnic boundaries of Hebrew canon challenged by, 9, 200–201; Islamic atomism represented in, 187–88; Layla Khouri, 178–79, 187, 190, 191; as minor literature, 196–99; narrator's and narrative portions of, 178–80, 183; narrator's status in, 178; negationist stance of, 177; Nur, 179, 190; oral sources of, 191–92, 201; Oz on Hebrew language and, 1, 176; politicization in, 198; reterritorialization of Hebrew in, 201–4; Shlomit, 190, 204; spatial patterning in, 189–90; time as represented in, 186–89; as truly Israeli novel, 177; two Anton Shammases in, 180; Uncle Yusef, 188, 190–92; women in, 190
Arab League, 212
Arabs: Ballas's Arab identity, 168; Canaanite representation of, 8, 105–17; in canonical Hebrew literature, 116; ethnic boundaries of Hebrew canon challenged by, 9; Israeli "fortress mentality" regarding, 175; and the Israeli state, 102; in Kahana-Carmon's "Heart of Summer, Heart of Light," 158; as manual laborers, 182, 195; military administration of Arabs abolished, 160; as never equal citizens in Israel, 181; otherness of, 3; in Oz's "Nomads and Viper," 149–50; in Shaham's *They Will Arrive Tomorrow*, 128, 129, 130, 135–39; writing in Hebrew, 201; in Yehoshua's "Facing the Forests," 145–46, 147; Yizhar's representation of, 113–14. *See also* Palestinian literature

About the Author

Hannan Hever is associate professor in the Department of Poetics and Comparative Literature at Tel Aviv University, where he teaches Hebrew literature, postcolonial theories, and theory and criticism of culture and nationalism. He has served as a visiting professor at Northwestern University, University of Michigan at Ann Arbor, and Columbia University.

Hever, who received his Ph.D. from the Hebrew University of Jerusalem, has published widely on the relationship between politics and literature. In his work, he presents postcolonial and post-Zionist readings of Hebrew and Israeli literature. His books in Hebrew include *Literature Written from Here: A Short History of Israeli Literature; Captive of Utopia: An Essay on Messianism and Politics in Hebrew Poetry in Eretz Israel between the Two World Wars;* and *Zealots and Poets: The Rise of Political Hebrew Poetry.*